CURRENT ISSUES IN INTERNATIONAL MONETARY ECONOMICS

CURRENT ISSUES IN ECONOMICS

General Editor: David Greenaway, University of Nottingham

Current Issues in International Monetary Economics

Edited by

David Llewellyn

Professor of Money and Banking
Loughborough University

and

Chris Milner

Reader in Economics
Loughborough University

St. Martin's Press
New York

4-3-95

First published in the United States of America in 1990

Printed in Hong Kong

ISBN 0–312–04755–X

Library of Congress Cataloging–in–Publication Data
Current issues in international monetary economics/edited by David
Llewellyn and Chris Milner.
p. cm.—(Current issues in economics; vol. 4)
Includes bibliographical references.
ISBN 0–312–04755–X
1. Foreign exchange. 2. International finance. 3. Monetary
policy. I. Llewellyn, David T. II. Milner, Chris. III. Series.
HG3851.C79 1990
332′.042—dc20
                                                90–8101
                                                CIP

Contents

List of Figures

List of Tables

Series Editor's Preface

The *Current Issues* Series has slightly unusual origins. *Current Issues in International Trade*, which Macmillan published in 1987 and which turned out to be the pilot for the series was in fact 'conceived' in the Horton Hospital, Banbury, and 'delivered' (in the sense of completed) in the Hilton International in Nicosia! The reader may be struck by the thought that a more worthwhile and enjoyable production process would start and finish the other way around. I agree! Be that as it may, that is how the series started.

As I said in the Preface to *Current Issues in International Trade* the reason for its creation was the difficulty of finding suitable references on 'frontier issues' for undergraduate students. Many of the issues which excite professional economists and which dominate the journal literature take quite a time to percolate down into texts, hence the need for a volume of Current Issues. The reception which *Current Issues in International Trade* received persuaded me that it may be worth doing something similar for other subject areas we teach. Macmillan agreed with my judgement, hence the series. Thus each volume in this series is intended to take readers to the 'frontier' of the particular subject area. Each volume contains ten essays, nine of which deal with specific current issues, and one which provides a general overview, setting the relevant current issues in the context of other recent developments.

As Series Editor the main challenge I faced was finding suitable editors for each of the volumes – the best people are generally the busiest! I believe however that I have been fortunate in having such an impressive and experienced team of editors with the necessary skills and reputation to persuade first-class authors to participate. I would like to thank all of them for their cooperation and assistance in the development of the series. Like me all of them will, I am sure, hope that this series provides a useful service to undergraduate and postgraduate students as well as faculty.

With regard to the present volume, we know that international monetary economics has been an area of profound change in recent years. As the Editors acknowledge in their introduction, this has been fashioned partly by institutional developments (such as the globalisation of asset markets and the shift to flexible exchange rates), and partly by 'technical change' in the economics profession. Consequently the issues which preoccupy analysts in this area, and the way in which they think about those issues has altered markedly. These changes are captured well in this volume. The issues covered include the modelling of exchange rate dynamics, empirical aspects of exchange rate movements, policy coordination, and international debt. The Editors are to be commended on their choice of topics. They have provided us with a well balanced blend of theory, empirics and policy analysis – a blend which conveys the richness and excitement of current issues in international monetary economics. The authors are also to be congratulated on producing essays of such a consistently high standard. The issues addressed are often complex yet the authors have still managed to provide us with a digestible volume. I have enjoyed working on this volume and have certainly learned from it. I hope others have a similar experience.

DAVID GREENAWAY

University of Nottingham

Notes on the Contributors

Robert Aliber is Professor of International Economics and Finance, University of Chicago.

Michael Beenstock is Professor of Economics, The Hebrew University of Jerusalem.

David Currie is Professor of Economics and Director of the Centre for Economic Forecasting, London Business School.

Andrew Dean is in the Balance of Payments Division of the Organisation for Economic Cooperation and Development.

Rudiger Dornbusch is Professor of Economics, Massachusetts Institute of Technology.

Colm Kearney is Lecturer in Economics, University of New South Wales.

David T. Llewellyn is Professor of Money and Banking, Loughborough University.

Ronald MacDonald is Professor of Economics, University of Dundee.

Chris Milner is Reader in Economics, Loughborough University.

Nick Snowden is Lecturer in Economics, University of Lancaster.

1 Introduction: Current Issues and the Structure of the Book

DAVID T. LLEWELLYN and **CHRIS MILNER**

INTRODUCTION

This book presents nine essays that review current issues in international monetary economics, including reviews of theoretical, empirical, policy and institutional issues. The essays have been prepared by acknowledged specialists in the subject area, but have been written specifically for the undergraduate student market. Undergraduates are increasingly faced with a large range of differentiated, but interrelated specialist (and often technical) references on their reading lists. This is especially so in the case of international monetary economics, given the rapid and substantial changes in the world economy in the last two decades and in macroeconomics to accommodate the analysis of expectations formation and of open economy conditions. Undergraduate students of international economics or international monetary economics cannot be expected to cope with either the full width or depth of this specialist material. But equally they should not be encouraged to think that a single text can adequately cover the rich diversity of theoretical and empirical analysis to be found in professional journals and similar publication outlets. This volume seeks to resolve this dilemma; to provide a companion reader to the standard textbooks of international monetary economics, without being a comprehensive textbook in its own right, and to provide a means of accessing specialist journal literature without seeking to survey in a comprehensive manner all aspects of a particular topic. The reader should use this volume as a guide to the issues raised by recent specialist research and writings.

1

Each essay is the particular author's personal interpretation of the issues and recent developments in a selected topic of international monetary economics. The selection of topics was partly determined by their topicality or policy relevance (e.g. the debt issue) and partly by our own view of the state of the subject called 'international monetary economics'.

'INTERNATIONAL MONETARY ECONOMICS': CHANGING PERSPECTIVES AND CURRENT ISSUES

International monetary economics cannot be satisfactorily defined in a short, terse manner. We can set down the type of issues and relationships that the subject is concerned with: the operation and functions of international financial markets; the mechanisms for settling inter-country payments imbalances; the endogenous and policy-induced changes in prices, incomes and outputs that may reduce or eliminate payments imbalances; and the global 'control' /management (or mis-management) of interrelated domestic monetary systems that results from national, regional and global 'rules' or policy instruments. But the issues that we list or the emphasis given to specific topics is not likely to remain constant through time. Our perspectives of the nature of the key topics tends to change as the characteristics of the 'system' change, as the problems facing international monetary relations change, and as the economist's technology or tools of analysis change. Of course there is a high degree of interdependence between these influences. The 'system' changes sometimes in response to exogenous shocks, such as the oil price rises of the early 1970s. On other occasions problems or issues arise because of endogenous changes in the nature and form of international monetary relations. The increased exposure of Euro-currency banks caused by the debt-problems of the developing countries was not independent of the declining role of official financing of payments imbalances after the oil crisis. Similarly the collapse of the Bretton Woods system of pegged exchange rates induced changes in the tools of economic analysis. The importance of market sentiment or attitudes in influencing the volatility of exchange rates inspired much theoretical interest in the modelling of expectations formation by economic agents.

The subject matter of international monetary economics has been particularly susceptible therefore to changing perspectives and emphases in the last two decades. In this period we have witnessed quite dramatic changes in the nature of the problems facing the world economy, in the characteristics of international monetary relations and in the rules of the 'system'. Let us briefly consider some of these changes and their implications for the student of international monetary economics.

More inflationary conditions from late 1960s onwards

The apparent fundamental changes in the traditional Phillip's curve trade-off between unemployment and inflation in the late 1960s, with increases in both unemployment and inflation being experienced, was associated with growing interest in the role of monetary factors in domestic price-level determination. But Friedman's statement of quantity theory principles in the context of closed economy macroeconomic models was only part of the growing interest among economists at this time in the role of monetary factors. Keynesian analysis of both the closed economy and of the balance of payments had tended to emphasise the autonomous expenditure–income relationship. The apparent failure of traditional policy instruments associated with this approach to control inflation and to avoid increasingly large payments imbalances inspired a burgeoning theoretical literature on monetary economics (see for example, Johnson, 1972). The monetary (not monetarist) approach to the overall balance of payments, for instance, sought to challenge the conventional income-absorption and elasticities approaches to the analysis of the current account. The classical link between reserve change and the money supply under fixed exchange rates and in the absence of accommodating monetary policies was resurrected. The long-run automatic nature of balance of payments adjustment and the role of inappropriate domestic monetary policies in causing payments problems in the short term were emphasised by this 'new' approach. In its more extreme manifestations this interest in monetary factors expressed itself in the form of a 'global monetarism'; inflation being seen as a global, rather than domestic, phenomenon determined by the aggregate world money supply. These developments have had a lasting influence on balance of payments and exchange rate theory, which like macroeconomics in general, is typified by much greater model-heterogeneity than was found during the era of Keynesian orthodoxy.

Increased exchange rate flexibility

Increasing and divergent inflation rates between industrial countries in the late 1960s and early 1970s meant that the pegged exchange rate regime of the Bretton Woods system became unsustainable. Adjustment of par-values or pegs had in general been resisted by deficit and surplus countries alike throughout the 1950s and much of the 1960s. Deficit countries feared the inflationary consequence of currency devaluation, while surplus countries feared the loss of competitiveness associated with revaluation. In particular the key currency country, namely the USA, resisted changes in the dollar price of gold in order to maintain confidence in the gold-exchange principle. The gold and dollar crises of late 1960s and early 1970s reflected this battle of wills between the US and the surplus countries of Western Europe and Japan. It was effectively brought to an end by the unilateral US decision to suspend dollar convertibility into gold in 1971. Although in global terms pegged exchange rates remained the most frequent form of exchange rate policy, with most developing countries maintaining their currencies pegged against a specific currency or basket of currencies, the key currency (the dollar) and a number of other major industrial currencies (including sterling) have been allowed to float relatively freely or within (unspecified) bounds since the early 1970s. Admittedly there has been a strong preference throughout for relatively managed exchange rates in the EEC – first under the 'snake' arrangements and more recently under the European Monetary System, but even in this case the scope for exchange rate adjustment is greater than that experienced during the Bretton Woods era. With this increased exchange rate flexibility, therefore, has come a shift of emphasis in the theoretical literature. Rather than seeking to explain the determinants of the balance payments for a given exchange rate or adjustments in particular sets of international transactions induced by exchange rate adjustment, theoretical concern has focused on the determinants of actual and equilibrium exchange rates and movements in each in the short and long run.

Increased capital mobility and importance of private capital flows

The equilibrium exchange rate would have been equated, initially at least, with balance in current transactions in the standard textbook treatment of the balance of payments during the 1960s. Balance of payments theory was predominantly concerned with current balance models; exchange rate adjustments influenced either the balance between income and absorption or the competitiveness of imports and exports. Increased integration and reduced policy barriers between the financial markets of industrialised economies has increased the international mobility of capital dramatically over the postwar period. Technological changes and the communications revolution have increased in turn the importance of (private) international capital flows of all types. Capital transactions or the threat of capital in- or outflow now tend to dominate current transactions in the highly industrialised economies. The current balance model is no longer adequate in its coverage of international transactions, or very relevant in terms of explaining shorter-term movements in exchange rates. Attention has shifted therefore from goods markets to assets markets. Asset market models, either with perfect substitutability between home and foreign assets in the case of the monetary approach or with imperfect substitutability in the case of the portfolio balance approach now dominate the literature in this area. Indeed the very nature of what might be viewed as 'autonomous' and 'accommodating' transactions in the balance of payments has tended to change. Academic discussion in the Bretton Woods era tended to focus on the manner in which exchange rate adjustment altered the balance of autonomous (commercial trading) transactions on the current account, with capital transactions (private or official) being viewed as accommodating any short-term current imbalance. By contrast it might be more accurate to represent autonomous changes in capital flows (induced by inter-country differences in savings and investment opportunities) as inducing changes in exchange rates, which are accommodated by changes in the current balance. This tends to oversimplify the issues and the terms 'autonomous' and 'accommodating' may in any case be somewhat misleading. Nonetheless the changing characteristics of international monetary relations in recent decades have necessitated a change in academic perceptions about the role of capital flows in exchange rate and payments models.

Increased openness and interdependence

The increasing importance of international capital flows and increasing share of imports and exports in a country's national output means that the typical industrialised country (and many industrialising countries) are increasingly sensitive to conditions beyond their boundaries. Closed economy models are now of little relevance, since they are likely to quantitatively and qualitatively mis-specify the effects of policy interventions. With the increased need for open-economy macroeconomics, the dividing line between the subject matter of macroeconomics and international monetary economics has become more blurred, even irrelevant. The ability of governments to influence the level of income or economic activity through domestic financial policies can no longer be viewed independently of the form of exchange rate policy being pursued. Similarly, the relative effectiveness of monetary and fiscal policy will be influenced by both the degree of exchange rate flexibility and the mobility of capital. Even where policy actions are in principle capable of altering the level of economic activity domestically, the ability to pursue independent policies may be severely constrained in an interdependent world. Thus increasing interdependence between countries has reduced the value of single-country models, and inspired an increasing literature on policy coordination in a multi-country setting.

Changes in the global pattern of economic power

The theory and practice of international policy coordination are, however, rather different. Optimising welfare in the context of a stylised, two-country model is rather different from the way in which international policy discussions are conducted in reality. Under the Bretton Woods regime the then main 'actors' of international monetary discussions were the USA and EEC. We have witnessed a steady decline in the relative economic power of the USA over the postwar period, but a corresponding rise in power for the EEC and for other countries (e.g. Japan) and other groups of countries (oil-surplus countries, the newly-industrialising countries, and the new highly-indebted developing countries). With many actors or players policy coordination has become more difficult to negotiate, as has the reform of the institutions and rules of the 'system'. Thus the control or management of the system has become more difficult. The effective banker under Bretton Woods, the US, is less able and inclined to fulfil the function in line with the needs of the system. This has had a number of significant implications for the evolution of international monetary relationships over the last two decades.

A decline in the role of official financing of payments imbalances

Governments and international agencies such as the IMF have become less important in the settlements process. With greater exchange rate flexibility and greater reliance on private capital flows, the private sector has become more important in 'recycling' funds from surplus to deficit countries. With this has come some loss of control of the system. The liberalisation of capital markets throughout the world and the move away from a rules-based international monetary system has reduced controllability. The lending of the Euro-currency markets, for instance to the developing countries in the post-oil crisis period, and the resulting enormous rise in these countries' external debt illustrates this control problem. The 'debt problem' confronts both debtor and lender alike, since for the former the servicing of debt is a severe burden or drain on current income and, for the latter, default threatens confidence in the banking sectors of many industrialised countries.

A fragmentation of the global monetary system

With declining official financing and control of the system there has been a tendency for the supply and composition of international liquidity to be endogenously determined. The US preference since Bretton Woods, for market convertibility of the dollar at a price or exchange rate determined by market forces, has reduced the attractiveness of the dollar as a key currency. It is still the dominant reserve currency, given the reluctance of other countries to allow their own currencies (e.g. Deutschemark and yen) to replace the dollar, but there has been a degree of currency deversification into these alternative 'strong' currencies. Thus a number of currencies now fulfil a 'polar' function, with currencies in the region tending to want to peg their currencies to these low inflation/high productivity economies. The yen has this position in Asia and the D-mark in Europe. Thus regional monetary systems are informally, or more formally (as in the case of European Monetary System) tending to emerge. In the absence of a global banker (the role previously played by the US) and of an effective supranational institution (a role which the International Monetary Fund has never fulfilled), there is a tendency to seek regional control mechanisms. Certainly the post-Bretton Woods era has been typified by greater flux and has been less 'rules'-based than the Bretton Woods system.

The growth of offshore banking and international financial intermediation

The origins of the Eurocurrency markets predate the decline in importance in official financing of payments imbalances and the demise of the Bretton Woods system. It would be wrong therefore to simply interpret the growth of international banking as either cause or consequence of the emergence of what some have called a 'non-system'. No doubt the growth of offshore banking has increased the control problems of both national policymakers and of the system as a whole. It is also the case that the decline in importance of official settlements mechanisms provided an opportunity for the private international banking sector to play a more important role in the financing of payments imbalances. The volume of Eurocurrency market transactions was, for instance, boosted considerably by the opportunity to 'recycle' the oil surpluses of OPEC to the oil-importing developed and developing countries during the 1970s. But it must be appreciated that the existence of international financial intermediation is not dependent on the existence of international payments imbalances. The funds of a surplus unit (creditor) in one country may be routed to a deficit unit (debtor) in another country more efficiently by a non-resident bank of either country, even if there is equilibrium in payments balances. The growth of international banking is not so much a product of slow or incomplete balance of payments adjustments, but rather part of a natural process of international specialisation; this process has been fostered by more liberal policies to international transactions and by technological changes which have revolutionised international communications.

The implications of this development for the subject matter of international monetary economics are fairly profound. International monetary economics is no longer only concerned with the operations of official agents (i.e. policymakers) in money and currency markets; it needs to understand the functioning of financial markets (the agents, institutions and instruments) that extend beyond national boundaries. We are, as a result, no longer interested in modelling only inter-country imbalances between income and expenditure: we need also to consider intra-country or sectoral imbalances and resulting flows of funds.

Domestic and international imbalances

Of course, all the changes we have been describing in this section must be viewed against the background of changes in the characteristics of the 'real' international economy. There have been substantial changes in the world economy (endogenous and policy-induced) in the last two decades: in relative prices of particular goods, in countries' shares of income or output, and therefore in savings capabilities and investment opportunities around the world. The rise in the price of oil has created a new group of surplus countries; Japan's share of world production has increased significantly; the investment requirements of the newly-industrialising countries of South East Asia and South America have increased substantially. With these changes have come changing perspectives about the nature of the problems (and their relative importance) that international monetary economics must address. With them has also come a clearer recognition of the fact that domestic and international imbalances should not be viewed separately. Thus the current US budget and trade deficits and the Japanese trade surplus are not wholly separate or distinct policy problems. The fact that a country's trade or current account imbalances must net out has long been recognised in the literature of international monetary economics. But the funding implications of a US budget deficit for flows of funds within and between countries is now recognised more explicitly in the literature.

THE STRUCTURE OF THE BOOK

We could not hope to provide a thorough coverage of all the issues raised in the previous section. We have tried, however, to deal with a number of the most important – those relating to exchange rate theory and determination, stabilisation policy, policy coordination, domestic and international imbalances and international debt. The essays selected can be organised under three broad headings; exchange rates, open-economy macroeconomics and global monetary issues.

On exchange rates

There are three essays that fall under this heading; one by Rudiger Dornbusch on exchange rate determination (Chapter 2), one by Michael Beenstock on exchange rate dynamics (Chapter 3) and one by Ronald MacDonald on empirical studies (Chapter 4).

The essay by such a prominent economist as Dornbusch provides an excellent starting-point for the book. It reviews the conceptual and empirical issues in the arguments for and against flexible exchange rates. It does so with the aid of an expectations-augmented, open economy. IS–LM model in the tradition of Mead, Fleming and Mundell. Not surprisingly, given the author's expertise in this area, the essay is wide-ranging, considering the link between exchange rates and prices, the political economy of exchange rate movements and a number of current policy issues such as target zones and exchange rate orientated monetary policy.

The second essay by Beenstock focuses on the rather narrower topic of the movement of exchange rates over time, and in particular short-term movements. It provides an alternative perspective to that in the first essay. The author's purpose is to restore a central role to exchange rate risk and, for analytical convenience, does so within a partial equilibrium or Marshallian framework. The essay explains exchange rate movements and the effects of exchange rate interventions within an integrated current and capital account model, which is offered as an alternative to the Dornbusch 'overshooting' model. Economic thought is rarely homogeneous!

The final essay in this group is a very comprehensive review of empirical studies relating to exchange rates. MacDonald is an experienced practitioner in this area, and he has succeeded in providing a clear exposition of the rigours of empirical work in this area. It reviews the extent to which the various models of the exchange rate can explain trend movements in, and the short-term volatility of, exchange rates. In particular the predictability or unpredictability of exchange rate movements and the role of 'news' in explaining unexpected exchange rate movements is investigated.

On open-economy macroeconomics

The three topics dealt with in this group of essays are by Colm Kearney on stabilisation policies in a single economy (Chapter 5), David Currie on policy coordination between interdependent economies (Chapter 6) and Andrew Dean on adjustment problems in a global setting (Chapter 7).

In Chapter 5 Kearney focuses on three key issues in open-economy macroeconomics. First, it considers how the flexibility or rigidity of exchange rates affects the efficacy of alternative instruments of domestic financial policy. Second, it considers the extent of and implications for the efficacy of stabilisation policies of increased international capital mobility. Third, it re-examines the relationship between a government's budgetary policies and the economy's current account position.

Currie shifts the focus of attention in Chapter 6 from national policy to inter-country policy coordination issues. The author considers whether policy coordination is desirable in principle, what form it should take in order to be beneficial and how it might be achieved in practice. In particular, attention focuses on some recent proposals (e.g. the extended target zone proposal by Williamson and Miller, 1987) for establishing coordinated policies by key currency economies.

In Chapter 7 Dean examines in detail the link between domestic and external imbalances. It seeks therefore to investigate global (balance of payments) adjustment policies and processes within a framework which considers both the sustainability and compatibility of internal and external imbalances. This perspective is used to examine the changing views of the adjustment process and alternative possible channels of adjustment. Finally some recent episodes of international imbalance (e.g. the effects of the oil price rises in the 1970s on OPEC countries, the developing countries and the industrialised countries) are explored. This discussion provides a useful link with the final three essays on some global monetary issues.

On global monetary issues

The final three essays are by Nick Snowden on international debt (Chapter 8), Robert Aliber on exchange rate arrangements (Chapter 9) and David Llewellyn on international monetary arrangements (Chapter 10).

The debt problem of the developing countries has become a central issue in international monetary relations. Snowden's essay investigates the causes of the international borrowing that resulted in the accumulation of debt. In particular Chapter 8 confronts the difficult issues of whether the 'debt crisis' was the outcome of 'excessive' borrowing and lending, or of the terms on which the loans were extended. There is some description of the major features of international lending, but the main aim is to provide an analytical framework for understanding the sources of the problem. Neoclassical analysis of optimising, 'rational' actors is contrasted, for instance, with more institutionalist models.

In Chapter 9 Aliber evaluates the impact of structural and monetary shocks on exchange rate arrangements. The historical experiences of, in particular, the pound sterling and the US dollar, are used to illustrate the influences on monetary authorities' ability to peg their currency. The importance of monetary shocks, inflationary or deflationary, in reducing the authorities' ability and willingness to maintain the pegging of its currency to an external asset is strongly argued by the author.

The historical perspective in Chapter 9 provides, therefore, a useful background to the discussion in Chapter 10 of current threats to global monetary stability and problems confronting the reform of international monetary relations. The various contributions to this volume tend to focus on specific, key aspects of international monetary arrangements. In the last chapter, Llewellyn brings some of the threads together and focuses upon the international monetary system as whole. He describes how the evolution of the system has implications for the issues discussed in other chapters, and indicates some of the interrelationships between the component parts. The focus of this chapter is upon the special considerations that arise in monetary relations between countries that do not arise within national financial systems.

2 Exchange Rate Economics[1]

RUDIGER DORNBUSCH

INTRODUCTION

The case for flexible rates as made by Friedman (1953) and Johnson (1969) rests on a double claim: flexible rates would provide a more efficient international system of adjustment and hence support a world of freer trade. At the same time they would free domestic monetary and fiscal policy instruments for domestic purposes. The counterargument, specifically by Nurkse (1944), is that flexible rates are tantamount to volatile, unstable rates, a source of disturbance and instability rather than efficient mechanism of adjustment.

When Johnson (1969) made the case for flexible exchange rates he rested it on the presumed policy autonomy that would be gained once balance of payments equilibrium was no longer absorbing the commitment of scarce policy instruments:[2]

The fundamental argument for flexible exchange rates is that they would allow countries autonomy with respect to their use of monetary, fiscal and other policy instruments, consistent with the maintenance of whatever degree of freedom in international transactions they chose to allow their citizens, by automatically ensuring the preservation of external equilibrium . . . the argument for flexible exchange rates can be put more strongly still: flexible exchange rates are essential to the preservation of national autonomy and independence consistent with efficient organization and development of the world economy.

Johnson also comments on the volatility issue:

> One of the common arguments under the heading of uncertainty
> is that flexible rates would be extremely unstable rates, jumping
> wildly about from day to day. . . . Abnormally rapid and erratic
> movements will occur only in response to sharp and unexpected
> changes in circumstances. . . . .

The discussion today is not far from the original debate, but some
lessons have been learnt: Flexible rates *are* more volatile than fixed
rates, there is no policy autonomy, and adjustment under flexible
rates is problematic. But these lessons notwithstanding, the fixed
versus flexible exchange rate debate is back to 1969. We review here
the conceptual and empirical issues in the debate and the policy
options that have been proposed.

In the past fifteen years, key exchange rates have moved in larger
and more persistent ways than advocates of flexible rates in the late
1950s and 1960s would have imagined. Certainly they did not
imagine constancy for nominal exchange rates. But real exchange
rate movements of 30 or 40 per cent were not suggested as a realistic
possibility. Moreover, where these large movements did ocur they
did not obviously appear to be connected with fundamentals, and
hence seemed difficult to explain in terms of the exchange rate
theories at hand. The persistence of rate movements was as surprising as the rapid unwinding of apparent misalignments when they did
ultimately occur. Research on exchange rate economics has grown
tired searching for risk premia determinants or for new macroeconomic models. With a shift of interest toward the microeconomic
effects of exchange rate movements, research is now turning in a
fresh direction. It is therefore a good time to take stock of what is
known of exchange rate economics, what has been learnt since the
early 1970s and where more research needs to be done.

The past fifteen years also provide a natural dividing line between
the Keynesian and monetary approaches of the 1960s, and the more
recent analysis that takes into account exchange rate expectations
and portfolio issues, which took off in the early 1970s, as well as the
brand-new approaches that concentrate on (partial equilibrium)
microeconomics. To review these ideas the paper starts with the
Mundell–Fleming model as a comprehensive framework of analysis.
A brief look at the experience with flexible exchange rates follows.

From there we proceed to linkages between exchange rates and prices, the political economy of exchange rate movements and the current policy debate.

THE BASIC FRAMEWORK

There are two standard models of exchange rate determination. One focuses on an expectations-augmented, open-economy IS–LM model in the tradition of Meade, Fleming, and Mundell. The other highlights the role of portfolio diversification and relative asset supplies. In choosing between them, an important question is to decide how relevant portfolio diversification effects are, as part of an explanation for exchange rate movements. In other words, are monetary and fiscal policy most of the story or do relative supplies of debts and other claims also play an important role?

The Extended Mundell–Fleming Model:

The textbook model today is an open-economy IS–LM model with perfect capital mobility, sluggish price adjustment, rapid asset market or interest rate adjustment, and rational expectations in asset markets.

A streamlined version is written in log-linear form and takes output as given. Complications stemming from output adjustments can easily be introduced but do not actually change the basic dynamics. In the same way we do not explicitly focus on wage–price interaction.[3]

$$m - p = \lambda i \tag{2.1}$$

$$i = i^* + \dot{e} \tag{2.2}$$

$$\pi = \alpha[\beta(e - p) + g + \gamma(i - \pi)] \tag{2.3}$$

Here m and p are the nominal money stock and prices, i and e are the nominal interest rate and the exchange rate respectively, and g is a variable representing fiscal policy. All variables other than interest rates are in logs.

Equation (2.1) represents monetary equilibrium or the LM schedule. Equation (2.2) states that with an adjustment for anticipated depreciation, assets are perfect substitutes. Perfect foresight is imposed by equating actual and anticipated depreciation. Equation (2.3) specifies that price adjustment is linked to the excess demand for goods, which in turn depends on the real exchange rate, fiscal policy and the real interest rate.

This model exhibits the familiar overshooting property: a one-time monetary expansion leads to an immediate depreciation of the exchange rate. The exchange rate overshoots its new long-run level – which is proportional to the increase in money. In the transition period, following the initial overshooting, the exchange rate appreciates while prices are rising. The process continues until the initial real equilibrium is restored.

Wilson (1979) has shown that this model also lends itself to the investigation of currently-anticipated disturbances or of transitory disturbances. This exercise highlights the flexibility of asset prices which move ahead of the realisation of disturbances. Exchange rates move immediately, driven entirely by anticipations, and bring about alterations of prices and interest rates before any monetary or fiscal changes are actually implemented.

The strong feature of the model is the contrast between instantly flexible assets prices which are set in a forward-looking manner, and the sluggish adjustment of product prices. The linkage of the domestic asset market to foreign rates of interest produces exchange rate dynamics which yield the required rate of return on home assets. Any 'news' will make the exchange rate jump instantly to that level where the expected capital gains or losses precisely offset the nominal interest differential. In this sense the structure is extraordinarily rigid, just as was the original Mundell–Fleming model.

There is room for some flexibility: output adjustment can be brought in, import prices can appear in the real money balances' deflator or a J-curve can be introduced to allow a more gradual response of demand to the real exchange rate. But these are niceties that do not add much to the basic flavour of the results.

Fiscal policy

A major insight comes from a different application: fiscal policy. A fiscal expansion in this model brings about currency appreciation. Fiscal expansion creates an excess demand for goods, leading to an expansion in output or prices and hence, with a given nominal money stock, to upward pressure on the interest rate. Incipient capital inflows bring about an exchange rate appreciation and full crowding-out. This is exactly the property captured by the Mundell–Fleming model. *Fiscal policy works in the way they described even when price adjustments and expectations are introduced.*

An interesting extension is to consider a transitory fiscal expansion. This corresponds, for example, to the US experience of the 1980s. Suppose that fiscal policy follows an adjustment process such as:

$$\dot{g} = -\eta(g - \bar{g}) \tag{2.4}$$

where $\bar{g}$ is the long-run level of government spending. According to (2.4) a fiscal expansion is being phased out over time at the rate η.

Now suppose that at time T_0 a fiscal expansion to level g_0 takes place and that from there on fiscal policy will follow the rule of (2.4). It is possible to solve for the path of the real exchange rate to establish the following results: there will be an immediate real appreciation. Then, under the impact of excess demand, prices will keep rising so that further real appreciation occurs. Over time the exchange rate overvaluation builds up even as the fiscal policy is being wound down. A recession develops which now forces deflation and hence gradually a return to the initial level of the real exchange rate.

If a future transitory fiscal expansion is anticipated or is gradually phased in, the adjustment process is somewhat more complicated. The adjustment path is shown in Figure 2.1. Upon the news of the fiscal programme there will be an initial nominal and real appreciation shown as a jump from A to B. Then the overvaluation exerts a deflationary pressure. As prices decline and real balances rise the nominal interest rate falls. To match the lower interest rate the exchange rate will be appreciating. That process continues until the fiscal expansion actually gets underway, and leads to excess demand and inflation. Only when real balances and hence interest rates have been pushed up beyond their initial level, does the corrective depreciation start. The depreciation then continues, along with the phasing out of the fiscal expansion, until the initial equilibrium is restored.

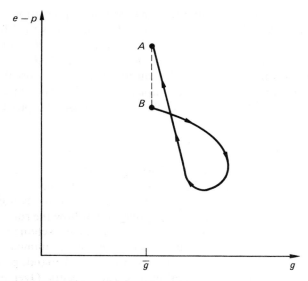

FIGURE 2.1   The real exchange rate effect of a transitory fiscal expansion

EXTENSION OF THE THEORY

Three features of the extended Mundell–Fleming model account for its strong and unambiguous predictions. First, the absence of any effects, dynamic or otherwise, associated with the current account. Second, that home and foreign assets are perfect substitutes. Third, that there are only two classes of assets, money and bonds, and no real assets. We consider now what alternative models might look like and what they imply for exchange rate economics.

Current account effects

A period of fiscal expansion leading to appreciation will also involve cumulative current account imbalances. The case of the United States stands out, as now more than 2 per cent of its GNP is borrowed from the rest of the world in financing the persistent deficit, adding in each year to a seemingly ever-growing external indebtedness. Some time in 1985 the US passed from net creditor to net debtor status.

The accumulated net external indebtedness will show up in the current account in the form of reduced income from net foreign assets. The reduction in net external assets means that following a period of deficits the current account cannot be balanced simply by returning to the initial real exchange rate. Now there will be a deficit stemming from the increased debt service. Therefore, to restore current account balance, an *over*depreciation is required.

The current account can be represented in the following manner. Let *d* be the net external asset stock and i^* the rate of return. A dot denotes the rate of change over time.

$$\dot{d} = f(a-p,g) + i^*d \tag{2.5}$$

The real exchange rate that yields current account balance will therefore depend on the rate of return on assets and on the cumulated history of fiscal policy and other shocks to the current account. A transitory fiscal binge requires a subsequent permanent real depreciation to yield the improvement in the non-interest current account that is necessary to service the debt.

Such a permanent response to transitory deficits is clearly not part of the standard model. The question is whether it represents a realistic, quantitatively important effect. This is the case addressed in trade theory under the heading of the 'transfer problem'. It depends in large part on the impact on demand for domestic goods of an international redistribution of wealth and spending, and on the production response to changes in relative prices.

The discussion of the transfer problem is not complete without a consideration of how the budget will be balanced. The fiscal expansion gives rise to a budget deficit which is financed by issuing debt. The debt in turn will have to be serviced at some point by increased taxes. The question then is whether the taxation yields an equal current account improvement at constant relative prices. If so then there is no need for terms-of-trade adjustments. At the going levels of output, disposable income and absorption by domestic residents decline but part of reduced spending falls on domestic goods rather than imports. To achieve the transfer *at full employment* ordinarily requires a real depreciation. The real depreciation will shift demand toward domestic goods.

The discussion of fiscal policy effects on real exchange rates clearly provides scope for an application of the Barro–Ricardo equivalence ideas to the open economy. A particularly complete rendition is offered in Frenkel and Razin (1986a).

Portfolio effects

A separate persistence effect can arise via the impact of fiscal and current account imbalances on the relative supply of assets. Suppose that, contrary to (2.2), assets are not perfect substitutes so that there is a risk premium:[4]

$$i = i^* + \dot{e} + \rho(b - b^* - e) \tag{2.6}$$

where b and b^* are the supplies of domestic and foreign debt in national currencies.[5]

If current account imbalances were financed by an increase in the relative supply of domestic debt, the cumulative imbalance would require an increase in the relative yield on domestic securities or a change in the relative valuation via exchange rate changes. A depreciation would be a means of correcting an increase in the relative supply of domestic securities by reducing their value in foreign currency, thus restoring portfolio balance at an unchanged yield differential. Other things being equal, we would therefore expect a period of debt accumulation to have a permanent effect on exchange rates, so as to bring interest differentials in line with the changed relative supply of assets.

The responsiveness of exchange rates to relative asset supplies has been addressed in a number of important papers by Frankel.[6] He concludes that relative asset supplies in fact do not provide a satisfactory account of relative yields, at least in the context of a capital asset pricing model. The impact of relative asset supplies is practically negligible. That is an uncomfortable conclusion for a whole strand of research which places major emphasis on the imperfect substitutability of assets as a major feature of open economy macroeconomics.

Real assets

The standard model remains oversimplified even when long-term issues of current account balancing and a risk premium are taken into account. The simplification lies in the omission of real capital from portfolios, and in disregarding the effect over time of invest-ment on the capital stock and thus the supply side of the economy.

Concurrently with the imbalance in the current account and the resulting shift in net foreign assets, capital accumulation takes place. Portfolio adjustments in response to the changing relative asset supplies bring about changes in the value of real assets and in relative yields. The flow of investment and the changes in the value of real capital potentially dominate the effects of current account imbalances. A good week on the stock market produces a change in wealth that is several times the magnitude of an entire year's deficit in the current account. While it is true that the current account is important because persistent imbalances cumulate, exactly the same argument must be made for investment.

Work by Gavin (1986) shows that the inclusion of the stock market in the standard model offers important additional channels for exchange rate dynamics. Unfortunately this inclusion removes at the same time the simplicity of the standard model. Now virtually anything is possible. And that result is arrived at by looking only at the portfolio implications of a money–debt–capital model and the ensuing yield and wealth effects, without even taking into account the accumulation of physical capital. Among the sources of am-biguity are two different effects: an expansion in demand will bring about both an increase in output and an increase in interest rates. The net effect on the valuation of the stock market is therefore uncertain. Thus wealth may rise or fall, and this is important in judging the induced effects on money demand and spending. The second important consideration is the relative substitutability of money and debt, and debt and capital. This is relevant for the extent of yield changes and hence for the direction and magnitude of exchange rate changes.

The money–debt–capital model is also important in highlighting the fact that current accounts are not necessarily financed by sales of domestic bonds or foreign bonds. There need not be a link between cumulative current account imbalances and yield differentials between home and foreign nominal bonds. There would be a significant distinction, for example, between fiscal deficits and investment deficits. The difference is also relevant from the point of view of the transfer problem. Deficits that arise as a result of increased investment have different implications from deficits that have their source in fiscal imbalances.

Hysteresis effects

A final channel for persistence effects is introduced by an industrial organisation approach to the consequences of extended rate mis-alignments. When an industry is exposed to foreign competition and entry by a persistent overvaluation, it may close down and perhaps even reopen in the low-wage country. Firms already producing in the low-wage country may make the necessary investment to enter the market where home firms are handicapped by overvalued labour. A period of overvaluation or undervaluation thus changes the industrial landscape in a relatively permanent fashion. These considerations are at the centre of a new literature that seeks to interpret the US experience following the five-year overvaluation.[7] The upshot of the literature is that overvaluation leads ultimately to the need for overdepreciation to remedy the accumulation of adverse trade effects.

Overvaluation, for example due to monetary contraction or fiscal expansion, brings in foreign firms and displaces domestic firms. When the overvaluation is ultimately undone the foreign firms are still there and the domestic firms may no longer exist. Worse yet, they may now even be producing abroad. A period of sustained undervaluation is required to bring forth the required re-investment. The possibility of entry and the choice of labour market from which to supply a particular market, thus opens an important dynamic theory of adjustment to the exchange rate. Expectations about the persistence of changes in relative labour costs become important for the determination of relative prices. Now pricing between firms not only involves current strategic interaction, which we consider below, but also the impact of pricing strategies on entry, location and investment.

There is some offset to these considerations from the side of factor prices. To the extent that an industry has a captive factor supply we would expect that wages come down with the exchange rate, thus maintaining a firm in existence. Conversely, in expanding countries, wages might rise and thus offset some of the gain in profitability arising from depreciation.

The recognition that real exchange rate changes have taken place on a massive scale, and that they have major and potentially persistent macroeconomic effects, points to several important directions for research:

Why do exchange rates move so much and so persistently?

Does the fact that real exchange rates remain misaligned so persistently imply that they must therefore ultimately overshoot to remedy the accumulated consequences of over- or undervaluation?

Does a review of available theories and evidence suggest that exchange rate movements are based on irrational speculation rather than fundamentals?

What are linkages between movements in the exchange rate and changes in relative prices?

Do the large and persistent movements lead to the inevitable conclusion that exchange rate management offers a chance for better macroeconomic performance? If so, what is the externality, and thus what is the appropriate policy instrument, exchange rate orientated monetary policy or a reduced scope for capital movements?

THE EXPERIENCE WITH FLOATING

The experience with flexible exchange rates has three outstanding characteristics: volatility of real exchange rates, persistent misalignments, and pervasive forecasting mistakes. We review these in turn.[8]

Volatility

Research shows that the variability of (bilateral) real exchange rates among the main industrial countries and the US is far higher under flexible exchange rates than under fixed rates. Figure 2.2 shows changes in the real exchange rate of the US and Canada in the past thirty years. The figure makes it clear that since the move to flexible rates in the early 1970s the variability of the real exchange rate has increased massively. Table 2.1 makes the same point for the real exchange rate between the US and various industrialised countries.

Misalignments

Figures 2.3 and 2.4 relate to the issue of exchange rate misalignment.

24

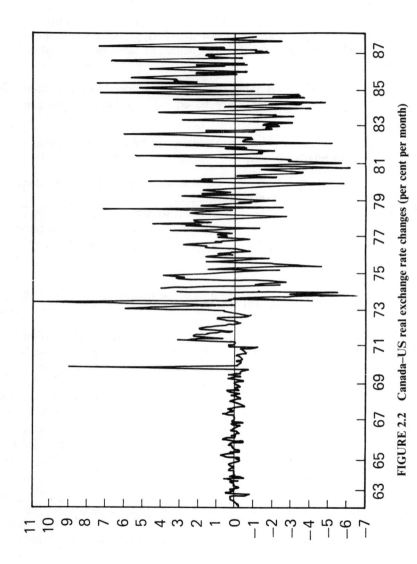

FIGURE 2.2   Canada–US real exchange rate changes (per cent per month)

TABLE 2.1 Variability of real exchange rates (coefficient of variation, monthly data)

	1958–72	1973–87
US real effective rate	0.04	0.11
US–Germany	0.07	0.21
US–Japan	0.14	0.15
US–UK	0.05	0.14
US–France	0.10	0.19
US–Sweden	0.08	0.21

Note Variability is measured by the coefficient of variation of the real exchange rate. The real exchange rate is the ratio of consumer prices measured in a common currency.

In Figure 2.3 we show the Canada–US real exchange rate in the past 100 years. The 1977–85 real appreciation of the US dollar stands out as the largest peacetime disturbance. In Figure 2.4, showing the US–German real exchange rate the appreciation and depreciation episode of 1979–87 stands out as an extraordinary and puzzling path of the real exchange rate.

One cannot infer that these large real exchange rate movements represent misalignments simply because they are sizable and ultimately are reversed. It is even less appropriate to assume that they reflect equilibrium relative prices although one cannot offer an explanation for the size and pattern of changes over time.

Forecasting

Poor forecasting performance of forward rates is the third property of the exchange rate experience in the past 15 years. Figure 2.5 shows the percentage forecast error (forward rates as a percentage of spot rates at maturity) implied in three-months forward exchange rates. Forecast errors are almost never zero; they are always large, although their sign varies sufficiently to give the impression of randomness.

In fact, however, forecast errors are not even random. A regression of forecast errors on *past* changes in the actual exchange rate yields significant explanatory power:

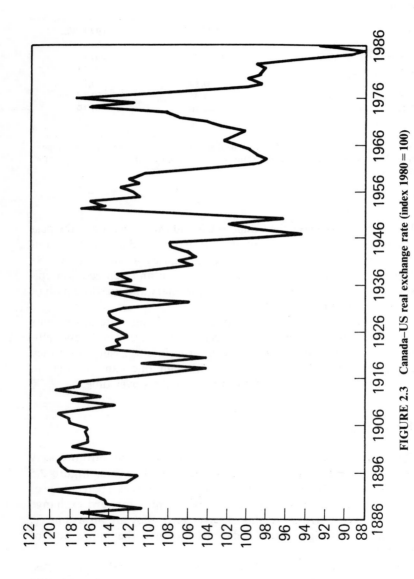

FIGURE 2.3   Canada–US real exchange rate (index 1980 = 100)

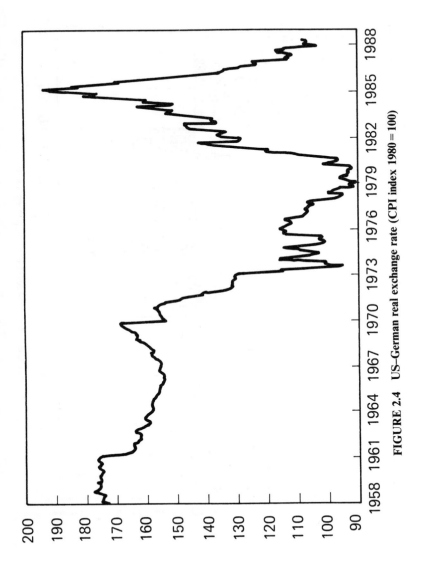

FIGURE 2.4 US–German real exchange rate (CPI index 1980 = 100)

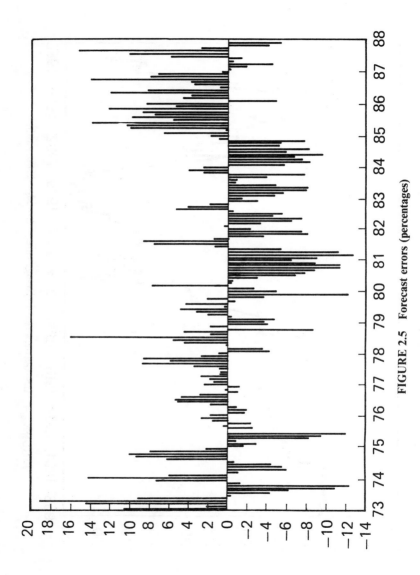

FIGURE 2.5 Forecast errors (percentages)

(1)   Error = 1.61 + 1.02 Depreciation
          (0.64)   (6.24)

$\bar{R}^2 = 0.61$ DW = 2.04   Rho = 0.88

where the terms in parentheses denote t-statistics.[9] The equation implies that when the DM/$ exchange rate is depreciating, as in 1980–85, the forward price of marks underestimates the actual price at maturity. This is a reflection of the fact that the forward rate (with small interest differentials) is basically equal to the current spot rate. Therefore when the spot rate is depreciating the forward rate is below the future spot rate. The fact that past depreciation predicts future forecast errors is a consequence of the lasting one-directional trips in the exchange rate.

Frankel and Froot (1986a) have shown extensive evidence of large discrepancies between forecasts gathered from market surveys, forward premia and realised depreciation. Table 2.2 shows some of their data for the case of the dollar/sterling exchange rate. It is apparent that forecast averages differ widely from forward rates and from realised depreciation.

We conclude this section by asking whether the standard models of exchange rate determination can give a satisfactory account of rate movements in the past decade.

Fiscal policy once more

In the Mundell–Fleming model explored earlier, fiscal expansion leads to real appreciation and fiscal contraction brings about real depreciation. In view of the massive shifts in US and foreign budgets

TABLE 2.2   Frankel–Froot dollar–yen data (per cent per year, sample average)

Period	Horizon	Actual	Survey	Forward discount
10/84–2/86	1 month	10.1	−11.91	−3.85
6/81–12/85	3 months	−6.43	3.66	−0.06
6/81–12/85	12 months	−9.47	3.38	0.36

Note   The 1 month forecasts are from one survey, the 3 and 12 months' forecasts from a different survey.
Source: Frankel and Froot (1986a).

Exchange Rate Economics

it is interesting to ask whether fiscal factors, together with monetary policy, can explain the behaviour of the US real exchange rate.

Feldstein (1986) and Hutchinson and Throop (1985) have documented that shifts in the full employment budget, along with real interest rates, do in fact explain the large shifts in real exchange rates that have occurred. Table 2.3 shows results by Hutchinson and Throop (1985). The real exchange rate, Rex (in logs), in these equations is explained by the real interest rate differential, r-r^*, and the structural budget deficits in the US and abroad, b and b^* respectively.

Interestingly for the regressions reported in Table 2.3 the empirical tests hold for the entire 1974–84 period and not only for the period of dollar appreciation in the period 1980–85. They work equally well when applied to multilateral exchange rates for the entire floating rate period. Fiscal expansion invariably leads to real appreciation. It is not clear, however, whether for a sample period including 1985–88 the performance of these equations continues to hold up.[10] Since 1985 real interest differentials, which had been in favour of the US by 3–4 percentage points in 1984–85 have declined and thus support the evidence of dollar depreciation. But full employment budgets have changed very little and thus cannot have played a major role.[11]

Fiscal policy, including the expectations of correction associated with Gramm–Rudman, provides one interpretation of the dollar movements in the 1980s. The alternative is to argue the case for at least partial irrationality as has been done by Frankel (1985), Frankel and Froot (1986b) and Krugman (1986).

TABLE 2.3 The effect of budget deficits on the current account
$(REX = a_0 + a_1 (r^* - r) + a_2 b + a_3 b^*)$

Period	a_0	a_1	a_2	a_3	$\bar{R}^2$	Rho
74–81:4	4.59 (85.4)	3.4 (3.7)	−4.3 (−3.05)	2.96 (2.11)	0.88	0.59
74–84:3	4.61 (191.4)	3.46 (4.49)	−4.48 (−7.6)	3.22 (3.12)	0.97	0.62

Source: Hutchinson and Throop (1985, p. 36)

EXCHANGE RATES AND PRICES

The monetary approach to the balance of payments used purchasing power parity (PPP) as an essential ingredient in explanations of exchange rate determination. Today PPP is certainly no longer a cornerstone for modelling. Attention has shifted to *changes* in equilibrium relative prices. The simple Keynesian model assumes that wages and prices in national currencies are given, so that exchange rate movements change relative prices one-for-one. A newer approach recognises the sluggishness of wages, but builds on a theory of equilibrium price determination along industrial organisation lines.[12]

The interest in research on price behaviour is apparent from Figure 2.6 which shows Japanese export prices in dollars and in yen as well as the \$/yen exchange rate. Figure 2.6 shows how the dollar price of Japanese exports increased far less than the dollar price of yen. The impact of exchange rate movements on prices can also be seen in Figure 2.7 which shows domestic and import prices (in dollars) of capital goods in the US. The import price follows the pattern of the exchange rate, but domestic prices do not. Hence exchange rate changes affect *relative* prices. The channels and the extent of these influences need modelling.

Relative prices

An interesting setting for exchange rate–wage–price relationships is a world of imperfect competition. Here firms are pricesetters. They may or may not interact strategically, but they certainly face the problem of how their pricing decision should react to a change in the exchange rate. Consider the simple case of an oligopoly.[13]

The typical setting would be the following. We look at the home market where n home firms and n^* foreign firms compete. The profits of the typical home and foreign firms, with constant unit labor costs in their respective currencies given by w and w^*, are:

$$H = (p_i - w)D_i(p_i, p_j) \tag{2.6}$$

$$H^* = (p_j - ew^*)D_j(P_i, P_j) \tag{2.7}$$

These profits are maximised subject to the strategic assumptions about the determinants of demand facing each firm and the

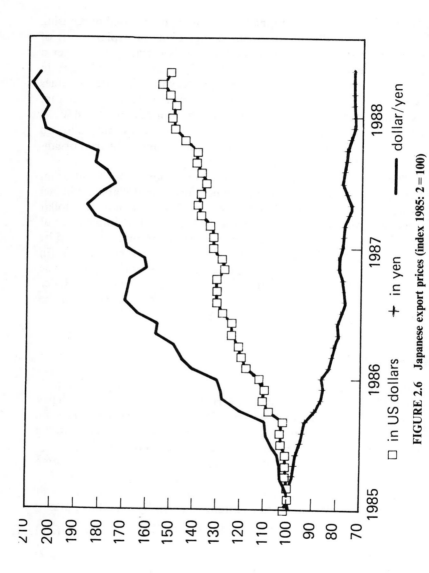

FIGURE 2.6   Japanese export prices (index 1985: 2 = 100)

□ in US dollars   + in yen   —— dollar/yen

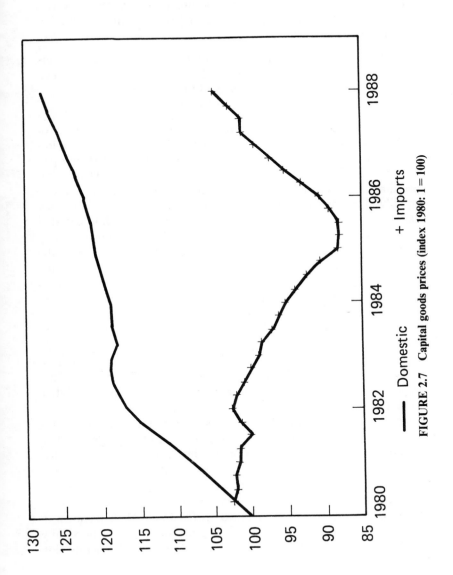

—— Domestic   + Imports

FIGURE 2.7   Capital goods prices (index 1980: 1 = 100)

responses of other firms in the market. It is clear that there is no general solution to the problem. The impact of an exchange rate change on equilibrium prices will depend on a number of factors. Specifically these include:

 −whether goods are perfect substitutes or differentiated products
 −the market organisation − oligopoly, imperfect competition, etc.
 −the relative number of domestic and foreign firms
 −the functional form of the market demand curve.

Even though there is no presumption about the effects of exchange rates on the changes in equilibrium prices, it is immediately clear that there is an important link between open economy macroeconomics and industrial organisation. There is no presumption that an exchange rate movement affects all markets equally. Some markets may involve a homogeneous good and, for example, a duopoly. Other markets may involve differentiated products and Chamberlinian competition. Yet other markets may be close to perfect competition. But whichever is the case, once the exchange rate changes, given wages, there will an adjustment in the equilibrium price. This pricing issue, depending on market organisation, may be repeated at different levels from import to retail. The same pricing issues arise on the export side.

For the case of differentiated products an appreciation tends to bring about a rise in the relative price of domestic goods. Imported variants decline in price both absolutely and relatively. For homogeneous products the industry price declines, with the decline being larger the less monopolised the market and the larger the relative number of foreign firms.

An interesting, and perhaps surprising, result appears here: currency appreciation, in certain cases, may lead to a more than proportionate decline in market price. This result occurs because the favourable cost shock for foreign firms makes expansion overly profitable and overcomes the tendency to preserve profits by restricting output. But these results are very specific to market structure and functional form. (In public finance, as Seade (1983) has shown, a similar result occurs: a tax on an oligopolistic industry may raise profits.) Even though this application of industrial organisation ideas to the effect of exchange rate movements does not emerge with firm results, it is quite apparent that it offers a major avenue for theoretical research and for applied studies. Exchange rate changes affect differentially home and foreign firms, to an extent which varies between industries. Focusing on the adjustment to major exchange rate movements may therefore help identify market structures and thus enrich industrial organisation research.

Commodity prices

One of the more interesting price effects of real exchange rate movements between major industrial countries occurs in the area of commodities. Figure 2.8 shows the IMF index of all (non-petroleum) commodities deflated by the US GNP deflator. The point here is to show that the movements of the real US exchange rate could have been an important determinant of the movements in real commodity prices.

It is readily established that a real dollar exchange rate depreciation (in terms of value-added deflators for manufactured goods) will lead to a rise in the dollar price of commodities, and a rise in their real price to US users. Conversely, abroad the real price declines as does the absolute price in foreign currencies.

This result can be seen by looking at the commodity market equilibrium condition where $J(.)$ is the excess demand for any particular commodity, say cotton:

$$J(p/P, p^*/P^*, ..) = 0 \qquad (2.8)$$

where p and p^* are the national currency commodity prices and P and P^* are the deflators. Excess demand is a declining function of the real prices in the two regions. In Figure 2.9 the market equilibrium schedule is shown as downward-sloping. Points above and to the right correspond to an excess supply. Let $R = P/eP^*$ be the real exchange in terms of manufacturing deflators rate, which is shown as the ray OR through the origin. Using the law of one price for commodities, $p = ep^*$, and the definition of the real exchange rate in (2.8) we obtain:

$$J(p/P, Rp/P, ..) = 0 \qquad (2.9)$$

or

$$p/P = \psi(R, ...), \ \psi' < 0 \qquad (2.9a)$$

A real appreciation of the dollar corresponds to a rise in R rotating downward the OR ray. The model predicts a decline in real

36

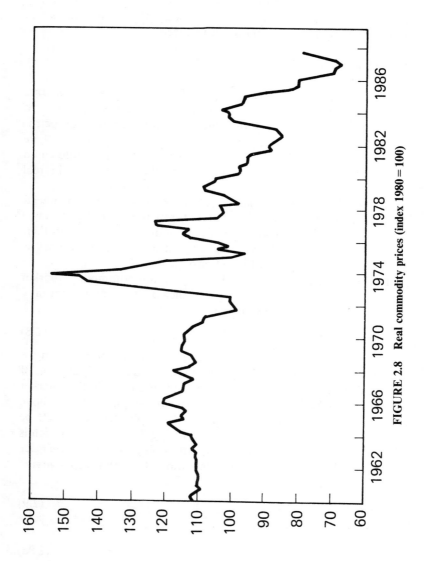

FIGURE 2.8   Real commodity prices (index 1980 = 100)

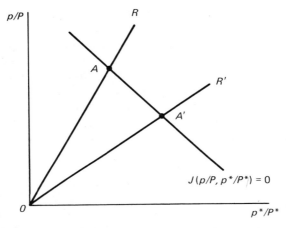

FIGURE 2.9 Real exchange rate movements and the real prices of commodities

commodity prices in the US as a result of dollar appreciation. Equation (2.9a) shows that a real appreciation of the dollar will lead to a decline in the real price of commodities to US users, and a real price increase abroad. Given the US deflator, P, the nominal commodity price quoted in dollars will decline. In this perspective the large dollar appreciation of 1980–85 helps to explain the sharp decline of dollar commodity prices in world trade. In fact, though, the dollar appreciation and world cyclical movements are not enough to explain fully the decline in these prices.

Exchange rates and inflation

The impact of exchange rates on inflation is well-established for any developing country and, indeed, for any industrial country. The experience of the 1980s makes it clear that it even applies to the United States. There are several channels through which exchange rates affect inflation. The least controversial concerns the prices of homogeneous commodities traded in world markets. Changes in commodity prices influence directly the rate of inflation for food and, hence, influence wages. They also affect industrial materials costs in manufacturing. But exchange rates influence inflation also via several other channels.

One channel working in addition to commodity prices involves the prices of traded goods and the prices of those goods directly competing with traded goods. The industrial organisation analysis considered above applies to determine the magnitude and speed of response for prices. The less monopolistic a market, and the lower entry costs, the more pervasive the price effects.

There are also inflation effects via wages. These can arise because wages respond to the competitive pressure of an appreciation or depreciation in affected industries. They also come about as wages respond to changes in the cost of living.

Adding together these various channels yields a pervasive pattern of cost and price effects that are directly or indirectly associated with exchange rate movements. It is interesting to note that in the US the magnitude of these effects is still under discussion. Estimates of the impact of a 10 per cent dollar appreciation on the price level range between one and two percentage points. The reason it is so difficult to establish the size of the impact is apparent. There have been only three recent episodes involving a major change in inflation. Each coincided with an oil price change, a large change in unemployment, and a major change in the dollar. As a result it is nearly impossible to extract a precise estimate for the size of each of these three elements in the inflation process.[14]

THE POLITICAL ECONOMY OF OVERVALUATION

The literature on political business cycles has drawn attention to the systematic pursuit of macroeconomic goals on a timetable dictated by political elections. The exchange rate fits very well into that scheme. It does so via its effects on output and inflation, but also as a highly visible indicator of confidence in policy.

The political business cycle implication of exchange rate movements is strongly enhanced by the relative timing of output and inflation results. A real appreciation quickly raises real wages in terms of tradeables and quickly reduces inflation. The impact on activity is much more gradual. The implication of these timing relationships is that a policy of real appreciation, conducted at the right time, can make an administration look particularly successful at controlling inflation, while at the same time delivering increases in real disposable income.

Diaz-Alejandro (1966) was the first to draw attention to the fact that devaluation in the short term may reduce activity, in addition to having inflationary effects. Only in the long term do output and employment expand. The reason is that in the short run a devaluation cuts real wages in terms of tradeables, thereby reducing purchasing power and the demand for home goods. These income effects dominate in the short run. The neoclassical substitution effects take time to build up. The short-term effects are sufficiently powerful to be highly relevant for political decision-making.

The reverse side of this coin is overvaluation. In the short term it involves less inflation and an increase in real income and hence it wins popularity contests. Only over time, as substitution effects become important and output declines due to the loss of competitiveness, do the costs emerge. No wonder that overvaluation is a very popular policy. It created broad short-term political support in Chile for Pinochet, in Argentina for the policies of Martinez de Hoz, for the Thatcher government in the UK, and in the US for Reaganomics.

Whether the policy-mix was deliberate or not, there is little doubt that for a while the real appreciation was celebrated as a mark of achievement, rather than being seen as a highly destructive misalignment. Only as the deindustrialisation effects became visible, and politically alarming, did the policymakers backtrack and start viewing overvaluation with concern. In the meantime it had bought a strong disinflation.

In the US case the oil-price decline of 1986 came just in time to offset the cut in real income and the inflationary impact implied by dollar depreciation. The timing of appreciation and depreciation thus looked like a masterpiece of political economy. The only cloud remains the very serious blow to industry, the effects of which do appear to persist even after an already significant depreciation. In addition, there is the cost of servicing the accumulated debt.

These episodes of overvaluation raise the interesting issue of why an electorate would favour exchange rate misalignment. Given the welfare costs associated with uneven tax structures over time, and the costs resulting from de- and reindustrialisation, one would expect voters to favour steady policies, rather than large fluctuations in the real exchange rate and the standard of living. Yet the evidence runs counter to this observation, overvaluation being one of the best tricks in the bag.

There is an international dimension to the issue of inflation stabilisation via overvaluation. Under flexible exchange rates a tightening of monetary policy exerts immediate disinflationary effects via currency appreciation. When used by a large country, such a policy amounts to exporting inflation. Investigation of policy coordination and of the game-theoretic implications of these effects has been an important part of international economics research.[15]

A study by Edison and Tryon (1986) makes an important point in this connection. The authors find that in simulations with the Federal Reserve MCM model an asymmetry is apparent. For the US – the large country – foreign repercussions and the particulars of foreign policy responses are relatively unimportant in their impact on inflation and growth. For foreign countries, by contrast, the details of US policy have a major impact. This asymmetry should be expected to influence the nature of Europe's policy responses to US actions.

CURRENT POLICY ISSUES

Extreme exchange rate volatility and persistent misalignments in the \$–DM–yen triangle lend all the support needed to the move for a better international monetary system. Naturally, participants in that debate follow the principle that 'the neighbours' grass is greener': given that we have flexible rates. In this section we consider policy issues that follow from the fact that macroeconomic disturbances exert significant *excess* effects on real exchange rates, trade flows, and on the standard of living. There are broadly two approaches: one is to accept the fact of international capital mobility and use monetary policy coordination to avoid exchange rate effects of disturbances. The other is to domesticate capital flows so as to free policy instruments for domestic macroeconomic objectives.

Target zones and exchange rate orientated monetary policy

A strong case for some form of managed exchange rates is returning in the aftermath of the extreme exchange rate fluctuations. In particular, among those arguing for more fixed exchange rates are Williamson (1983), McKinnon (1984, 1988) and Miller and Williamson (1987).

The McKinnon position for a fixed exchange rate has at its centre the assumption that international portfolio shifts are behind exchange rate movements. In an initial version of this argument shifts between M_1 in one country and another were the source of disturbance. Monetary authorities, being committed to *national* monetary targets, would not accommodate these money demand shifts, and exchange rate volatility was seen as the inevitable consequence. More recent versions of the hypothesis recognise that international portfolio shifts are more likely to take the form of shifts in the demand for interest-bearing assets denominated in different currencies. But the recommendation remains to fix exchange rates, using exchange rate orientated monetary policy to hold rates and accommodate money demand shifts. In other words *unsterilised* intervention is to be used.

This policy recommendation prescribes exactly the wrong kind of intervention. To offset the exchange rate impact of shifts in the demand for bonds the currency denomination of the world bond portfolio should be allowed to change. That means sterilised intervention is the correct answer. In response to exchange rate appreciation the authorities should intervene, leaving money supplies unchanged but increasing the supply of home bonds and reducing the supply of foreign currency bonds, i.e. sterilised intervention. The case for sterilised intervention is well-established, and has been a basic principle of asset market management ever since Poole's (Poole, 1970) authoritative analysis of the choice between interest rate and monetary targets. The remaining problem is to determine whether it is portfolio shifts or shifts in fundamentals that are moving rates.

The case for fixing exchange rates whatever the source of disturbance is advanced by those favouring target zones. Their position is that exchange rates do not necessarily reflect fundamentals but rather irrationality, bandwagons, and eccentricity. The large movements in exchange rates interfere with macroeconomic stability, but they can and should be avoided by a firm commitment to exchange rate targets. On the surface it is difficult to see any difficulty with this prescription, but on further inspection two serious difficulties emerge. First, one might argue (perhaps without much conviction) that it certainly is not an established fact that exchange rates move irrationally and without links to fundamentals. Nor, if they do move in this way, is it clear that they do so more than stock prices or long-

term bond prices. Why single out one price for fixing if it may mean
that the other prices have to move even further away from their
fundamental equilibrium levels?

The second objection concerns a lack of instruments. Governments are unlikely to agree on coordinating their fiscal policies. But
if real exchange rates are to remain fixed in the face of uncoordinated fiscal policy changes, monetary accommodation is required.
In the context of the dollar appreciation of 1980–85, for example,
that would have meant a more aggressively expansionary monetary
policy in the US and hence no disinflation. It is questionable whether
the objective of fixed rates is sufficiently important to warrant bad
monetary policy.[16]

Policies toward excess capital mobility

Most of the shortcomings of our exchange rate experience stem from
excessive, overly volatile capital mobility. The stickiness of wages
relative to exchange rates creates a macroeconomic externality
which possibly justifies closing or restricting some markets. Rather
than fix exchange rates, the alternative is to limit the consequences of
capital mobility.

It can be argued that it is too late for reversing the trend toward
international integration of capital markets and the near-total
deregulation of financial flows. One response to these facts is to
break the tight link between asset-market-determined exchange rates
and the macroeconomy which is bounced around by volatile
exchange rates colliding with sticky wages and prices. An operational way of doing this is to use a managed rate for current account
transactions so as to achieve stability of inflation and of real activity
and at the same time employing a separate or dual exchange rate for
capital account transactions. If capital markets are irrational and
primarily speculative, it might be as well to detach them altogether
from an influence on real activity. Rather than use scarce macropolicy tools to adapt the real sector to the idiosyncrasy of financial
markets, a separate exchange rate would detach the capital account
and deprive it from distorting influences on trade and inflation.

Another possibility is to throw some sand in the wheels, but this is
no longer sufficient. Tobin (1982) has argued that it is desirable to
reduce the overwhelming influence of capital flows over productive
activity and trade. The proposal, known as the 'Tobin tax', involves

a uniform tax on all foreign exchange transactions, to be levied in all countries of the world. The consequence of the tax is to make short-term hot money roundtrips unprofitable. Under this system capital flows would therefore be more nearly geared to considerations of the long-term profitability of investment rather than the overnight speculation which now dominates.

There is no reason to tax only foreign exchange transactions. Since asset market instability suggests short-horizon speculation in all asset markets the response should be a worldwide financial transactions tax. A moderate, worldwide tax on all financial transactions would force asset markets to take a long-run view of the assets they price. As a result there would be more stabilising speculation. The case for such a tax is becoming more and more apparent after the crash of 1987.

There are two major objections to such a tax. One is the resource cost of implementing yet another tax. That cost would have to be held against the costs of large asset price volatility and misalignment and the resulting resource cost. On that basis, presumably it comes out to be small. The second is the argument that with the tax implemented in only one or a few countries business would merely shift to offshore centres. In this context it is worth noting that both Japan and Switzerland do have a financial transaction tax. An appropriate response to the offshore problem is to develop such a tax (rather than exchange rate targets) in cooperation with other countries. In the meantime there is not much cost in moving ahead and designing mechanisms that implement the tax in an efficient, pervasive manner.

3 Exchange Rate Dynamics[1]

MICHAEL BEENSTOCK

INTRODUCTION

The study of exchange rate dynamics is concerned with the movement of exchange rates over time. Exchange rate movements, in common with other economic variables, can be classified into movements induced by temporary equilibrium phenomena, or by permanent equilibrium phenomena. The former tend to be inherently short term while the latter are more concerned with longer-term trends in exchange rate movements. Here, we are primarily concerned with the former although we shall also have something to say about the latter.

Even before the widespread adoption of floating exchange rates in the early 1970s economists had focused their attention on exchange rate dynamics, e.g. Friedman (1953), Kemp (1964) and Britton (1970). However, once currencies were floated, the literature on the subject grew at an exponential rate as economists tried to shed light on the behaviour of exchange rate movements. Here I pick out certain themes that have caught my attention on the subject of exchange rate dynamics and which I hope will enlighten and perhaps even inspire the reader.

My selection will cover the exchange rate dynamics that are incurred by current account and capital account transactions, by speculation and rational expectations, and by wealth effects that are generated in the balance of payments. In doing so I will address all the main hypotheses including Purchasing Power Parity (PPP), Portfolio Theories and Asset Theories. I will argue that all of these models are restrictive and are special cases of a general model. The latter provides the basis of what might be called a 'General Theory of Exchange Rate Dynamics'.

The theory of exchange rate dynamics has developed within two distinct intellectual traditions which might usefully be summarised as the Marshallian and Walrasian traditions respectively. The former has dealt with exchange rate dynamics within a partial equilibrium framework, i.e. markets ancillary to the foreign exchange market (e.g. labour, money, goods, capital) have been assumed given, and spillover effects between these markets ignored. The latter, by contrast, has been concerned with exchange rate dynamics within a general equilibrium setting, i.e. where the inter-dependence between the foreign exchange market and other markets is explicitly taken into consideration.

On the whole, Walrasian models have tended to cut corners in order to arrive at models that are simple enough to be analytically tractable. This not only applies to the foreign exchange market but also to the specification of other markets that form part of the general equilibrium system. In the case of the foreign exchange market, corner-cutting has largely consisted of the assumption of interest parity and abstraction from considerations of exchange rate risk that reflects man's general inability to forecast exchange rate movements accurately. This in turn has meant that the exchange rate is dominated by capital account activity and that the current account has no short-term influence on the exchange rate. Therefore, part of my purpose here is to restore a central role to exchange rate risk, but since this is not an inconsiderable task, the arguments below are developed within the Marshallian tradition. A plausible account of the dynamics of the foreign exchange market is a consuming enough task in its own right without having to consider the dynamics of other markets as well.

The layout of the paper is as follows. In the next section the 'Dornbusch Model' is presented and critically appraised. This will be the only Walrasian element of the paper, although see Bhandari (1982) for numerous modifications to the basic model. It is concluded that the Walrasian tradition, for the present, is unlikely to serve as a fruitful basis for exchange rate dynamics since until the dynamics of labour, product, capital, money and other markets have been specified little can be concluded about the dynamics of exchange rates.

The third section introduces the current account as a factor in exchange rate dynamics and addresses problems associated with the so-called J-curve. The section after this introduces the capital account as a factor in exchange rate dynamics and the role of expectations of exchange rate movements. These sections set the scene for a section on the dynamic implications if the current account and the capital account are integrated into what might be called a general (Marshallian) theory of exchange rate dynamics. This also provides an analytical framework for explaining the role of exchange rate intervention on exchange rate dynamics as well as shocks to the current and capital accounts of the balance of payments. The next section concludes with some policy observations.

The analytical tools of the trade consist of linear stochastic difference equations whose manipulation is usefully described by e.g. Sargent (1979, Chs 9 and 11). In the section on exchange rate dynamics, I have tried to make a virtue out of a necessity by taking the opportunity of demonstrating how these techniques may be applied in the context of rational expectations under conditions of imperfect foresight.

THE DORNBUSCH 'OVERSHOOTING' MODEL

The theory of exchange rate dynamics first proposed by Dornbusch (1976) has become the stock-in-trade not only for a generation of textbook-writers but also for theoreticians, e.g. Buiter and Miller (1981). The so-called 'overshooting' model is premised on the following basic relationships.

$$E(\dot{S}/S) + r = r* \tag{3.1}$$

$$M_d/P = F_1 (Y^+, \bar{r}) \tag{3.2}$$

$$Y^d = F_2 (S\bar{P}/\bar{P}_*, \bar{r}) \tag{3.3}$$

$$\dot{P}/P = F_3 (Y_d - Y_m) \tag{3.4}$$

$$M_d = M_s \tag{3.5}$$

where

S = exchange rate (foreign currency per unit of domestic currency)

r = domestic rate of interest
r^* = overseas rate of interest
P = domestic price level
M = quantity of money
P^* = overseas price level
Y^d = aggregate demand
Y^m = aggregate supply
$E(\ )$ = expected value of $(\ )$

Since the model is so well known only the minimum of exposition is provided here. The first equation states that the return on domestic assets is equal to the return on overseas assets after allowing for the expected rate of change in the exchange rate. Equation (3.2) is the Keynesian demand for money function while equation (3.3) is an aggregate demand schedule in which demand varies inversely with domestic relative prices and the rate of interest. The signs of partial derivatives are indicated over the variables to which they refer. Equation (3.4) hypothesizes that inflation depends on the pressure of excess demand while equation (3.5) is the familiar equilibrium condition in the money market.

Consider what happens in this model when the quantity of money is permanently reduced to say 10 per cent. In the long run the price level will fall by 10 per cent and the exchange rate will rise by 10 per cent on account of PPP. Equations (3.5) and (3.2) imply that interest rates will rise by e.g. 2 percentage points p.a. But equation (3.1) implies that this will trigger an expected rate of depreciation of 2 per cent p.a. If the exchange rate is expected to be 10 per cent higher than it originally was, the initial jump in the exchange rate must have been 12 per cent. So the exchange rate must overshoot its long-run value.

Had the price-level instantaneously fallen by 10 per cent, the interest rate would not have risen in the first place since the demand for money would also have fallen by 10 per cent. Then none of this would have happened. But equation (3.4) implies that prices are sticky so the overshooting is unavoidable.

This characteristic depends crucially on equations (3.1) and (3.4) but together they imply that exchange rates react more quickly than prices to monetary disturbances. The specification of equation (3.4) can be criticised however. The New Classical Macroeconomics, e.g. Minford and Peel (1983), challenges both the theoretical and empirical validity of equation (3.4) whose disequilibrium characteristics are inconsistent with optimising behaviour.

The specification of equation (3.1) implies either that investors are risk neutral or that exchange risk does not exist. In the general case when investors are risk-averse and when they perceive exchange rate risk (i.e. they know that they cannot forecast currency movements with complete accuracy) equation (3.1) becomes

$$E(\dot{S}/S) = \lambda_0 + \lambda_1 \ (r* - r)$$

where λ_0 and λ_1 are coefficients that reflect currency risk premiums. Dornbusch assumes $\lambda_1 = 1$. At the other extreme of $\lambda_1 = 0$ (because very high currency risk implies zero asset substitution), the exchange rate will not be affected by interest rates. This demonstrates the obvious point that 'overshooting' depends on the degree of international asset substitution and in this context Niehans (1977) has demonstrated that the exchange rate is as likely to 'undershoot' as it is to 'overshoot'.

In short, the 'overshooting' model may be a useful pedagogic tool but its relevance to conditions in which currency risk is not zero and in which international assets are imperfect substitutes for each other must be questionable (see e.g. Minford (1978) and Beenstock (1978) for empirical estimates for international currency substitution).

THE CURRENT ACCOUNT AND THE J-CURVE

A complete account of exchange rate dynamics requires the simultaneous analysis of current and capital account influences on the exchange rate. The balance of payments identity is

$$CA + CAP \equiv Z \tag{3.6}$$

where

    CA   = current account balance
    CAP = capital account balance
    Z   = central bank purchases of foreign exchange.

Equation (3.6) may be regarded as a market-clearing condition in the foreign exchange market since it implies that the net excess demand/supply for foreign exchange is always zero. When the exchange rate is fixed the central bank is required to vary Z in order to support the exchange rate. When $Z=0$ the exchange rate is perfectly flexible, and in each time period the exchange rate (and other variables) varies to satisfy (3.6) and balance the supply and demand for foreign exchange. Incipient balance of payment shocks $(CA + CAP < 0)$ generates excess demands for foreign exchange which induce lower exchange rates.

To isolate the implications of the current account for exchange rate dynamics we assume that there are no capital flows and that there is no foreign exchange intervention, i.e. $CAP = Z = 0$. Equation (3.6) therefore implies that the current account must balance, i.e. $CA = 0$.

In the present context Britton (1970) demonstrated that exchange rate dynamics will be induced if exports and imports do not respond instantaneously to changes in international price competitiveness. Indeed (see e.g. Winters (1981)), the empirical evidence suggests that there are substantial lags in these relationships in which case these dynamic considerations are likely to be of practical importance. These lags imply the existence of the so-called 'J-curve' which under most relevant circumstances induces dynamic instability.

The J-curve phenomenon may be stated as follows. Suppose that the current account is in an incipient deficit so that the exchange rate falls by say 1 per cent. At that instant export volumes and import volumes do not change because of adjustment lags. However, the lower exchange rate will raise the value of imports by 1 per cent while the volume of exports does not change. Therefore the current account will deteriorate even further, resulting in further destabilising falls in the exchange rate, and so on. A once-and-for-all fall in the exchange rate will cause the current account to worsen in the short run until higher export volumes and lower imports eventually generate the conventional favourable current account response, assuming that the Marshall–Lerner conditions hold. Thus the dynamic pattern of the current account traces out a J-curve.

To elaborate these dynamics we introduce the following notation and simple model of the current account. The current account balance may be written as

$$CA = XP_X - MP_m/S = 0 \qquad (3.7)$$

where

X = volume of exports
M = volume of imports

P_X = price of exports (home currency)
P_M = price of imports (foreign currency)
S = exchange rate (foreign currency per unit of domestic currency).

Using lower-case letters as logarithms we may rewrite equation (3.1) as

$$x + p_X = m + p_m - s \tag{3.8}$$

We assume, for simplicity, that export and import prices are given and that exports and imports respond with a first-order adjustment lag to relative prices:

$$x = -\frac{\lambda_1}{D + \lambda_1} \varepsilon_1 \ (p_x + s - p_x*) \tag{3.9}$$

$$m = -\frac{\lambda_2}{D + \lambda_2} \varepsilon_2 \ (p_m - s - p) \tag{3.10}$$

where

P = domestic price level
$P*$ = price of competitor's exports (foreign currency)
D = d/t (differential operator).

ε_1 is the long-run price elasticity of demand for exports and ε_2 the corresponding elasticity of demand for imports. λ_1 and λ_2 are exponential lag parameters. Fulfilment of the Marshall–Lerner conditions implies $\varepsilon_1 + \varepsilon_2 > 1$.

If the exchange rate is flexible it must move over time to balance the current account. Thus the balance of payments identity given in equation (3.8) acts as a market-clearing condition in the foreign exchange market. Incipient current account deficits depress the exchange rate and vice-versa. To determine the dynamic implications for the exchange rate we may substitute equations (3.9) and (3.10) into (3.8) and solve the second-order differential equation that is obtained. We do so under the assumption that P_X and P are perfectly correlated, that P_m and $P*_X$ are similarly related and that P and $P*_M$ are constants. The differential equation of the system is

$$(-D^2 + \alpha_1 D + \alpha_0)S = -\alpha_0 \ (P - P*_X)$$

where

$$\alpha_1 = \lambda_1 (\varepsilon_1 - 1) + \lambda_2 (\varepsilon_2 - 1) \geqslant 0$$

$$\alpha_0 = \lambda_1 \lambda_2 (\varepsilon_2 + \varepsilon_1 - 1) > 0$$

The general solution that describes the dynamic path of the exchange rate is

$$S(t) = A_1 e^{r_1 t} + A_2 e^{r_2 t} + p*_x - p$$

where A_1 and A_2 are arbitrary constants and r_1 and r_2 are the roots of the system

$$r_1 = [-\alpha_1 \pm \sqrt{\alpha_1^2 - 4\alpha_0}]/2$$

Necessary and sufficient conditions for stability are that both α_1 and α_0 be negative. However, the Marshall–Lerner conditions that $\alpha_0 > 0$ rule this out. The J-curve phenomenon sends the exchange rate into a nose-dive from which it never recovers. For example, a fall in the exchange rate worsens the current account in the short run which in turn causes the exchange rate to fall further. Although export volumes rise continuously and import volumes fall continuously, import values grow faster than export values and thus the exchange rate instability persists.

Later in our general model, we show how this instability may be neutralised by speculative behaviour that reflects 'rational expectations'. Here we discuss other possibilities that may offset the destabilising influences of the J-curve.

The main candidate has been Britton's (1970) proposal that export prices are unlikely to remain constant. He endogenised them as follows:

$$P_X + S = \frac{\varphi \delta S}{D + \varphi}$$

This hypothesis states that exporters set their prices in terms of foreign currency rather than domestic currency, so that revaluations only gradually raise export prices when measured in international prices. It also implies that in the first instance devaluations trigger proportionate increases in export prices when measured in domestic currency. Thereafter P_X falls and in this way exports become more competitive. Britton shows that such export pricing behaviour may neutralise the instability generated by the J-curve. However, it does so by assuming away the existence of the J-curve since P_x varies inversely with the exchange rate in the first instance.

This export pricing hypothesis is, however, unreasonable since what we know about export prices suggests quite a different dynamic specification. At the moment of devaluation P_x does alter so that exports become more competitive to the full extent of the devaluation. Thereafter, the competitive edge is eroded so that the benefits of the devaluation are lost over time. This suggests that a more realistic specification for export price dynamics is

$$P_x = \frac{-\varphi\delta S}{D+\varphi}$$

which implies once more that the J-curve necessarily destabilises the exchange rate.

THE CAPITAL ACCOUNT AND WEALTH

In the previous section our intention was to demonstrate that exchange rate dynamics may be generated by current account behaviour. In this section we show how the capital account of the balance of payments (CAP in equation (3.6)) can induce exchange rate dynamics in its own right. We present the analysis in terms of the 'Portfolio Approach' proposed for example by Branson (1980); whereas the 'Asset Theory' (represented in equation 3.1) abstracts from exchange risk, the 'Portfolio Approach' takes explicit account of it.

We denote by W_t the net stock of domestic assets held by the overseas sector at the end of period t. Thus net capital flows during period t are defined as

$$CAP_t = W_t - W_{t-1}$$

We assume that the portfolio demand function for these assets is given by

$$W_t = \alpha \ (r_t - r*_t + E_t \ (S_{t+1}) - S_t) \tag{3.11}$$

where $E_t \ (S_{t+1})$ denotes the expectation, as of the end of time t, of the exchange rate one period hence. Equation (3.11) states that the overseas sector will only agree to hold more domestic securities in its portfolio provided that the expected return on the securities is higher relative to the return on competing securities abroad ($r*$). If domestic interest rates (r) are given, equation (3.11) implies that as foreign-owned domestic securities increase, the expected rate of exchange rate appreciation must rise. For given expectations this implies that the current exchange rate must fall.

Equation (3.6) implies that current account deficits will raise W via the capital account and it is in this way that a current account deficit will weaken the exchange rate. This is no more than a restatement of the 'Portfolio Approach', which implies that the world is only prepared to invest more in domestic currency if it is induced to do so by higher-risk premiums on these assets.

The current account is hypothesised here to depend upon wealth-effects (we reinstate price-effects later); increased wealth induces expenditure increases which adversely affect the current account. Thus we may write

$$CA_t = \beta_0 - \beta_1 \, W_{t-1} \qquad (3.12)$$

as the relationship between the current account and wealth.

Equations (3.11) and (3.12) generate exchange rate dynamics via the interplay between the current and capital accounts of the balance of payments. To explore them we assume that interest rates, etc. are given and that only the exchange rate and balance of payments variables vary. We also assume that exchange rate expectations are formed rationally, hence $E_t(S_{t+1})$ is equal to the solution of the model. To aid exposition we assume perfect foresight, although this contradicts the assumptions about risk that are implicit in the behaviour of α. If foresight is perfect there can be no exchange rate risk and so $\alpha = \infty$ as in the 'Asset Theory'.

Since

$$CAP_t = -CA_t = W_t - W_{t-1}$$

we may write equations (3.11) and (3.12) as:

$$\begin{bmatrix} 1-(\beta_1+1)L & 0 \\ & \alpha(1-L^{-1}) \end{bmatrix} \begin{bmatrix} W_t \\ S_t \end{bmatrix} = \begin{bmatrix} \beta_0 \\ \alpha \, (r_t\text{-}r*_t) \end{bmatrix}$$

where L is a lag operator.

Solving this system for the exchange rate generates the following second-order difference equation:

$$-\alpha S_{t+1} + \alpha(2+\beta_1)S_t - \alpha(1+\beta_1)S_{t-1} = -\alpha\beta_1(r-r*)_t + \beta_0$$

The auxiliary equation of this difference equation is

$$\lambda^2 - (2 + \beta_1)\lambda + (1 + \beta_1) = 0$$

which factorises to generate roots λ_1 and λ_2. The stability conditions, see Samuelson (1966, p. 436), are

(a) $1 - 2 - \beta_1 + 1 + \beta_1 > 0$

(b) $1 - 1 - \beta_1 > 0$

(c) $1 + 2 + \beta_1 + 1 + \beta_1 > 0$

Although condition (c) must hold conditions (a) and (b) cannot hold since in equation (3.12) β_1 is positive. Therefore, as it stands, the system is unstable. However, this instability is common to all rational expectation models and does not form part of the solution of the model, see e.g. Beenstock (1978, Ch. 4). It is well known that latent speculative bubbles[2] are inherent in all rational expectation models, but because they are irrational they must be excluded, by assumption, from the model solution. Hence one of the roots will exceed unity (the unstable root) while the other will be less than unity. If the former is say λ_1, we set its arbitrary constant to zero and the difference equation becomes

$$S_t - \lambda_1 S_{t-1} = \beta_1 (r - r*)_t + \beta_0/\alpha$$

If interest rates are constant the general solution for the exchange rate is

$$S_t = A\lambda_1{}^t + (\beta_1(r - r*) + \beta_0)/(1 - \lambda_1)\alpha \tag{3.13}$$

where A is an arbitrary constant. When domestic and world interest rates are equal (in the absence of inflation) equation (3.13) states that in the long run the exchange rate tends to $\beta_0/(1 - \lambda_1)\alpha_1$, i.e. it reflects trends in the current account as suggested earlier.

A GENERAL MODEL OF EXCHANGE RATE DYNAMICS

In this section we integrate the current account and capital account implications for exchange rate dynamics. In doing so we allow for J-curves, wealth effects on the current account and portfolio-balance effects. Therefore the model is perfectly general in that it allows for stock (capital account) and flow (current account) equilibria in the foreign exchange market. In doing so we distinguish between temporary equilibria and permanent equilibria in which the former are dominated by capital account transactions and associated asset effects while the latter are dominated by current account considerations and associated PPP effects. This model therefore accords with the idea that PPP does not apply in the short run but applies instead in the long run.

As in previous sections we continue in the Marshallian tradition of investigating exchange rate dynamics in a partial equilibrium setting. Hence, we ignore problems associated with the behaviour of prices, interest rates, etc., and the spillover effects between foreign exchange, capital and product markets. A general equilibrium analysis would carry us too far afield. As will become apparent, Marshallian exchange rate dynamics are sufficiently absorbing in their own right.

Following previous notation and specifications our model is as follows:

$$CA_t = -\beta W_{t-1} + \tau_0 S_t - \tau_1 S_{t-1} + u_t \tag{3.14}$$

$$W_t = \alpha(E_t(S_{t+1}) - S_t) + v_t \tag{3.15}$$

$$Z_t = CA_t + W_t - W_{t-1} \tag{3.16}$$

Equation (3.14) allows for the wealth effects on the current account that were introduced in equation (3.12) and it allows for the effects of the exchange rate that we introduced in Section 3. The inclusion of terms in S_t and S_{t-1} is intended to capture simple J-curve effects; if $\tau_0 > 0$ the impact effect of the exchange rate on the current account is perverse. If $\tau_1 > \tau_0$, the Marshall–Lerner conditions are fulfilled and the current account eventually responds appropriately to the exchange rate. The term u_t represents other time-dependent forces (e.g. the volume of world trade) that affect the current account.

Equation (3.15) is based on (3.11), except that we assume for simplicity of exposition that $r = r^*$ and v_t represents other time-dependent factors that affect the net international portfolio position. Finally, equation (3.16) is based on (3.6) where Z_t may be regarded as central bank intervention in the foreign exchange market. This forms the basis of the model proposed by Beenstock (1978) and Minford (1978) where α varies inversely with the degree of risk aversion and perceptions of exchange rate risk defined as $E_t(S_{t+1} - E_t(S_{t+1}))^2$. When exchange risk is zero and/or when risk aversion is zero (risk neutrality) α is infinite, capital flows are perfectly elastic and the assumption of the Dornbusch Model are fulfilled. However, the empirical evidence, for instance Beenstock et al. (1986), suggests that exchange risk as measured by the variance of exchange rate forecast errors tends to be substantial, in which case the standard assumption must be that α is finite.

To explore the implications of this general model for exchange rate dynamics the equations are solved for the exchange rate in terms of the exogenous variables:

$$\alpha E_t(S_{t+1}) + (\tau_0 - \alpha)S_t - (1 + \beta)\alpha E_{t-1}(S_t) + ((1 + \beta)\alpha - \tau_1)S_{t-1} = x_t \tag{3.17}$$

where

$$x_t = Z_t + (1 + \beta)v_{t-1} - v_t - u_t$$

Equation (3.17) is a first-order difference equation in the exchange rate (since it contains terms in S_t and S_{t-1}) which depends on the exogenous variables and expectations of the exchange rate ($E_t(S_{t+1})$ and $E_{t-1}(S_t)$). If expectations are rational they must be consistent with the structure of the model. The solution procedure follows that of Sargent (1979, especially Ch. 9 and pp. 268–71). This procedure involves the application of the 'law of iterated expectations', namely that $E_{t-1}(E_t(S_{t+1}) = E_{t-1}(S_{t+1})$, to equation (3.17), and the lagging of the resulting expression by one period. The latter is a second-order difference equation in the expected exchange rate with roots λ_1 and λ_2. One of these roots, say λ_1, is less than unity while the other, λ_2, is greater than unity. The stable root based on λ_1 is solved backwards and the unstable root based on λ_2 is solved forward in order to derive the saddle-path equilibrium. This implies that the current exchange rate depends on its own past as well as expectations and their revisions of the future values of the exogenous variables. The result we obtain is

$$S_t = \lambda_1 S_{t-1} + \delta \sum_{i=0}^{\infty} (\frac{1}{\lambda_2})2(E_t(X_{t+1}) - \frac{1+\beta}{\lambda_2}E_{t-1}(x_{t+1})) \tag{3.18}$$

where

$$\delta = 1/(\alpha(\lambda_1 - 1) + \tau_0)$$

Equation (3.18) provides a complete Marshallian account of

exchange rate dynamics. It states that the current exchange rate depends on the exchange rate in the previous period, via λ_1 which reflects all the parameters in the model, i.e. equations (3.14–3.16). Since $\lambda_1 < 1$, the exchange rate tends to be a first-order autoregressive process (under the present very simple specification). It also states that the evolution of the exchange rate depends on expectations of the exogenous variables and revisions to these expectations. However, expectations that refer to more distant forecast horizons have a smaller effect on the exchange rate than expectations that apply to less remote forecast horizons.

The dynamics of the model may be analysed under perfect and imperfect foresight assumptions. In the former case $E_{t-1}(\lambda_{t+1}) = E_t(x_{t+2}) = x_{t+2}$, in which case equation (3.19) becomes

$$S_t = \lambda_1 S_{t-1} + \frac{\delta(\lambda_2 - \beta - 1)}{\lambda_2} \sum_{i=0}^{\infty} (\frac{1}{\lambda_2})^2 x_{t+1} \qquad (3.19)$$

Like equation (3.18), equation (3.19) describes the sequence of temporary equilibria in the foreign exchange market. The long run or stationary state equilibrium (i.e. when $S_t = S_{t-1}$ and $x_t = x_{t-1}$) may be calculated from (3.19) as

$$S_* = \frac{\delta(\lambda_2 - \beta - 1)}{(\lambda_{2-1})(1 - \lambda_1)} x_* \qquad (3.20)$$

The reader may verify numerically that the coefficient of x_* is negative in which case e.g. permanent benign shocks to the current account (i.e. U_t in equation 3.14) strengthen the exchange rate in the long run. The opposite happens if Z increases permanently, but this can be ruled out on practical grounds since permanent one-way official intervention in the foreign exchange market is not a feasible policy option. However, in principle an endless supply of reserves would enable the Central Bank to raise the long-run exchange rate by ensuring the Z remained negative.

Just as benign current account shocks will strengthen the long-run exchange rate (e.g. North Sea oil in the case of the UK) so benign capital account shocks that are permanent will strengthen the long run exchange rate. In the model, such shocks are represented by ▲ v. Thus ▲ $v > 0$ implies a permanent inflow of capital (e.g. US foreign borrowing in the early 1980s which strengthened the dollar), which raises the exchange rate for as long as it is expected to last. An increase in β will tend to weaken the exchange rate in the long run, because it implies a secular deterioration in the current account via adverse wealth effects.

To illustrate the dynamic implications of the model we make the following numerical assumptions about its parameters:

$$\lambda_1 = 0.7, \ \lambda_2 = 1.8, \ \delta = -1, \ \beta = 0.2$$

These assumptions imply that the coefficient of $x*$ in (3.20) is -2.5, hence a permanent unit increase in x will lower the exchange rate by 2.5 units in the long run. Given the definition of x above in equation (3.15) the increase in x can be interpreted as a foreign exchange sale by the central bank ($Z_1 = -1$). If the model were loglinear this response would have the dimension of an elasticity.

Our exercise begins in time $t = 0$ in a state of long-run equilibrium, i.e. where all expectations are fulfilled, the exogenous variables are constant and the exchange rate is constant too at an arbitrary index value of zero. Suppose that during $t = 1$ there is an unanticipated unit fall in x that is temporary, i.e. for $t > 1$ $x_t = 0$ once more. This occurs for instance (given equation 3.15) if there is a favourable shock to the current account ($u_t = 1$). Shocks to the capital account (see below) are more complicated because x_t depends on v_{t-1} as well as v_t.

The dynamic path for the exchange rate that is implied by equation (3.18) is shown as case A in Table 3.1. The exchange rate rises by one unit (percent in a loglinear model) after which it falls geometrically back to its initial value. In case B the fall in x is anticipated one period before it occurs (during $t = 2$) so that the exchange rate jumps by 0.55 in advance of the shock itself. The exchange rate peaks at 0.72 when the shock occurs, after which it falls geometrically back to its initial value. In simulation C we assume that the shock is anticipated two periods in advance, i.e. it occurs during $t = 3$ and the exchange rate jumps to 0.31 two periods ahead of the event itself. Notice that the exchange rate tends to peak when the shock itself occurs, but the scale of the peak diminishes the longer the period of anticipation.

In simulation D, expectations are asymmetric in the sense that the fall in x is anticipated but agents do not expect the reverse to occur during period 3 but during period 4. Hence, they correctly anticipate the fall in x but they incorrectly assess the timing of its reversal. This causes the exchange rate to jump initially by more than in case B,

TABLE 3.1   Illustrative exchange rate dynamic ($S_0 = 0$)

Time/case	A	B	C	D	E	F	G
1	1*	0.55	0.31	0.86	0.36*	0.44*	0.25
2	0.7	0.72*	0.4	1.12*	−0.16	−0.02	0.31*
3	0.49	0.51	0.62*	0.12	−0.11	−0.01	−0.11
4	0.34	0.35	0.43	0.08	−0.08	−0.01	−0.08
5	0.24	0.25	0.3	0.06	−0.06	−0.01	−0.05
6	0.17	0.18	0.21	0.04	−0.04	−0.01	−0.04
	—	—	—	—	—	—	—
	—	—	—	—	—	—	—
	—	—	—	—	—	—	—
∞	0	0	0	0	0	0	0

A   Unanticipated fall in x
B   Anticipated fall in x
C   As B but with the fall in x unanticipated two periods in advance.
D   As B but with reversal in x unanticipated
E   Unanticipated increase in v
F   Unanticipated exchange rate intervention (Z, see p. 61)
G   Anticipated exchange rate intervention (Z, see p. 61)
*   Period in which the shock occurs.

because agents expect the fall in x to last into period 3. When it does not, the revision to expectations are all the more severe and the exchange rate falls back sharply in period 3 when they discover their mistake.

Finally, in case E, we consider the effects of shocks to x that occur in the capital account of the balance of payments, i.e. when there is a temporary increase in v by one unit. Thus $x_0 = 0$, $x_1 = -1$, $x_2 = 1.2$, $x_3 = 0$ etc., in which case there is an inflow in period 1 followed by an enlarged outflow in period 2. This has the effect of boosting the exchange rate in period 1 and weakening it in period 2 as indicated in Table 3.1.

Changing the assumptions of the parameter values obviously changes the value of λ_1, λ_2, δ and β and naturally alters the dynamics of the model. Space prevents a complete sensitivity analysis but certain special cases are worth noting. Consider what happens when $\beta = \tau_1 = 0$ and $\alpha = \infty$, i.e. there are no wealth effects on the current account, the current account has no J-curve and capital flows are infinitely elastic (implying that exchange risk is zero). The polynomial in the lag operator L becomes

$$1-2L + L^2 = (1-L)^2$$

in which case the roots λ_1 and λ_2 converge on unity. This implies that $S_t = S_{t-1}$ which in turn implies that the exchange rate has no dynamics at all, i.e. the long-run and short-run equilibria are identical. But this implies that the exchange rate jumps from one long-run equilibrium to the next without any lags; there is no adjustment path. This is the property of the 'Dornbusch Model' which contributes to the 'overshooting' phenomenon. More generally, λ_1 is less than unity and the exchange rate does not jump from one equilibrium to the next. Instead it presents an autoregressive adjustment path. As λ_1 approaches zero, the adjustment will be slow, in which case 'undershooting' is just as likely as 'overshooting'.

It is also worth noting that even if the J-curve happens to be destabilising, as discussed in Section 3, the exchange rate may still be dynamically stable if expectations are rational, as noted by e.g. Levin (1985). Indeed, left to itself, the J-curve would be unambiguously destabilising in our present model since the current account becomes

$$\tau_0 S_t - \tau_1 S_{t-1} = u_t$$

in which case the root is $\lambda = \tau_1/\tau_0$. The J-curve implies that τ_1 and τ_0 are both positive while the Marshall–Lerner conditions imply that $\tau_1 > \tau_0$, i.e. devaluations strengthen the current account. However, the latter implies that $\lambda > 1$, in which case, as noted in Section 3, the exchange rate is inherently unstable. But the J-curve is not left to itself, the dynamics of the foreign exchange market are also governed by expectations and the capital account. Rational expectations implies that agents understand the dynamics of the J-curve and allow for it in their speculative behaviour. They know that the current account gets worse before it gets better. It is this knowledge that eliminates the potentially destabilising influence of the J-curve.

EXCHANGE RATE POLICY

In discussing the implications of our analysis for the design of exchange rate policy it is easier to be negative rather than positive. The specific implication is that the 'overshooting model' is unlikely to provide a basis for the design of exchange rate policy, although as a pedagogic device it may be invaluable. More generally it will be impossible to proffer policy advice until we have reliable, empirically-estimated models of exchange rate behaviour. This seems a long way off.

At a less ambitious level it may be worth drawing attention to the implications of the model described in the previous section for exchange rate policy. (This issue has been discussed in greater detail by Beenstock 1983).

If the objective of exchange rate policy is to insulate the exchange rate against random shocks then it follows from equation (3.17) that the path of exchange rate intervention must be

$$Z_t = v_t + u_t - (1 + \beta)v_{t-1} \tag{3.21}$$

This path guarantees that $x_t = 0$ and so complete stabilisation is achieved. If, however, v and u are not stationary random variables (they are trended), or their means change permanently (i.e. the long-run equilibrium exchange rate changes) the implied path for intervention will not be feasible. Nevertheless, if the authorities can isolate the stationary components of u and v, they will be able to reduce the variance of the exchange rate.

Exchange rate intervention cannot be one-way for very long. Indeed it is argued that exchange rate intervention is designed to 'smooth' the market by buying foreign exchange when it is cheap, and selling it when it is expensive. Successful smoothing should therefore be profitable to central banks. However, Taylor (1982) claims that central banks' spot exchange rate intervention policies are typically unprofitable while Beenstock and Dadashi (1986) conclude that the Bank of Canada did not profit from its forward market intervention. This suggests that in practice central banks do not get things right and that, although in theory intervention can be stabilising, in practice it is not.

In this context we may consider what happens according to equation (3.18) when exchange rate intervention occurs. Because the central bank balances its book over time we assume that $Z_1 = -1$ and $Z_2 = 1$, i.e. it supports the exchange rate in period $t = 1$. In case F on Table 3.1 this policy is unanticipated, while in case G it is anticipated. However, even in case F, Z_2 is anticipated once the cat has been let out of the bag in $t = 1$. In case F the exchange rate rises by 0.44 in the first period. However, had agents not anticipated the unwinding of the central bank's position the increase would have been 1.0. Thus the influence of rational expectations considerably moderates the efficacy of the policy. By the time the position is unwound in period 2 the net effect on the exchange rate is virtually zero. The moderation effect varies inversely with λ_2. If for example $\lambda_2 = 1.1$ instead of 1.8 as assumed the impact effect in column F would have been only 0.09.

Column G assumes that agents anticipated the exchange rate intervention policy. Here the efficacy of exchange rate policy is further reduced so that when the shock occurs the exchange rate only rises to 0.31 instead of 0.44.

CONCLUSIONS

The majority of textbooks on open economy macroeconomics analyse exchange rate dynamics in a Walrasian, general equilibrium setting. The most popular of such models is the 'overshooting model' which, however, abstracts from currency risk. To take account of the latter, exchange rate dynamics were explored within a Marshallian, partial equilibrium setting and even though the proposed model was very simple, a rich variety of dynamics were implied by the current account, the capital account, J-curves, foreign exchange intervention and suchlike.

Clearly, the real world is a general equilibrium (or disequilibrium) phenomenon and so our Marshallian proposals cannot provide a complete theoretical account of exchange rate dynamics. Perhaps future theoretical efforts might concentrate on integrating it into the broader macroeconomic framework to which it naturally relates. But hopefully it will constitute a more reliable basis for such endeavours than the ubiquitous risk-neutrality assumption that pervades the textbooks.

The shortcomings of the theory of exchange rate dynamics have to be judged in reference to the absence of sound empirical work on the subject. To proffer policy advice it is necessary to have good theory and supporting empirical work. At present, we seem far removed from such a happy state, albeit in an area which is fraught with difficulty.

4 Empirical Studies of Exchange Rate Determination

RONALD MacDONALD

INTRODUCTION

In contrast to the predictions of the early proponents of flexible exchange rates,[1] the actual experience with floating exchange rates has been characterised by large fluctuations of both nominal and real exchange rates. The main task of the theoretical literature on exchange rate determination has been to determine the causes of such volatility in terms of the economic fundamentals. The main task, in turn, of the empirical research on exchange rate determination has been to test whether the theoretical literature is valid. It would be wrong, however, to give the impression that theory has always outpaced the empirical evidence. Rather, the two have had something of a symbiotic relationship in that the jettisoning of a favourite theory by the evidence has led to the formulation, development and refinement of alternative theories to be tested. Running alongside the research using economic fundamentals has been a somewhat separate research strategy to determine the efficiency of foreign exchange markets and, in particular, the efficiency of the forward market for foreign exchange.

The purpose of this paper is to try to explain some of the empirical regularities of exchange rates from the recent float using the exchange rate models that have been developed since 1973. In the next section we outline some of the salient empirical regularities of exchange rates since 1973. In the third section we briefly outline the theoretical development of models of exchange rate determination. Then we survey some of the reduced form evidence on exchange rate models in order to see if they explain the trend movement in exchange rates over time and also whether they help to explain the volatility of exchange rates. In the next section the unpredictable nature of exchange rate movements is considered by discussing the usefulness of 'news' in explaining unexpected exchange rate movements. The empirical evidence on the efficiency of foreign exchange markets and the empirical evidence on purchasing power parity is considered in the final two sections.

THE BEHAVIOUR OF EXCHANGE RATES

Consider, first, the issue of exchange rate volatility. In Table 4.1 we present some minimum and maximum monthly percentage changes for a number of prominent bilateral exchange rates. The striking features are the magnitude of the volatility and the fact that volatility has not diminished as the experience with floating has increased. Such volatility is also much greater than for the 1960s period, as is evidenced by the fact that the average monthly change for the seven major currencies increased from 0.20 per cent in 1961–70 to 1.18 per cent in 1974–83 (see Llewellyn and Sutherland (1987)). Nominal effective exchange rates[2] have in general also been more volatile for the 1970s and 1980s relative to the 1950s and 1960s (the average for seven major currencies increased from 0.25 for the period 1963–70 to 1.15 per cent for the period 1974–83), although the volatility for the former period is of a lesser magnitude relative to the comparable bilateral volatility.

But is this volatility meaningful? Clearly it can only be meaningful if it is related to the fundamental factors which are regarded as determining exchange rates. That is, is exchange rate volatility *excessive* or, to put it slightly differently, do exchange rates have a tendency to overshoot the fundamental factors that determine exchange rates? The answer to this question is important since if exchange rates are continually overshooting, the monetary authorities may have an important role to play in attenuating such exchange rate movements (by foreign exchange intervention) and thus reducing the deleterious implications of excessive exchange rate volatility. If, on the other hand, exchange rates are volatile because underlying

TABLE 4.1 Minimum and maximum monthly percentage exchange rate changes

	1973	1974	1975	1976	1977	1978	1979
France	-9.87/5.66	-5.54/2.75	-4.01/8.27	-0.45/4.01	-3.15/0.54	-7.93/10.63	-3.91/3.30
Germany	-11.17/7.12	-5.42/2.36	-4.01/9.43	-3.58/2.31	-5.51/1.49	-10.42/10.75	-4.66/3.68
Japan	2.63/2.01	2.76/3.02	2.86/3.05	2.87/3.04	2.39/2.89	1.76/2.41	2.01/2.43
Switzerland	-13.67/5.69	-6.48/2.11	-4.48/8.44	-2.85/1.31	-7.60/1.40	-6.27/16.73	-7.39/5.94
UK	-4.33/4.09	-3.69/2.58	-2.02/5.16	-3.17/5.82	-4.77/0.94	-5.64/7.22	-5.44/5.85

	1980	1981	1982	1983	1984	1985
France	-6.14/7.84	-4.39/5.99	-4.24/11.81	-1.76/5.88	-6.74/4.73	-8.75/5.19
Germany	-7.22/9.55	-4.38/5.36	-4.44/4.89	-2.51/3.99	-7.39/4.91	-8.89/4.88
Japan	2.03/2.49	2.04/2.39	2.30/2.79	2.32/2.46	2.25/2.51	2.00/2.59
Switzerland	-8.89/8.55	-7.05/5.56	-6.70/5.36	-2.89/3.00	-2.36/5.72	-10.98/5.75
UK	-4.38/5.16	-6.35/8.23	-0.38/3.81	-5.28/5.11	-5.74/5.02	-12.31/3.44

Source: MacDonald (1988)

fundamentals are volatile the policy response would be quite different, if in fact any response is possible. In order to illustrate whether exchange rates have been excessively volatile we present in Table 4.2 the standard deviations of exchange rates and a number of key macroeconomic variables which are viewed in the literature as important determinants of exchange rates. The story to emerge from this table is that exchange rates are more volatile than factors like money supplies and price levels but (generally) less volatile than other asset prices like the interest rate and share price.

The greater volatility of exchange rates than price levels noted in Table 4.2 does tend to suggest that real exchange rates have not been constant during the recent float. For example, the average monthly change of the real effective exchange rates for the seven major currencies is 0.38 per cent for 1961–70 and 1.22 per cent for 1974–83. But volatility is not the only relevant concept when dealing with real rates – the concept of misalignment is also important, since real effective rates are relevant for current account equilibria (see Llewellyn and Sutherland for a further discussion). Misalignment refers to the situation where an exchange rate, although it may be a market clearing rate, moves for some time away from its long-term *sustainable* level. By sustainable we often mean the rate which would equilibrate the current account. In Figure 4.1 we present the real effective exchange rates (RER) and their associated trends for three prominent currencies – the US dollar, the UK pound and the German mark. It is clear that there have been trend movements in all three currencies. In the case of the US, for example, the RER fell by 35 per cent between 1968 and 1978 and rose by 40 per cent in the period 1980–85 (see MacDonald (1988) for a further discussion). Note also the sharp 40 per cent rise in the sterling RER between 1978 and 1982. Of course such trend movements in real exchange rates that have existed during the recent float need not necessarily imply misalignment. For example, Forsyth and Kay (1980) argue that the sharp real appreciation of sterling in the late 1970s was required to maintain current account balance due to the discovery of North Sea oil in the UK's offshore sector (this view has, however, been contested by Buiter and Miller (1983) who cite real interest differentials as the cause of the appreciation). The trends in real rates are also clearly evident in the behaviour of nominal effective rates presented in Figure 4.2. Both real and nominal charts also give a

TABLE 4.2 Standard deviations of monthly percentage changes in the exchange rate and other macroeconomic variables

		USA	UK	France	West Germany	Japan	Switzerland
1973	Exchange rate	—	2.499	4.863	5.644	3.623	5.403
	Price level	0.383	0.512	0.248	0.353	1.042	0.680
	Money supply	0.351	1.384	1.310	1.537	1.516	0.469
	Share price	3.510	5.658	4.470	5.273	3.651	4.312
	Interest rate	7.984	18.041	5.218	132.251	5.266	237.302
1974	Exchange rate	—	1.983	2.506	3.033	2.488	2.828
	Price level	0.258	0.819	0.708	0.225	0.990	0.842
	Money supply	0.161	0.879	0.927	0.675	1.349	0.572
	Share price	5.348	4.205	5.836	3.227	4.771	4.788
	Interest rate	16.354	1.684	4.351	27.628	3.878	343.594
1975	Exchange rate	—	2.173	3.485	3.544	1.638	3.939
	Price level	0.219	1.134	0.092	0.281	0.856	0.262
	Money supply	0.552	2.185	0.968	0.682	1.124	0.592
	Share price	4.897	13.253	4.818	5.803	3.825	3.898
	Interest rate	7.683	5.008	4.194	48.808	5.840	1051.896
1976	Exchange rate	—	3.324	1.574	1.418	1.062	1.116
	Price level	0.128	0.413	0.206	0.204	0.918	0.217
	Money supply	0.305	1.841	0.672	1.134	0.544	1.267
	Share price	2.063	5.468	4.795	3.586	2.067	2.865
	Interest rate	5.701	9.014	6.975	18.978	3.055	47.106

TABLE 4.2 cont.

Year	Variable						
1977	Exchange rate	—	1.932	0.998	1.752	1.779	2.243
	Price level	0.248	0.607	0.505	0.192	0.838	0.226
	Money supply	0.167	1.148	1.175	0.764	1.126	0.856
	Share price	1.405	4.952	5.478	2.173	2.255	2.146
	Interest rate	4.671	17.385	3.414	6.230	7.498	45.905
1978	Exchange rate	—	3.758	4.709	5.997	5.743	6.814
	Price level	0.192	0.252	0.230	0.222	0.675	0.182
	Money supply	0.302	0.771	1.329	0.467	0.913	2.287
	Share price	3.636	4.223	6.821	1.781	1.453	2.943
	Interest rate	4.151	8.087	6.794	12.579	7.116	54.157
1979	Exchange rate	—	3.431	2.304	2.538	2.916	3.342
	Price level	0.147	1.189	0.219	0.158	0.747	0.452
	Money supply	0.387	1.474	1.457	0.269	0.987	1.922
	Share price	2.828	6.079	6.445	2.250	1.569	1.722
	Interest rate	7.547	7.861	5.248	9.678	4.792	232.019
1980	Exchange rate	—	2.761	3.470	4.146	3.898	4.387
	Price level	0.349	0.881	0.223	0.297	0.693	0.312
	Money supply	1.092	1.244	0.955	0.978	1.132	1.414
	Share price	4.744	3.591	4.777	2.486	1.516	3.227
	Interest rate	18.192	4.172	3.574	5.272	10.039	368.831
1981	Exchange rate	—	4.268	3.185	3.312	4.022	4.352
	Price level	0.342	0.708	0.306	0.157	0.586	0.574
	Money supply	0.490	2.824	1.006	1.048	1.037	1.561
	Share price	3.280	5.145	8.176	2.579	3.157	2.903
	Interest rate	14.925	8.740	12.734	7.192	3.600	359.924

1982	Exchange rate	—	1.567	4.320	2.893	4.756	3.300
	Price level	0.492	0.583	0.320	0.321	0.705	0.425
	Money supply	0.672	1.081	1.050	0.578	0.521	1.411
	Share price	5.188	2.802	12.221	2.398	3.109	3.163
	Interest rate	11.988	7.096	4.599	3.857	2.904	242.059
1983	Exchange rate	—	2.778	2.243	1.884	1.721	1.593
	Price level	0.219	0.343	0.256	0.153	0.663	0.247
	Money supply	0.469	0.796	0.658	0.673	0.682	1.052
	Share price	2.249	3.157	3.133	3.556	1.612	3.938
	Interest rate	5.169	2.433	1.155	4.362	4.141	594.102
1984	Exchange rate	—	2.914	3.154	3.426	2.108	2.469
	Price level	0.294	3.498	0.154	0.215	0.695	0.308
	Money supply	0.451	1.101	3.652	1.363	0.669	2.480
	Share price	4.509	3.930	4.829	2.433	3.507	3.178
	Interest rate	5.826	10.509	2.086	1.064	4.312	106.021
1985	Exchange rate	—	4.864	3.869	3.719	2.959	4.111
	Price level	0.108	0.605	0.221	0.207	0.706	0.363
	Money supply	0.344	1.754	1.898	1.177	0.598	2.82
	Share price	2.699	2.966	5.992	3.066	2.602	4.069
	Interest rate	4.398	6.557	1.702	3.604	4.847	24.323

The exchange rates are defined as the home currency price of a dollar; the price level is the CPI; the money supply is M1; the share prices are all share indices; and the interest rates are treasury bill rates.

Source: OECD Main Economic Indicators; MacDonald (1988)

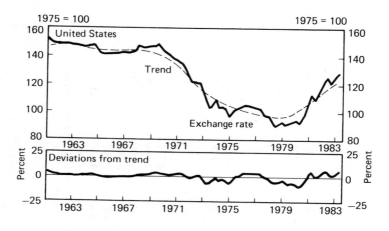

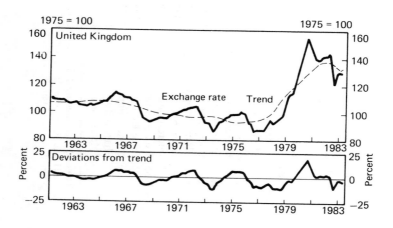

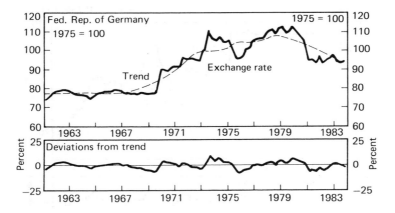

FIGURE 4.1 Major industrial countries: quarterly real effective exchange rates, 1961–83
Source: IMF (1984).

further indication of the increased volatility of exchange rates in the 1970s and 1980s compared to the 1960s referred to above.

The volatility of exchange rates, and particularly the predictability of such volatility, may be gauged in a further way. It is often argued that in the absence of risk the forward exchange rate is a representation of foreign exchange market participants' expectations of the future spot exchange rate. That is:

$$s^e_{t+n} = f^{t+n}_t \tag{4.1}$$

where s^e_{t+n} is the spot rate expected to prevail in time period $t+n$ (home currency per unit of foreign currency), f^{t+n}_t is the forward rate with a $t+n$ maturity set in period t and a lower-case letter denotes that the variable is expressed as a natural logarithm. If we assume expectations are formed rationally:

$$s_{t+n} = s^e_{t+n} + u_{t+n} \tag{4.2}$$

where $s_{t+n} = E(s_{t+n}/I_t)$; i.e. expected (E) spot rate given the available information at time $t(I_t)$ and u_{t+n} is the rational expectations

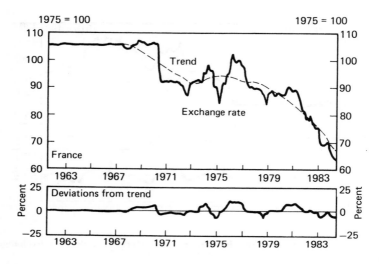

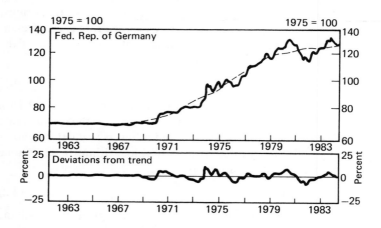

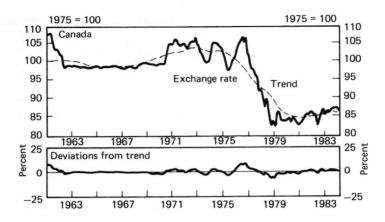

FIGURE 4.2 Major industrial countries: monthly nominal effective exchange rates, 1961–83
Source: IMF (1984).

forecasting error due to news between period $t+1$ and $t+n$. On using (4.2) in (4.1) we obtain:

$$s_{t+n} = f_t^{t+n} + u_{t+n} \qquad (4.3)$$

and on subtracting s_t from s_{t+n} and f_t^{t+n} we have

$$s_{t+n} - s_t = f_t^{t+n} - s_t + u_{t+n} \qquad (4.4)$$

Equation (4.3) posits that the forward rate should be a good predictor of the spot rate to the extent that u_{t+n} is small, and (4.4) says that the forward premium should be a good predictor of the corresponding change in the spot rate, again to the extent that u_{t+n} is small. In Figures 4.3 and 4.4 we plot levels of the spot and forward rates for the mark-dollar and the pound-dollar and in Figures 4.5A and B we plot the relationship between the premium and the change in the exchange rate for the same two currencies. Both sets of figures indicate that the forward rate is not a particularly good predictor of the future spot rate and this is particularly evident in Figure 4.5 where the volatility of the spot rate dominates the (relatively constant) forward premium: exchange rate movements are essentially unpredictable, that is, the u_{t+n} term dominates equations (4.2) and (4.3).

One of the strong impressions gained from the above discussion is the volatility of floating rates. This may lead to a sub-optimal allocation of goods and capital in the international economy. First, to the extent that volatile nominal exchange rate movements result in real exchange volatility (as we have seen they do) this will have an effect on the distribution of goods internationally via current account imbalances. The latter arises both via the effects of changes in competitiveness but also because the volatility may affect the behaviour of exporters/importers. They may regard involvement in international trade as increasingly risky in periods of high exchange rate volatility (despite the existence of forward markets, which may only be adequate at the short end of the maturity spectrum). Second, those who hold their wealth in an internationally diversified portfolio will have an incentive to expend resources in order to minimise the revaluationary effects of exchange rate changes on their wealth: such resource use must clearly be sub-optimal.

The remainder of the chapter attempts to use the empirical evidence on exchange rate models to try to explain the trend movement in exchange rates, the volatility of exchange rates and the unpredictable nature of exchange rate movements. Before presenting the empirical evidence we turn first to a brief survey of the development of exchange rate theories.

BRIEF THEORETICAL AND HISTORICAL ACCOUNT OF EXCHANGE RATE DETERMINATION

Purchasing Power Parity (PPP)

Perhaps the earliest, and certainly one of the most enduring, views of the determination of the exchange rate is that of purchasing power

FIGURE 4.3   Contemporaneous spot and forward rates: (a) dollar–pound; (b) dollar–mark
Source: MacDonald (1988)

(a)

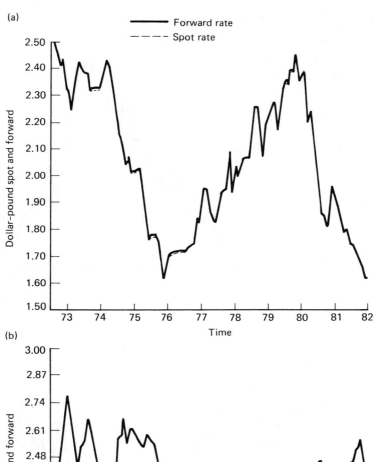

(b)

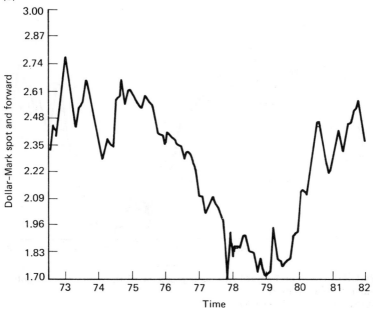

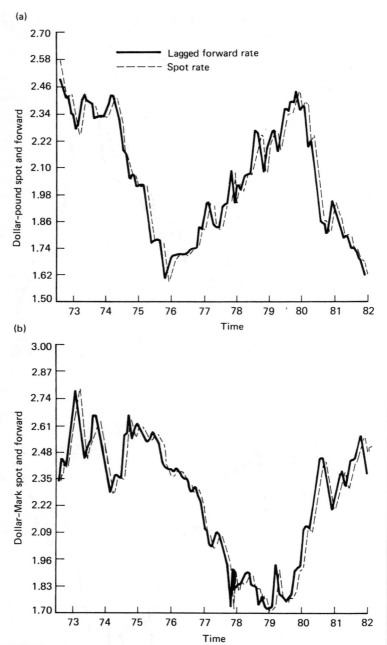

FIGURE 4.4 The forward rate as a predictor of the spot rate: (a) dollar–pound; (b) dollar–mark
Source: MacDonald (1988)

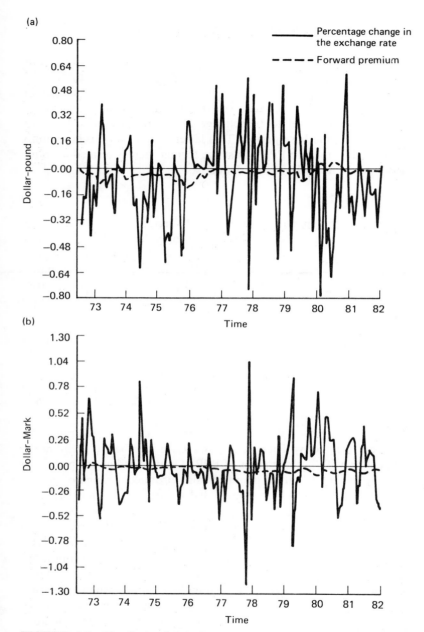

FIGURE 4.5 The forward premium and the percentage change in the exchange rate: (a) dollar–pound; (b) dollar–mark
Source: MacDonald (1988)

parity (PPP). This asserts that the exchange rate is equal to the ratio of some domestic price level to a comparable foreign price level. Additionally, in terms of rates of change, the doctrine posits that the change in the exchange rate is equal to the ratio of the change in the domestic price level to the change in the foreign price level, all relative to some base period. This latter view of PPP is commonly described as relative PPP whilst the former view is termed absolute PPP. Absolute PPP may be defined as

$$S = P/P^* \tag{4.5}$$

where S is the spot price of a unit of foreign exchange, P is 'the' domestic price level, P^* is 'the' foreign price level. Thus if the price level in the UK (home country) is £50 and the corresponding price level in the US (foreign country) is \$100, the pound/dollar exchange rate will be 50 pence per dollar of \$2 per £1. Since few countries report price levels, PPP is usually defined in relative terms using price indices, i.e.

$$S_{t,b} = P_{t,b}/P^*_{t,b} \tag{4.6}$$

where $S_{t,b}$ is the spot exchange rate in period t relative to its value in the base period (i.e. $S_{t,b} = S_t/S_b$) and $P_{t,b}$ and $P^*_{t,b}$ are the home and foreign price indices, respectively, based on period b, where b is assumed to be a period in which absolute PPP held.

The main appeal of PPP as a theory of the exchange rate is its inherent simplicity. There are, however, a number of well-known difficulties with both versions of PPP.[3] Only traded goods prices are usually included, but all countries also produce a range of goods, such as services, which are non-traded and enter the computation of price indices. Is it, however, legitimate to use such price measures in the calculation of PPP? A controversy exists over this issue. Some international economists have strongly argued that if one only uses traded goods in a derivation of PPP, it amounts to nothing more than a tautology (that is, that the price of a bundle of home goods is the same as an identical foreign bundle of goods when converted into a common currency), and, therefore, only non-traded goods should be used.[4] If a price index which includes both traded and non-traded goods is used this can impart a bias into the calculation of PPP if there are productivity differences between countries (this is known as the Balassa–Samuelson thesis).[5]

Flexible Price Monetary Approach (FLMA)

Perhaps the simplest extension of the PPP doctrine is the flexible price monetary approach (FLMA) to the exchange rate. Although this model sidesteps some of the problems associated with PPP, it does have some useful features in that it appends a theory of the price level to a PPP relationship and formalises the role expectations of the future exchange rate play in determining the current exchange rate. The reduced form of FLMA is given in natural logarithms by equation (4.7):

$$s = m - m^* - \alpha_1 y + \beta_1 y^* + \alpha_2 i - \beta_2 i^* \qquad (4.7)$$

This equation has a number of well-known predictions. In particular, it states that an x per cent increase in the domestic money supply (m) leads to an x per cent depreciation of the spot exchange rate (s) – the exchange rate is homogeneous of degree 1 in the money supply. An increase in domestic income (y) leads to an exchange rate appreciation by an amount equal to the change in y times the income elasticity, α_1. This result is in sharp contrast to the traditional 'balance of payments' view of the exchange rate where an increase in income leads to an exchange rate depreciation. The income effect in the FLMA reflects its influence on the demand for money: an increase in income increases the transactions demand for money which, for a given money supply and strict PPP, necessitates an exchange rate appreciation to equalise real money demand and supply. Similarly an increase in the domestic interest rate reduces the demand for money which, for a given money supply and PPP, requires an exchange rate depreciation equal to the change in the interest rate (i) times the interest elasticity (α_2). Since the familiar Fisher equation is assumed to hold in the FLMA, the cause of interest rate changes is, in turn, a reflection of changes in inflationary expectations. Thus if i and i^* are given by (4.8)

$$i = r + \Delta p^e \qquad (4.8)$$

$$i^* = r^* + \Delta p^{e*} \qquad (4.8a)$$

r is the real interest rate and Δp^e is the expected inflation rate. By assuming that real interest rates are constant and equal across countries we may substitute the expected inflation rate for i and i^* in (4.7).

The interest rate/expected inflation terms in (4.7) may be pushed further by saying a little about expectations. To see this it is useful to introduce the final building-block of the FLMA, namely perfect capital mobility which is represented here by the Uncovered Interest Parity (UIP) condition:

$$(i\text{-}i^*)_t = \Delta s^e = s^e_{t+1} \text{-} s_t \tag{4.9}$$

By further assuming that expectations are formed rationally:

$$s^e_{t+n} = E(s_{t+n} | I_t) \tag{4.10}$$

where E is the mathematical expectations operator and I_t is the information set available to agents in period t. On using (4.10), applying it to next periods exchange rate, s_{t+1}, using the fact that $E_t(E_{t+1}(s_{t+1}) = E_t(s_{t+2})$ and applying this procedure iteratively for all future periods, we obtain after further substitution:

$$s_t = \frac{1}{1+\delta_2} \sum_{j=o}^{\infty} \left(\frac{\delta_2}{1+\delta_2}\right)^j E_t[m_{t+j} - m^*_{t+j}] -$$

$$\frac{\delta_1}{1+\delta_2} \sum_{j=o}^{\infty} \left(\frac{\delta_2}{1+\delta_2}\right)^j E_t[y_{t+j} \text{-} y^*_{t+j}] \tag{4.11}$$

where $\delta_1 = \alpha_1 = \beta_1$ and $\delta_2 = \alpha_2 = \beta_2$. In obtaining (4.11) it has been assumed that the transversality (or terminal) condition is satisfied. This assumption is vital, since if it is violated the actual exchange rate could, in principle, move away indefinitely from the value determined by fundamentals – the exchange rate is driven by a speculative bubble. We shall return to this concept below.

Equation (4.11) makes clear the dependence of the current exchange rate (asset price), s_t on the expected future levels of the exogeneous variables, $(m - m^*)$ and $(y - y^*)$. Notice (4.11) predicts that, if for some reason, agents' expectations of future variables change, this can have a direct effect on the current exchange rate even if *current actual values have not changed*. Equation (4.11), although derived within the context of the FLMA, has more general applicability, in that if other variables, such as the current account or real interest rates, are believed to determine the exchange rate, then a reduced form similar to (4.11) could be derived with the additional expectational variables added.

Sticky Price Monetary Model (SPMA)

The assumption of continuous price flexibility is perhaps the FLMA's most unappealing feature. Hence in the short term it seems more reasonable to assume that prices are sticky. PPP is violated, at least in the short run. Dornbusch (1976) has presented a version of the monetary model which features short-run price stickiness combined with the equilibrium PPP properties of the FLMA in the 'long run'. The model, discussed in more detail in Chapter 2, is noted here in the briefest detail in order to derive a reduced form equation which has been estimated by a number of researchers for the recent floating experience.

In the sticky price monetary model (SPMA) PPP does not hold in the short term and therefore an alternative equation is required to describe the evolution of the price level over time. The price level in the home and foreign country is assumed to evolve according to

$$\Delta p_t = \eta(d - y)_t \qquad (4.12)$$

where $\Delta p_t = p_{t+1} - p_t$ and d represents aggregate demand. Excess demand is assumed to depend upon competitiveness, real income and the interest rate. Assuming that this holds for both countries, the resulting relative price relationship can be used to derive a reduced form equation representation of the Dornbusch model. If it is assumed that exchange rate expectations evolve according to a simple regressive expectations scheme and that the long-run exchange rate is proportional to the relative money supply term, then the following reduced form equation may be obtained (following Driskell, 1981):

$$s_t = \pi_0 + \pi_1 s_{t-1} + \pi_2 m'_t + \pi_3 m'_{t-1} + \pi_4 P'_{t-1} + \pi_5 y'_t + \pi_6 y'_{t-1} \qquad (4.13)$$

where

$$\sum_{i=1}^{4} \pi_i = 1, \ (\pi_1 < 0, \ \pi_2 > 1, \ \pi_3 < 0, \ \pi_4 < 0, \ \pi_5 < 0, \ \pi_6 < 0)$$

and $x' = (x - x^*)$, $x = m, p, y$.

The first constraint simply states that PPP must hold in the long run in this model. The sign of π_2 is representative of the key element of the Dornbusch model: a change in the money supply has a more than proportionate impact on the exchange rate – overshooting.

Thus estimates of (4.13) should give insight into whether exchange rate overshooting has been a prominent feature of the recent float. One interesting feature of equation (4.13) is that it may be derived using a capital flow function like (4.14) instead of (4.9).

$$C = \beta(i - i^* - \Delta s^e)_t, \qquad \beta > 0 \qquad\qquad (4.14)$$

where C denotes the capital account of the balance of payments. Equation (4.14) allows for a variety of options regarding capital mobility. Thus if $\beta = 0$, capital is completely immobile whilst if $\beta = \infty$ capital is perfectly mobile and (4.14) collapses to (4.19): UIP is continually maintained. However, for values of β between 0 and ∞, (4.14) posits that capital is imperfectly mobile which is a reflection of the slow adjustment of agents' portfolios. Although using (4.14) instead of (4.9) results in a reduced form identical to (4.13), the signs of the coefficients differ (see Driskell (1981) for a proof); i.e.

$$\sum_{i=1}^{4} \pi_i = 1, \ (\pi_1 < 1, \ \pi_2 > 0, \ \pi_3 < 0, \ \pi_4 > 0, \ \pi_5 < 0, \ \pi_6 < 0)$$

Thus, in common with the perfect capital mobility version, the PPP constraint holds; however, other constraints, such as the overshooting result, are ambiguous. Tests of equation (4.13), therefore, should provide discrimination between the Dornbusch model and versions thereof which explicitly recognise imperfect capital mobility (i.e. Frenkel and Rodriguez (1982) or Bhandari *et al.* (1984)).

Real Interest Differential Model (RID)

Although the SPMA model is an improvement over the FLMA in describing short-run adjustment, it does have a deficiency in that it ignores short-run inflation differences between countries. Frankel (1979) has derived a reduced form which combines elements of both the FLMA (i.e. interest rates reflect inflationary expectations) and the SPMA (interest rates reflect the *real* implications of monetary policy). Such a reduced form is useful, as we shall see, since it allows discrimination between the SPMA and FLMA. This reduced form is christened the real interest differential (RID) model. The RID model is derived in the following way. First, assume that PPP holds in the long run. Second, we modify the regressive expectations scheme to include secular inflation rates. Thus in long-run equilibrium, the exchange rate is expected to change by an amount equal to the expected inflation differential, i.e.

$$\bar{s} - s = \frac{1}{\lambda}[(i - i^*)] - (\Delta p^e - \Delta p^{e*})] \tag{4.15}$$

This states that in a world in which PPP does not hold in the short run, the current exchange rate differs from its long-run equilibrium (a bar denotes a long-run value) in proportion to the real interest differential. The estimatable reduced form for the RID model is as follows:

$$s = m - m^* + \alpha_1(y - y^*) + \alpha_2(\Delta p^e - \Delta p^{e*}) + \alpha_3[(i - i^*) - (\Delta p^e - \Delta p^{e*})] \tag{4.16}$$

where, for simplicity, it is assumed that equilibrium values are given by their current levels. Notice that (4.16) is identical to the FLMA reduced form but for the addition of the real interest rate term $[(i - i^*) - (\Delta p^e - \Delta p^{e*})]$. In principle, this additional term allows discrimination between the FLMA and the SPMA. Thus if the FLMA is correct, the coefficient α^2 should be positive and α_3 should be zero. If, alternatively, the SPMA is correct, α_3 should be negative and α_2 should equal zero. If the RID model is correct, however, both terms should be significant. The hypothesised signs can be summarised, therefore, as follows:

FLMA	$\alpha_2 > 0$	$\alpha_3 = 0$
SPMA	$\alpha_2 = 0$	$\alpha_3 < 0$
RID	$\alpha_2 > 0$	$\alpha_3 < 0$

Portfolio Balance Approach (PBA)

In all of the models discussed hitherto, emphasis has been given to relative excess money supplies as determinants of the exchange rate: other, non-money, assets do not have a role to play in determining the exchange rate. This is despite the fact that the monetary models considered allow domestic residents to hold domestic and foreign bonds. Why then do the supplies of these non-money assets not count? The justification for not looking at these assets in the monetary model is that they may be viewed as perfect substitutes and therefore there are effectively only three assets in the monetary model: domestic money, foreign money and a 'bond' (B). By appealing to Walras Law, attention may therefore be legitimately placed on the money supplies since if the money markets are in equilibrium, then, via the domestic wealth constraint, the 'bond' market must also be in equilibrium. But is it legitimate to assume that bonds are perfect substitutes? A number of researchers have argued that because of the existence of factors like exchange rate risk, political risk and default risk, risk-averse agents will not view bonds issued in different countries as perfect substitutes and indeed will require a risk premium, in addition to the expected net yield, to induce them to hold foreign bonds. Thus:

$$i = i^* + \Delta s^e + \lambda \qquad (4.17)$$

where λ is a risk premium. Hence if international investors decide that a currency has become riskier, they are likely to reallocate their bond portfolios in favour of the less risky assets. The moral of this story is that if bonds are regarded as imperfect substitutes then they will have a role to play in determining the exchange rate. Models of the exchange rate which include non-money assets in the menu of assets determining the exchange rate are classified as portfolio balance models.

   In order to empirically implement the portfolio model, researchers have adopted basically two approaches. First, a very short-run specification of the exchange rate may be derived by postulating that in the short term only asset supply shocks affect the exchange rate. If non-money assets are imperfect substitutes, and therefore potentially have a role to play in determining the exchange rate through the risk premium avenue, a simple reduced form for the exchange rate may be thought of as:

$$s = f(M, M^*, B, B^*) \qquad (4.18)$$

This is the approach favoured by Branson *et al.* (1979) where B denotes the supply of bonds. An alternative approach, due to Hooper and Morton (1982) and Frankel (1983) has been to incorporate a risk premium term into the RID model, i.e.

$$s = m - m^* + \alpha_1(y - y^*) + \alpha_2(\Delta p^e - \Delta p^{e^*}) + \alpha_3[(i - i^*) - (\Delta p^e - \Delta p^{e^*})] + \lambda. \qquad (4.19)$$

The trick is then to substitute in factors which are believed to be determinants of λ. We shall return to such determinants in the following section.

SOME EMPIRICAL EVIDENCE

Asset approach reduced form econometric evidence

In this section we consider some of the reduced form evidence pertaining to the models described in the previous section (we consider PPP tests in the following section).

Evidence on FLMA

Equation 4.7 has been estimated by a large number of researchers for the recent floating experience.[6] For the early part of the recent float (until the end of 1977) reasonably satisfactory reduced form estimates of the FLMA were reported by a number of researchers. A representative ordinary least squares result, due to Hodrick (1978), for the US dollar–German mark exchange rate is:

$$s = 1.520m - 1.390m^* - 2.230y + 0.2070y^* + 2.530i + 1.930i^* + 7.850$$
$$\quad (2.98) \quad (2.48) \quad (2.16) \quad (0.18) \quad (2.16) \quad (2.88) \quad (3.03)$$

$$R^2 = 0.66 \quad DW = 1.61 \quad SER = 0.37 \quad \text{April 1973–September 1975}$$
$$(4.20)$$

where t ratios are in parenthesis. Notice that the home and foreign money supply terms are statistically significant and are close to plus and minus unity (indeed the hypothesis that they *are* equal to plus and minus unity cannot be rejected at the 95 per cent level). The coefficient on the home and foreign income terms are correctly signed, but only the US term is statistically significant. The interest rate coefficients are both statistically significant, although the German interest rate has the wrong sign. The overall in-sample explanatory power of the equation appears to be reasonably good in that the coefficient of determination is above 0.5 and the Durbin–Watson statistic, DW, indicates an absence of first-order autocorrelation.

Evidence on RID

Equation (4.11), has been implemented by Frankel (1979) for the German mark–US dollar for the period July 1974–February 1978 and a representative result is:

$$s = 0.97(m - m^*) - 0.52(y - y^*) - 5.40[i - i^*) - (\Delta p^e - \Delta p^{e^*})]$$
$$\quad (4.62) \qquad\qquad (2.36) \qquad\qquad (7.65)$$

$$+ 29.40(\Delta p^e - \Delta p^{e^*}) + 1.39$$
$$\quad (8.83) \qquad\qquad (11.58)$$
$$R^2 = 0.91 \tag{4.21}$$

Comparing the coefficient signs with those predicted by the RID model, we note that all are correctly signed and statistically significant. Of particular interest are the coefficients on the real interest differential and the expected inflation differential which allow rejection of both the FLMA and SPMA models in favour of the RID. Usefully the estimates in equation (4.21) allow calculation of the response of the exchange rate to a once-for-all 1 per cent increase in the money supply. Frankel calculated that the effect of the money supply increase on the real interest differential and long-term inflation differential would lead to an exchange rate overshoot of 1.58 per cent.

Evidence on SPMA

A version of the SPMA reduced form has been tested by Driskell (1981) for the recent floating experience and his result for the Swiss franc–US dollar is:

$$s_t = 0.43 s_{t-1} + 2.37(m - m^*)_t - 2.45(m - m^*)_{t-1} + 0.93(p - p^*)_{t-1}$$
$$\quad (3.65) \qquad (5.73) \qquad\qquad (5.60) \qquad\qquad (2.23)$$

$$R^2 = 0.99 \quad \text{Data period: 1973 quarter 1–1977 quarter 1.} \tag{4.22}$$

which was estimated using the Cochrane–Orcutt procedure to account for first-order autocorrelation. As predicted by the theory $\sum_{i=1}^{4} \Pi_i$ equals 1.28 which is insignificantly different from unity at the 95 per cent level and thus PPP holds as a long-run phenomenon in this model. Interestingly, although the coefficient on $(m - m^*)$ is greater than unity (i.e. overshooting), which is clearly supportive of the perfect capital mobility version of the SPMA model, the coefficients on s_{t-1} and $(p - p^*)_{t-1}$ are both positive, which is supportive of the imperfect capital mobility version of the model.

The equation also seems to have a high in-sample explanatory power, judging by the R^2.

The above empirical results tend to cast the monetary approach, in its three different versions, in a favourable light. However, we must stress that these results are (very) special cases. Thus when researchers have extended the sample beyond 1978 and examined a variety of exchange rates (both bilateral and effective), highly unsatisfactory results have been obtained in terms of poor in-sample explanatory power and the fact that coefficients are often wrongly signed and insignificant (for the RID/FLMA models, see the results presented in Dornbusch (1980), Haynes and Stone (1981), Frankel (1984), Backus (1984) and Hacche and Townend (1981) and for the SPMA model see Hacche and Townend (1981) and Backus (1984)).

How then may the generally poor performance of the monetary approach equation be explained? A number of answers to this question have been offered in the literature. First, notice that the coefficients in all of the above reported equations have been constrained to have equal and opposite signs. This situation is usually justified on the grounds of multicollinearity, but it has been demonstrated (see Haynes and Stone (1981)) that such constraints may lead to biased estimates and sign reversals. Second, underlying the derivation of all the reduced form equations considered above is the (albeit implicit) assumption that money demand functions are stable. However, one of the salient features of the recent floating experience has been the instability of money demand functions (see Artis and Lewis (1981) for a discussion). Related to the breakdown of money demand functions for the period has been the failure of PPP to hold during the 1970s/1980s period and this certainly would go some way to explaining why updates of the FLMA have not held for the full floating sample.[7] Related to this issue is the fact that most of the estimated equations lack any dynamics in that variables enter contemporaneously. Such lack of dynamics is currently unfashionable in the light of the work by Hendry and Mizon (1978).

Evidence on PBA

Tests of the portfolio balance model have proceeded along essentially three lines. The first has been to take a very short-term view of the determination of the exchange rate and examine the effects of asset stocks, such as money supplies and bonds. Thus, for example,

Branson et al. (1979) estimated a log-linear revision of equation 4.18 for a number of currencies from the recent float and reported some evidence in favour. Some coefficients have the correct sign and are statistically significant; however, autocorrelation is a persistent problem suggesting model and/or dynamic misspecification.

The second line of research on the PBA has attempted to improve the model specification by estimating the hybrid monetary/portfolio reduced form, introduced earlier as equation (4.19). In order to empirically implement such an equation, a measure has to be found for the risk premium term, λ. One of the simplest ways to proceed is to use a two-country model and assume that the residents in each country have the same portfolio preferences (the uniform preference assumption). This allows a researcher to write the risk premium as a function of net domestic government indebtedness, B, and net foreign government indebtedness, β^*. A number of researchers have used this approach and in some cases results which are favourable to the hybrid model are reported. One particularly interesting feature of some of the results for the hybrid reduced form is the absence of autocorrelation, which is suggestive that this specification is an improvement over either the standard monetary approach or the simple (short-run) portfolio model.

The third way in which researchers have attempted to test the portfolio model is by simply regressing the risk premium, λ, on factors believed to be determinants of the risk premium. This type of test may be outlined in the following way. Thus the investor may be assumed to balance his portfolio among the assets of different countries as a function of their expected return. If the supply of, say, home country assets increases, either the domestic rate of interest will have to rise or the currency will be expected to appreciate for the asset to be willingly held. Hence if assets are imperfect substitutes they should be systematically related to returns. This hypothesis may be expressed in a form suitable for econometric estimation as

$$(i - i^* - \Delta s) = \Phi(B/SB^*F) + u \qquad (4.23)$$

Versions of (4.23) have been estimated by a variety of researchers for the recent floating experience.[8] The main conclusion to emerge from such research is usefully summarised by Frankel (1982a) who reports that 'many regressions were run ... [but] no coefficients appeared significantly different from zero'. The verdict to be drawn from the above tests of the PBA is somewhat unclear, but on balance we would argue that the battery of tests that have been performed are somewhat unfavourable to the approach: bonds seem approximately to be perfect substitutes and therefore the monetary model seems to be more appropriate – albeit a monetary model with a richer specification than many of those posited in the literature.

Before leaving the monetary/portfolio balance reduced form evidence it is worth noting the results of an important study by Meese and Rogoff (1983). They tested the out-of-sample forecasting performance of a number of the asset-reduced forms (which we have discussed) against a simple random walk representation of the exchange rate for the dollar–deutschmark, the dollar–yen and the trade-weighted dollar using the data period March 1973 to June 1981. The out-of-sample forecasts were computed in the following way. First, the equations were estimated using data from the beginning of the sample to November 1976 and four forecasts were made for periods of one, three, six and twelve months ahead. The data for December 1976 was then added to the original data set, the equations re-estimated and a further set of forecasts made for the four time-horizons. This procedure was repeated until the end of the sample. The devastating result to emerge from the work is that none of the asset-reduced forms considered outperformed the simple random walk. This conclusion is all the more striking because the reduced-form forecasts have been computed using *actual* values of the various assets. In an attempt to improve on the performance of the asset-reduced forms, these authors alternatively attempt estimating the models in first differences, allow home and foreign magnitudes to enter unconstrained, include price levels as additional explanatory variables, use different definitions of the money supply, and use a variety of proxies for inflationary expectations. But all to no avail: the modified reduced-form equations still fail to outperform the simple random-walk.

One feature of all the reduced-form studies considered hitherto is that they make no attempt to model expectations. However, in our discussion of the FLMA we saw the important role expectations could play in telescoping the future into the present. But does the explicit modelling of expectations in the econometric implementation of a monetary reduced form make any difference? A number of researchers have answered this question in the affirmative. Thus Hoffman and Schlagenhauf (1983) econometrically test equation 4.13 (a rational expectations version of FLMA, i.e. REFLMA) for three-dollar bilateral exchange rates over the period 1974,6 to 1979,12 (monthly data). Interestingly, they cannot reject the restrictions implied by the rational expectations hypothesis and further their coefficient estimates are consistent with the monetary model. Woo (1985) pushes the estimation of the REFLMA further by testing its out-of-sample forecasting performance for the dollar–deutschemark rate, 1974–81 (in contrast to the simple FLMA model, he uses money demand functions with a partial adjustment mechanism). One striking result reported by Woo is that he finds that the REFLMA outperforms a simple random-walk model using standard forecasting criteria. Thus the incorporation of expectations seems to overturn the more negative findings of a number of researchers reported above. Perhaps the better performance of the REFLMA may be traced to the fact that, in implementing expectations, researchers introduce more complex dynamics than that in the simple monetary reduced forms discussed earlier.

Evidence on purchasing power parity

Perhaps the simplest test of whether PPP has held during the recent float involves examining the relationship between the real and nominal exchange rate. Thus if PPP holds continually, these two exchange rates should be independent: changes in prices should call forth an equal and offsetting exchange rate change. But to the extent that there are factors other than relative prices driving exchange rates, and also if prices are relatively inflexible, then we would not expect to observe an independence between nominal and real exchange rates. To the extent that the two series are related, this must imply a violation of PPP. In Figs 4.4 and 4.5 we plot the real and nominal exchange rates for the UK pound–US dollar and German mark–US dollar nominal and real exchange rates.[9] It is clear for the period and currencies considered that nominal and real exchange rates move closely together. Thus the nominal appreciation of the sterling rate from mid-1976 to the end of the 1970s is seen also to be a real appreciation and the nominal depreciation thereafter is also seen to be a real depreciation.[10]

The violation of PPP has been demonstrated in a somewhat different way by a number of researchers, such as Isard (1977) and Kravis and Lipsey (1978). For example, Isard takes the most disaggregated groupings of manufactured goods for which US, German and Japanese prices are readily available, and demonstrates that for the period 1970–75 the 'law of one price' fails to hold –

changes in exchange rates result in relative price changes. Kravis and Lipsey's study is similar to Isard's, and they come to similar conclusions. Thus, it would seem to be impossible to construct aggregate price indices, which would be expected to obey the law of one price.

The latter conclusion is reflected in a number of studies which use regression-based tests of PPP. In particular, a number of researchers have estimated equations of the form

$$s_t = a + b_0 p_t - b_1 p_t^* \qquad \text{(absolute PPP)} \qquad (4.24)$$

$$s_t = a + b_0 \Delta p_t - b_1 \Delta p_t^* \qquad \text{(relative PPP)} \qquad (4.24a)$$

Where the prices used are aggregate series, and if PPP holds, it is expected that $b_0 = b_1 = 1$ and the a terms should equal zero. The tests have resulted in a resounding rejection of PPP for a number of currencies for the recent floating period.[11]

The final way that researchers have sought to test PPP is by examining the time-series properties of the real exchange rate. This version of PPP, due to Roll (1979), is christened the efficient markets view of PPP (EMPPP). If UIP holds (equation 4.9), nominal interest rates in the UIP condition are given by the Fisher relationship (4.8 and 4.8a), and expectations are formed rationally we obtain by substitution

$$r - r^* = \Delta \rho^* - \Delta p + \Delta s + e \qquad (4.25)$$

where e is the composite error from assuming rational expectations. From (4.25) we see that if the real interest differential is constant over time then the logarithmic change in the real exchange rate should follow a random walk. Few proponents of PPP (see Officer (1976) for a discussion) would deny that in the short term there may be shocks which push the exchange rate away from its PPP value. But this phenomenon will only be temporary; over time the real exchange rate will return to its equilibrium value and therefore the change in the real exchange rate should be serially correlated. If, then, the random-walk model of the real exchange rate is supported by the data, it must call into question the traditional view of PPP. The majority of evidence does in fact find that the change in the real exchange rate follows a random walk.[12]

The main implication, for our purposes, of the failure of PPP to hold is that any model of exchange rate determination, such as the

FLMA, which uses PPP as a building block must be called into question. The failure of PPP to hold calls into question the forecasts of those who use PPP as an exchange rate forecasting device.

Exchange Rate Volatility and Variance Bounds Tests

The aforementioned empirical studies are concerned with trying to explain the trend movement of exchange rates over time. But what of exchange rate volatility? Can the models outlined in Section 3 be used to explain the volatility of exchange rates? A number of researchers have answered in the affirmative. Such tests have their origins in the finance literature (see Shiller, 1981). If agents are rational in the context of FLMA it must follow that the volatility, or variance (VAR), of the predicted or forecast spot exchange rate, $\hat{s}$, is given by:

$$VAR(\hat{s}_T) = VAR(s_t) + VAR(u_t) \tag{4.26}$$

where u_t is the forecast error.

Now since variances cannot be negative it must therefore follow that $VAR(s) \leq VAR(\hat{s})$; that is, that the variance of the actual spot exchange rate should be less than or equal (i.e. it is bounded) to the spot exchange forecast. A number of researchers have tested this requirement for a selection of currencies over the recent float. For example, Huang (1981) finds that actual exchange rates are too volatile to be consistent with the assumptions of the monetary model and rational expectations. But is the failure of the variance bounds test due to the failure of rational expectations or the unrealism of the monetary approach (i.e. continuous money market clearing and PPP)? Honohan (1986), using the SPMA, finds that the variance bounds inequalities are not rejected by the data: hence when continuous price flexibility is relaxed the variability of exchange rates can be 'explained' in terms of fundamentals. But Diba (1987) argues that the various inequalities are satisfied even for the simple FLMA model if a 'correct' measure of the semi-interest elasticity is utilised.[13]

Although the above volatility studies do not necessarily establish that the monetary model has empirical support, they do tend to indicate that exchange rates are not excessively volatile relative to monetary fundamentals.

The efficiency of the forward market for foreign exchange

We now turn our attention away from exchange rate determination *per se* to the efficiency of foreign exchange markets and, in particular, the efficiency of the forward market for foreign exchange. The two topics are not entirely unrelated as can be seen by considering one of the key building-blocks of the asset approach, namely uncovered interest parity (UIP). If a researcher wanted to test UIP he would need some measure of s_{t+1}^e, the expected exchange rate. As we have seen (equation 4.1), one pervasive view is that the forward exchange rate is a representation of the expected future spot rate. In a world of uncertainty, this will hold only if foreign exchange market participants are risk-neutral. If, however, they are risk-averse, and therefore require an additional risk premium in order to persuade them to hold forward foreign exchange, covered interest parity requires that:

$$RP_t + s_{t+1}^e = f_t^{t+1} \tag{4.27}$$

where RP is a risk premium. Clearly in the absence of RP_t, covered interest parity and uncovered parity will be equivalent. However, in the presence of RP_t the two relationships differ. The existence of risk is clearly of crucial importance in determining which view of the exchange rate is 'correct'. Hence if UIP holds continually this implies that non-money assets are perfect substitutes and therefore the monetary class of models are appropriate. If, however, risk is important then the portfolio balance model is the more appropriate. Since each class of model has differing policy implications (see Chapter 2) it is clearly of some importance to determine whether we may legitimately substitute the forward rate *f* for the expected future spot rate s^e.

A market, such as the forward foreign exchange market, is said to be efficient if prices fully and instantly reflect all available information and no profit opportunities are left unexploited. The efficient markets hypothesis (EMH) is a joint hypothesis in the sense that it contains some view of what determines equilibrium prices, and the hypothesis that agents act rationally (that is, they avoid making knowable forecasting errors on the basis of the current information set). If we take equation (4.1) as our representation of the 'equilibrium process', (given rational expectation) the model may be tested econometrically by estimating an equation of the form

$$s_{t+n} = a + bf_t^{t+n} + \varepsilon_{t+n} \qquad (4.28)$$

Thus if the market efficiency proposition is valid, then a should differ insignificantly from zero, b should be insignificantly different from unity and the error term should be random (the joint hypothesis of unbiasedness). Furthermore, if agents are rational, and therefore exploit all the information in I_t, there should be no correlation between ε_{t+n} and I_t. If there is, then this implies that agents could have used available information to make a better forecast of the forward exchange rate. (This latter property is, somewhat inelegantly, known as the error-orthogonality property).

In the early empirical research of forward market efficiency researchers tended to utilise equations like (4.28). However, there is an important technical problem that concerns the stationarity of the variables. By stationarity we basically mean that a variable has had its trend component removed. Classical econometric inference relies on the stationarity of the variables under consideration. However, both s and f are likely to be highly trended (see Fig. 4.3) and exhibit non-stationarity behaviour for the kind of observation frequency typically used by researchers, such as weekly or monthly. In a bid to overcome this problem researchers have implemented equation 4.4 in regression form:

$$s_{t+n} - s_t = a + b(f_t^{t+n} - s_t) + n_{t+n} \qquad (4.29)$$

where if the EMH is valid a should equal zero and b should equal unity. The transformations underlying equation (4.29) result essentially in differenced variables which are stationary, and therefore proper inferences may be drawn from equations containing these variables.

What then of the econometric estimates of (4.28) and (4.29)? A representative estimate for equation (4.28) for the dollar/pound exchange rate, due to Frenkel (1981), is:

$$s_t = 0.033 + 0.956f_{t-1} \quad R^2 = 0.96 \quad DW = 1.72$$
$$(1.94) \quad (39.83) \qquad \text{June 1973–July 1979} \qquad (4.30)$$

where t values are in parenthesis.

Note that the coefficient estimate on f is statistically significant and very close to unity, which is supportive of the model; the constant term, though, is statistically significant, which is a violation of the EMH (although when the hypothesis $a = 0$ and $b = 1$ was tested jointly using an F test, the joint hypothesis could not be rejected). Furthermore, note that the Durbin–Watson statistic is insignificant, which is supportive of the EMH. The significant constant term is a common finding in estimated versions of (4.28) and may be rationalised by an appeal to a risk premium term.[14]

Estimates of equation (4.29) have also been conducted by a large number of researchers and we report a representative result by McAvinchey and MacDonald (1987):

$$s_{t+1} - s_t = -0.009 - 4.418 \ (f_t - s_t)$$
$$(2.25) \quad (3.25)$$

$$DW = 2.28 \quad SER = 0.034 \qquad LM(12) = 1.13 \qquad (4.31)$$

[UK pound–US dollar, 1979(3)–1986(5) monthly.]

where t values are in parenthesis.

In this case the joint hypothesis is clearly violated in that the constant and slope coefficients differ widely from their *a priori* values. Although the significantly negative constant may be rationalised by appealing to a constant risk premium, how may the more troublesome negative b coefficient be rationalised? Fama (1984), for example, has argued that a value of b which differs significantly from unity is evidence of risk premium varying over time. A large number of researchers have pursued this hypothesis by trying to capture the risk premium using variables which are believed to be important determinants of risk.[15] However, the view that a value of b significantly different from unity is a reflection of a risk premium is based on the assumption that agents behave rationally. But what if they do not? What instead, if agents are risk-neutral but irrational. A number of researchers have taken this alternative view in interpreting the results.[16]

The choice of interpretation would therefore in a sense seem to boil down to whether a researcher believes that market operators are risk-neutral/risk-averse or rational/irrational – hardly very scientific! The problem we are faced with, then, is identifying which part of the joint hypothesis is failing. Recently, the availability of market survey data on agents' expectations of the future exchange rate has allowed researchers to make single hypothesis tests. Thus given access to information on agents' expectations, we do not need to *impose* rational expectations on the data, thus allowing a direct test of whether it is irrational behaviour or risk that generates results like equation 4.31.

In both the US and the UK a number of financial companies have, since the floating period began, conducted regular surveys of foreign exchange market dealers' expectations of future exchange rates. Interestingly, the results for both the UK and the US tend to indicate that both legs of the joint hypothesis are at fault.[17] But care must be taken in interpreting this result. It may not mean that agents are irrational processors of information, rather it could reflect certain popular notions of foreign exchange market behaviour such as rational speculative bubbles (Frankel, 1985a) or the peso problem (Krasker, 1980), which may result in exchange rate expectations and exchange rates moving in opposite directions.

A speculative bubble is a sophisticated rationalisation for the perceived behaviour of foreign exchange market speculators. Thus, it is often argued that exchange rate movements are governed by technical trading rules adopted by foreign exchange market traders: a speculator deems a currency worth buying if he expects to pass it on at a higher price in the future, even if this means moving the exchange rate in an opposite direction from fundamentals. Technical trading rules are usually regarded as governing the short-term movement of exchange rates (on an hour-to-hour/day-to-day basis). A speculative bubble is usually interpreted as a longer-term extension of the trading rule phenomenon, and is regarded as perfectly consistent with rational expectations as long as they are self-validating. The problem, though, with the rational speculative bubble concept is that it must eventually come to an end – it must eventually burst. This being so, why do rational bubbles get started in the first place? Blanchard (1979) argues that since the probability of collapse in any period is likely to be small, there will be some rate of appreciation plus an interest differential which will be sufficient to persuade speculators to hold the currency, despite the possibility of a collapse. The appreciation of the US dollar, 1980–85, is often cited as one example of a speculative bubble, but the empirical evidence tends to negate this assertion – 'the appreciation has gone on for too long to represent a single rational bubble!' (Frankel, 1985a). However, in tests of this phenomenon Meese (1986) finds evidence of bubbles for the dollar/deutschemark, over the period 1973–82 (monthly data base).[18]

The 'peso problem' (see Krasker, 1980) concerns the probability of a large exchange rate change, say a depreciation, which does not actually occur during the sample period of interest. This phenomenon can be used to explain the finding by researchers using survey data that market participants are irrational. Thus, say a currency is appreciating for time period t to $t+n$ but speculators expect the currency to depreciate in the future, say $t+n+1$. During the sample period t to $t+n$ speculators attach a small probability to their expectation of a depreciation and the currency continues to appreciate. A researcher who therefore regresses the actual change of the exchange rate on the expected change for period t to $t+n$ will find that agents get the direction of the exchange rate change completely wrong (see MacDonald and Torrance (1988) for a further discussion).

The 'news' approach to exchange rate modelling

Another feature of the recent float which we illustrated in section 1 has been the unpredictable nature of exchange rate changes. Thus to the extent that the forward rate is to be taken as the market's expectation of the future spot rate, Figs. 4.3 and 4.4 illustrate that most of the movement in exchange rates must be due to the arrival of new information in foreign exchange markets. A number of researchers have attempted to implement the models discussed in Section 3 in a 'news' format, in order to determine if they can be used to explain unexpected exchange rate movements. The 'news' approach to exchange rate determination may be illustrated with the following reduced-form equation:

$$s_t - f_t^{t-1} = \alpha(z_t - z_t^e) + v_t \tag{4.32}$$

where z denotes a vector of variables regarded as determinants of the exchange rate, an e superscript denotes a rational expectation and therefore the term in parenthesis represents the 'news'. The main task facing a researcher who tries to implement this model lies in obtaining an estimate for the expected values of the determinants of the exchange rate. In the literature there are two popular ways to proceed. First, a researcher may run a regression equation for z using variables which he believes are important determinants of z. The fitted value from this estimated equation is then taken as the expected value and used in a second stage of estimation. The second main way is to use expectational data culled from a survey data base.

This latter approach has the advantage that the expectational series should reflect the information set specified by the economist/econometrician. Here we illustrate the news approach using an estimated equation from MacDonald (1983). MacDonald uses the regression-based approach in deriving estimates of expected money supply for a number of OECD countries and a representative result is:

$$s_t - f_{t-1} = -0.015 - 2.017(\dot{m} - \dot{m}^e)_t$$
$$(1.85) \quad (3.27)$$

$$+ 3.173(\dot{m}^* - \dot{m}^{e*})_t \quad R^2 = 0.43$$
$$(2.68) \qquad \text{Currency: mark–dollar}$$

(4.33)

where t ratios are in parenthesis. Variables have their usual interpretation, a dot above a variable denotes a growth rate, and the $\dot{m}^e$ values have been derived by regressing actual $\dot{m}$ on a set of variables believed to be important determinants of $\dot{m}$, such as lagged m, lagged current account surpluses and lagged government deficits.

Notice that the coefficients on the surprise terms are both statistically significant, but they have signs which contradict the simple FLMA. Perhaps, though, the perverse signs are explicable in terms of a policy anticipation effect (see Cornell (1983) for a discussion). That is, if a surprise increase in the home money supply results in a belief that this monetary expansion will be more than offset in the future, the current exchange rate will appreciate. The reported R^2 coefficient for (4.33), although relatively low by conventional standards, is perhaps acceptable in the exchange rate context given Mussa's (1979) dictum that any exchange rate model which can explain 10 per cent of exchange rate movements should be deemed a success!

A number of other researchers have also empirically implemented news equations, using a variety of news variables, for the recent float and the results are deemed to be supportive of the news approach (see MacDonald (1988) for a further discussion). One problem, though, with the extant estimated news equations is that the volatility of exchange rates is much greater than the volatility of the actual news variables used by researchers in their news equations. But perhaps this is unsurprising given that a great deal of news is by its very nature unquantifiable (i.e. the importance of rumours, etc.) and indeed non-economic news (i.e. political announcements) may at times dominate any economic news, moving the exchange rate by more than that reflected by the economic fundamentals.

CONCLUSIONS

In the second section of this chapter we highlighted a number of empirical regularities of exchange rates during the recent float, such as the volatility and trend movement of nominal and real exchange rates, and the unpredictable nature of exchange rates. A number of conclusions may be drawn from our survey of the empirical evidence on the validity of various economic models which seek to explain such exchange rate behaviour.

The first conclusion to emerge from our study is that reduced form equations which relate the exchange rate to fundamental variables, such as relative excess money supplies and prices, have been largely unsuccessful for the recent float. In particular, such equations exhibit poor in-sample and out-of-sample explanatory power, have coefficients which often conflict with theoretical priors and exhibit numerous instabilities. But, as we pointed out, such findings are hardly surprising given the rather *ad hoc* way reduced form asset approach equations have been implemented. Therefore a fruitful avenue for future research would be the 'correct' specification and empirical implementation of asset approach exchange rate equations (particularly since better-specified equations, such as those using forward-looking expectations, have proved successful).

A second conclusion to emerge is that exchange rates do not appear to be excessively volatile compared with other asset prices (such as share prices and interest rates) or relative to the fundamentals suggested by the monetary model; however, the use of survey data or exchange rate expectations tends to indicate that speculation has been excessive.

A third finding to emerge is that the joint hypothesis of market efficiency in the forward market for foreign exchange is strongly rejected by the data. Perhaps the most appealing explanation for this failure, and one which numerous researchers have adopted, is that since the 1970s and 1980s have been periods of immense uncertainty in foreign exchange markets, foreign exchange market operations have required a risk premium in return for holding open positions in foreign currencies.[19] However, the use of survey data, which allows single hypothesis tests of the joint hypothesis, suggest that both risk-aversion and irrationality (in that exchange rate movements appear excessive) are to blame. This finding in turn has important policy implications since, if speculators' behaviour is in itself excessive, then there may be a role for government intervention in the foreign exchange market of a coordinated type along the lines suggested by the Plaza accord. To the extent that risk premia are important, then such intervention may be of a sterilised nature since non-monetary assets are not perfect substitutes in the presence of risk.[20]

Further areas in which the future research strategy on the empirical modelling of exchange rates is likely to be developed is in terms of the modelling of speculative bubbles relative to fundamentals and the extension of the news model both in terms of the news variables included and the estimation techniques utilised.

5 Stabilisation Policy with Flexible Exchange Rates

COLM KEARNEY

INTRODUCTION

Economists' understanding of how stabilisation policy operates in economies which are open to foreign trade in commodities, services and financial assets has developed dramatically over the past quarter of a century. One source of this development has stemmed from structural changes which have occurred in the world economy over the intervening period. Examples of this are the rapid growth of the international financial system which has resulted in high mobility of capital across political frontiers and the movement away from the Bretton Woods system of fixed exchange rates in the early 1970s towards the present system of generalised floating rates. Another important source has stemmed from improvements which have occurred in understanding how economic agents make decisions, together with advancements in modelling the macroeconomy. Examples of this latter source are to be found in the rational expectations paradigm and the currently fashionable approach to deriving macroeconomic relationships from the microeconomic first principles of optimising behaviour.

It is not surprising that a large, complex and dynamic field of study such as macroeconomic stabilisation policy has been previously surveyed by other researchers. The classic surveys of Johnson (1962) and Barro and Fischer (1976) spring immediately to mind in this regard. More recently, Marston (1985), Blanchard (1988) and Fischer (1988) have surveyed open economy stabilisation policy, monetary economics and macroeconomics respectively. It is interesting to note, however, that while Marston's (1985) survey does not include the more recent developments which have occurred in analysing the microfoundations of open economy stabilization policy, Blanchard (1988) focuses exclusively on monetary matters and Fischer (1988) ignores open economy issues. The present chapter fills this gap by considering in turn the models of open economies which are based upon 'postulated' macroeconomic relationships, together with their more recent counterparts which derive the important macroeconomic relationships from the microfoundations of optimising behaviour.

It is worth emphasising at this point that our purpose here is not to provide an exhaustive survey of the relevant literature but to focus upon key issues which currently confront the student of open economy stabilisation policy. These issues can readily be interpreted as stemming from a realisation that the system of floating exchange rates which was adopted in many Western economies in the early 1970s has not performed in the manner which was envisaged by its original proponents. Both real and nominal exchange rates have exhibited unprecedented volatility which has been accompanied by a high degree of international capital mobility. As Purvis (1985) observes, the result of this has been that the large swings which have occurred in exchange rates have often become the source of need for domestic policy adjustment rather than serving as an expedient mechanism for facilitating adjustment of the economy to various disturbances. This development has prompted renewed investigation of a number of issues in open economy macroeconomics and in what follows, we focus upon three key issues which currently confront the student of open economy stabilisation policy. *First*, how do alternative exchange rate regimes affect the ability of macroeconomic policymakers to influence domestic economic activity through monetary and fiscal policies? *Second*, given the importance of international capital movements, to what extent has capital become perfectly mobile across political frontiers? *Third*, to what extent does there exist a 'twin deficits' relationship between the government's fiscal policy stance and the performance of the economy on current account of the balance of payments?

We shall see that these issues are closely related, they occupy pivotal positions in current policy discussions and they remain largely unsettled on both theoretical grounds and on the basis of available empirical evidence.

An outline of the remainder of this chapter is as follows. The second section surveys recent developments in the modelling of open economy stabilisation policy which are based upon 'postulated' macroeconomic relationships. The next section introduces the more recent microfoundation analysis of open economies and points to the relevant results which have been obtained. Taken together, these two sections provide an up-to-date account of current thinking on the first key issue which concerns the role of alternative exchange rate arrangements in determining the effectiveness of stabilisation policy. The chapter then focuses on the remaining two issues concerning the international mobility of capital and recently popular 'twin deficits' analysis. The final section summarises the chapter's main findings and points to the areas of future research interest.

RESULTS FROM 'POSTULATED' MACROMODELS

Recent research into the potency of open economy stabilisation policy which utilises 'postulated' macroeconomic relationships is readily recognisable as being based upon developments and extensions of the Mundell–Fleming model which constitutes an open-economy version of the Hicksian IS–LM model. Given the importance, popularity and wide usage of this model, we begin by providing a brief description of a 'bare bones' version of it. This will subsequently serve as the basis for discussing recent research and the results which have been obtained.

The equations of the model are numbered (5.1)–(5.13) in Table 5.1, the first six of which describe the demand for domestic output (Y) as the sum of private consumption (C) and investment (I) expenditures together with government expenditures (G) and net exports ($X - M$). These expenditures are functions of domestic income, taxes (T), the domestic interest rate (r), the foreign interest rate adjusted for expected exchange rate depreciation ($r^* + \Delta s^e$) and the real spot exchange rate ($s.P/P^*$) with s defined as the domestic currency price of foreign exchange. Equations (5.7)–(5.8) describe the demand for domestic money (L) and bonds (B) as depending upon domestic income and the expected yield to holding domestic and foreign currency denominated bonds. The own yield on money which is defined narrowly is set to zero. Equation (5.9) models the capital account of the balance of payments in a very simple fashion

TABLE 5.1   A simple 'postulated' open economy macromodel

$C = c(Y)$	$c'_y > 0$	(5.1)
$I = i(r)$	$i'_r < 0$	(5.2)
$G = \bar{G}$		(5.3)
$T = t(Y)$	$t'_y > 0$	(5.4)
$X = x(s.P/P^*)$	$x'_s > 0$	(5.5)
$M = m(Y, s.p/P^*)$	$m'_y > 0,\ m'_s < 0$	(5.6)
$H + R = L = l(Y, r, r^* + \Delta s^e)P$	$l'_y > 0,\ l'_r < 0,\ l'_{r^*} < 0$	(5.7)
$B = b(Y, r, r^* + \Delta s_e)P$	$b'_y > 0,\ b'_{r^*} < 0$	(5.8)
$\Delta F = f(r - r^* + \Delta s^e)$	$f'_r > 0,\ f'_{r^*} < 0$	(5.9)
$Y - T - C - I = \Delta\bar{H} + \Delta B - \Delta F$		(5.10)
$T - G = \Delta R - \Delta\bar{H} - \Delta B$		(5.11)
$M - X = \Delta F - \Delta R$		(5.12)
$Y = C + I + \bar{G} + X - M$		(5.13)

Notes

1. The model as presented constitutes a simplified version of Mundell (1963) and Fleming (1962).
2. $(X - M)$ denotes the balance of trade. By ignoring net income and transfers, we shall refer to this also as the current account of the balance of payments.

by relating net capital flows (ΔF) to the interest rate differential adjusted for expected depreciation of the spot exchange rate. Other symbols which require explanation are as follows: H denotes domestic high-powered money, a bar over a variable indicates that it is determined by the authorities as a matter of policy and an asterisk denotes the foreign magnitude of a variable.

Identities (5.10)–(5.13) complete the model specification. The first two of these define the private and government budget constraints while the third defines the change in foreign exchange reserves as the sum of the current and capital accounts of the balance of payments. The final identity (5.13) requires no explanation. Note that only two of identities (5.10)–(5.12) are independent. Denoting private domestic savings by $S = Y - T - C$, we can see that the sum of these identities is zero and we can write.

$$(M - X) = (I - S) + (G - T) \tag{5.14}$$

Proponents of the Ricardian equivalence theorem as restated by Barro (1974) argue that increases in $(G - T)$ will be offset by increases in S insofar as the private sector fully discounts the future tax liabilities associated with financing the fiscal deficit. If foreign residents purchase the government's debt at unchanged interest rates, Dwyer's (1985) capital inflow hypothesis will yield a close association between the current account and fiscal deficits. Proponents of the recently popular 'twin deficits' analysis such as Laney (1984), argue that the private sector tends to run a stable $(I - S)$ relationship so that current account deficits tend to mirror fiscal deficits. The relationship which exists between the variables in identity (5.14) is obviously crucial for the analysis of open economy stablilisation policy, and we shall have more to say about this in the context of both 'postulated' and optimising models of the open economy.

In order to simplify the present model to its 'bare bones' essentials, wages and prices are assumed to be fixed at unity so nominal magnitudes are equal to their real counterparts. The economy being modelled is assumed to be small, so all foreign variables are fixed and omitted from the analysis for convenience. This means that the Marshall–Lerner condition applies when $x_s + m_s > 1$. In addition, expectations are assumed to be formed in a static fashion so $\Delta s^e = 0$. The model is solved by first applying Walras Law to identify (5.10) in order to make domestic bonds the residual in private portfolios so that equation (5.8) drops out of the explicit analysis. We then substitute equations (5.1)–(5.6) into (5.13)–(5.6) together with (5.9) into (5.12) and totally differentiate the resulting two equations along with (5.7) to get equations (5.15)–(5.17) respectively.

$$dY = (c_y - c_t t_y - m_y)dY + i_r dr + (x_s - m_s)ds + d\bar{G} \qquad (5.15)$$
$$dR = -m_y dY + f_r dr + (x_s - m_s)ds \qquad (5.16)$$
$$d\bar{H} + dR = 1_y dY + 1_r dr \qquad (5.17)$$

Given the fiscal and monetary policy variables, $\bar{G}$ and $\bar{H}$, the model solves for three endogenous variables: Y, r and s (with $dR = 0$) under floating exchange rates and Y, r and R (with $ds = 0$) under a fixed exchange rate regime. The formal solution of the model for both exchange rate regimes along with the policy multipliers is not dwelled on here. The discussion here will focus rather upon the standard diagrammatic presentation of the model.

Figure 5.1 presents equations (5.15)–(5.17) as the *IS, FF* and *LM*

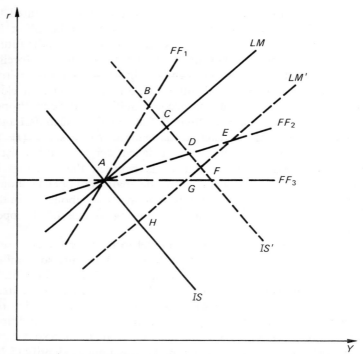

FIGURE 5.1   Stabilisation policy in the simple 'postulated' model

schedules which depict loci of combinations of domestic income and interest rates which yield equilibrium in the domestic goods market, the balance of payments and the market for domestic money respectively. The FF_1–FF_3 schedules depict the cases of low, high and perfect capital mobility respectively. Some researchers (notably Boyer (1978), Henderson (1979) and Marston (1985)) replace this schedule with one which depicts equilibrium conditions in the domestic bond market. Although the two methods are equivalent and give similar analytical results, they prompt the reader to note that perfect capital mobility implies the dual condition of *perfect substitutability* between domestic and foreign currency denominated bonds (which is an assumption about the characteristics of financial assets and/or the preferences of the market participants who trade them), and *perfect capital markets* (which is an assumption about the absence of restrictions on the behaviour of market participants).

The intersection of the *IS* and *LM* schedules determines the instantaneous equilibrium position of the economy at any given moment in time. If this does not coincide with the *FF* schedule the balance of payments is non-zero. Under fixed exchange rates, the monetary authorities must accumulate or run down their stock of foreign exchange reserves. If the monetary consequences of this intervention behaviour are not sterilised, the money supply will expand or contract and the *LM* schedule will shift in a manner which moves the instantaneous equilibrium position of the economy along the *IS* schedule towards the *FF* schedule. When all three schedules intersect at a point such as *A* in Figure 5.1, the balance of payments is zero, the monetary authorities cease to accumulate or lose foreign exchange reserves, the stock of money no longer changes and the economy is in full equilibrium. This is the classical monetary mechanism of balance of payments adjustment which is bypassed by exchange rate changes under a regime of market-determined rates. One of the enduring issues in open economy stabilisation policy concerns the relative merits of fixed versus flexible exchange rates and we shall return to consider this after outlining the basic results which emanate from our simple 'postulated' model.

Consider first the effects of a bond-financed fiscal expansion which shifts the *IS* schedule to IS_1 and the economy from *A* to *C*. The higher domestic income raises imports and causes the current account of the balance of payments to turn into deficit, while higher interest rates attract inflows of foreign capital which cause the capital account to turn into surplus. The net effect of these influences on the overall balance of payments is ambiguous – with relatively immobile capital (FF_1) the tendency will be towards deficit, while with mobile capital (FF_2 and FF_3) the overall tendency will be towards surplus. What happens next depends upon the type of exchange rate regime which the authorities operate. With fixed exchange rates and low capital mobility (FF_1), the balance of payments deficit will result in lost foreign exchange reserves and the *LM* schedule will shift back towards point *B* unless the authorities engage in successful sterilisation behaviour. With fixed exchange rates and high capital mobility (FF_2 and FF_3), the balance of payments surplus will result in the accumulation of foreign exchange reserves and, in the absence of successful sterilisation behaviour, the *LM* schedule will shift right towards points *D* and *F* respectively. With floating exchange rates and low capital mobility, the tendency for fiscal expansion to result in the loss of foreign exchange reserves will now be replaced by exchange rate depreciation. This will cause the *IS'* schedule to shift further rightwards through the operation of the Marshall–Lerner condition, and this will be joined by a similar movement in FF_1 with the economy ending up at some point to the right of *C* along the original *LM* schedule. With floating exchange rates and high capital mobility (FF_2 and FF_3), fiscal expansion will appreciate the foreign exchange value of the domestic currency and the resulting loss in international competitiveness will reduce net exports which will drag the *IS'* schedule back towards *IS*. The economy will end up on the original *LM* schedule somewhere between points *A* and *C* with imperfectly mobile capital (FF_2), and it must return to point *A* with perfectly mobile capital (FF_3)

Consider next the effects of expansionary monetary policy. An open market purchase of domestic bonds by the monetary authorities will shift the *LM* schedule rightwards to LM_1 and the economy will move from point *A* to *H* where both the current and capital accounts of the balance of payments will tend to move into deficit. With fixed exchange rates, the resulting loss of foreign exchange reserves will reduce the supply of domestic money and drag the *LM'* schedule back towards *LM* unless the authorities can successfully engage in sterilisation behaviour. When exchange rates are free to float in response to market conditions, however, the monetary expansion will unambiguously depreciate the exchange rate and the resulting improvement in current account performance will shift the *IS* schedule to the right of point *H* – at *G* with perfect capital mobility (FF_3), between *H* and *E* with high capital mobility (FF_2) and possibly further along the LM' schedule with low international mobility of capital.

It is appropriate at this stage to summarise the main conclusions about open economy stabilisation policy, which emerge from our simple 'postulated' macromodel of the Mundell–Fleming vintage. This will serve as the basis for assessing the significance of more recent theoretical advancements which can usefully be interpreted as stemming directly from respecifications of the basic model in order to overcome its weaknesses. The *first* conclusion concerns the commendable nature of the model for highlighting the importance of explicitly modelling the capital account of the balance of payments while allowing for varying degrees of international capital mobility. The previously popular 'insular economy' models of Harberger (1950) and Meade (1951) did not model the capital account of the balance of payments so the current account was forced to be zero under floating exchange rates. In terms of the model presented here, $X - M = 0$ in equation (5.10) and all entries in equation (5.11) were equal to zero so that stabilisation policy operated just as it would in a closed economy with flexible exchange rates 'insulating' the domestic economy from foreign disturbances. By introducing the capital account into the model, however, Mundell–Fleming allowed the current account to be non-zero under floating exchange rates. This destroyed the 'insulating' properties of flexible rates while determining the potency of stabilisation policies in a manner which depends importantly upon the degree to which capital is internationally mobile.

Second, the power of fiscal and monetary policies to influence domestic economic activity is crucially dependent upon the exchange rate regime as well as the degree of international capital mobility. More specifically, if we consider point C to be the closed economy response to a fiscal stimulus of the type considered above, the conclusion is reached that in an open economy with floating exchange rates, fiscal policy will be more (less) effective with low (high) capital mobility than in a closed economy, and vice versa for fixed exhange rates. If we consider point H to be the closed economy response to a monetary policy initiative like that considered above, the conclusion is reached that monetary policy in an open economy with floating (fixed) exchange rates will be more (less) effective than in a closed economy. By ignoring the case of low capital mobility (FF_3), these conclusions can be taken together to imply that fiscal policy is more effective under fixed than under floating exchange rates while monetary policy is more effective under floating than under a fixed exchange rate regime. These are perhaps the best-known of Mundell's (1963) conclusions.

Third, in the polar case of perfect mobility of capital across political frontiers, fiscal policy will become powerless to influence domestic income when the exchange rate is market-determined. This happens because the resulting exchange rate movements will ensure that the entire fiscal stimulus is transmitted abroad through the current account of the balance of payments. This is the so-called 'twin deficits' case which has gained recent popularity since the 'blow-out' in the United States' fiscal and current account deficits under the Reaganomics of the 1980s.

Fourth, monetary policy will become a powerless tool of stabilisation policy in a world of perfect capital mobility and fixed exchange rates except to the extent that the authorities can successfully sterilise the monetary implications of its foreign exchange market intervention behaviour. Although there exists some scope for this in the short run, it will not persist over time, as eventually the monetary base will have no domestic component or the authorities will run out of foreign reserves. Limited scope for successful short-term sterilised intervention behaviour has been demonstrated to exist for Germany and the UK by Obstfeld (1983) and Kearney and MacDonald (1986) respectively.

Having spelt out the major conclusions about open economy stabilisation policy which emanate from the Mundell–Fleming model, it is interesting to consider the extent to which subsequent developments in the specification of the model have resulted in revisions to these conclusions. The main weaknesses in the model as presented here are fivefold: namely, it contains an inappropriate stock-flow specification of the capital account of the balance of payments; it omits consideration of wealth effects; it models only the demand side of the macroeconomy while keeping wages and prices fixed; it models the formation of expectations in a naive static fashion; and it omits consideration of the issues which arise from the existence of uncertainty. As alluded to above, the developments which have occurred in 'postulated' macroeconomic models of open economy stabilisation policy have largely been directed at overcoming these weaknesses, and it is interesting to examine how these developments have resulted in revised conclusions.

The Mundell–Fleming model specifies capital *flows* rather than *stocks* as depending upon the level of interest rates with the result that changes in the latter will induce permanent *flows* of capital across political frontiers. As a number of authors have pointed out, this feature of the model is not consistent with portfolio balance because it allows the current account to be permanently non-zero, while implying that domestic residents are willing to allow non-residents to accumulate indefinite amounts of claims and/or liabilities on them. By making all asset *stocks* dependent upon interest rate levels, the portfolio balance approach overcomes this weakness while emphasising the degree of substitutability between domestic and foreign currency denominated assets along with wealth effects as important determinants of the potency of stabilisation policy. In terms of the financial sector of our simple 'postulated' model, the portfolio balance model involves adding wealth to the consumption equation (5.1) and replacing equations (5.7)–(5.10) with (5.18)–(5.21) respectively:

$$L = 1(Y,W,r,r^* + \Delta s^e)P \tag{5.18}$$

$$B = b(Y,W,r,r^* + \Delta s^e)P \tag{5.19}$$

$$F = f(Y,W,r,r^* + \Delta s^e)P \tag{5.20}$$

$$W = L + B + s.F \tag{5.21}$$

where W denotes wealth and F is now measured in foreign currency so pre-multiplying by s will convert it to domestic currency.

Although the qualitative effects of stabilisation policy under floating exchange rates remain as before, the quantitative effects will be less certain insofar as there now exists a more complete range of cross-substitution effects, while the *IS, FF* and *LM* schedules will all be affected by changes in wealth. It is interesting to note that when domestic and foreign currency denominated assets are perfectly substitutable, the portfolio balance model predicts the same short-run effects of stabilisation policy as does the Mundell–Fleming model with perfect capital mobility. As Rodriguez (1979) and Sachs (1980) demonstrate, however, these effects can be reversed over time in the portfolio balance model if expansionary fiscal policy reduces the net foreign asset position of the economy due to current account deficits. In this case the achievement of long-run equilibrium may necessitate the achievement of lower domestic output in order to generate trade account surpluses to match deteriorating debt-service obligations.

The inclusion of domestic bonds (B) in the wealth identity (5.17) prompts consideration of the application of Ricardian equivalence as restated by Barro (1974) to open economies. The conditions under which this equivalence theorem will operate in an open economy context will match the closed economy case if the foreign interest rate which is faced by the domestic private and public sectors is the same. In this case, as Leiderman and Blejer (1987) point out, the domestic private sector internalises the government's debt regardless of the extent to which it is held by domestic or foreign residents. There exists a well-documented set of conditions under which Ricardian equivalence will not hold – Stiglitz (1983) provides examples of market imperfections such as price rigidities and incomplete markets for intergenerational risk-sharing, Barro (1979) and Razin and Svensson (1983) illustrate the effects of distortionary taxes, Greenwood and Kimbrough (1985) illustrate the effects of capital controls and Blanchard (1985) illustrates how finite horizons drive a wedge between private and public discount rates. Helpman and Razin (1987) employ Blanchard's (1985) insight to provide an important example of Ricardian inequivalence in a flexible exchange rate open economy context. Inspired by the experiences of some Latin American countries in the late 1970s and Israel in the early 1980s, these researchers examine the implications of a policy-induced slowdown in the rate of devaluation of the foreign exchange rate which is not matched by an accompanying fiscal contraction. This results in the loss of foreign reserves and greater foreign borrowing which should not influence domestic private wealth under the conditions of Ricardian equivalence. In the countries examined, however, consumption expenditures actually increased and deteriorating current account performance was accompanied by appreciation of the real exchange rate.

What implications does this have for stabilisation policy? Consider, for example, the effects of a bond-financed fiscal expansion which, in the Mundell–Fleming model with high capital mobility and flexible exchange rates, was seen to move the economy to somewhere between points A and C on the original LM schedule in Figure 5.1 – with zero effectiveness under perfect capital mobility at point A. In the portfolio balance model with highly substitutable domestic and foreign currency denominated assets (FF_2 and FF_3 in Figure 5.1), a similar fiscal policy initiative will move the economy to somewhere within the triangular area ACF if the economy is a net creditor in foreign currency denominated assets. This occurs because the exchange rate appreciation shifts the LM schedule rightwards by reducing the domestic currency value of financial wealth and moderating the demand for financial assets. Note that if domestic and foreign currency denominated assets are perfectly substitutable, the economy will end up on the FF_3 schedule between points A and F but not at A. This destroys the *third* prediction of the Mundell–Fleming model alluded to above concerning the impotency of fiscal policy with perfectly mobile capital and flexible exchange rates. It also implies the non-existence of a 'twin deficits' relationship whereby the entire fiscal deficit is exported through the resulting current account deficit. It is worth noting that similar results to this were obtained by

Branson and Buiter (1983) who amended the Mundell–Fleming model by allowing the exchange rate to influence the domestic price level. Expansionary fiscal policy which appreciates the exchange rate will also shift the *LM* schedule in this case because the lower prices will raise the real supply of money in the economy.

When wage and price flexibility is added to the existence of wealth effects in our 'postulated' portfolio balance model, the Mundell–Fleming conclusions about the potency of stabilisation policy under alternative exchange rate systems require further modification. Marston (1985) provides a good account of how this comes about. The primary effects of fiscal expansion with high capital mobility will be to raise the real exchange rate (*s.P/P**). With fixed nominal exchange rates, this will occur wholly through higher domestic prices and the resulting drop in real wages will ensure that extra output is generated. When exchange rates are market-determined, however, the higher real exchange rate will partly consist of nominal appreciation, and the resulting wealth effects will ensure that output expands more than under fixed rates. This contrasts with the *second* of Mundell–Fleming's conclusions. In addition, monetary policy loses its potency in a flexible exchange rate regime in this version of the model because the higher prices reduce real wealth and generate less output, together with a surplus on current account of the balance of payments which raises wealth over time until its initial level is restored in full equilibrium. Note that if purchasing power parity holds in this version of the model, the exchange rate and domestic prices will move in tandem to eliminate any short-term output effects of monetary policy. This result corresponds to that obtained in the monetary models of exchange rate determination – MacDonald (1988) provides an excellent survey.

When the agents whose economic behaviour is being modelled are assumed to form their expectations in a rational manner, some interesting conclusions emerge, depending upon the specification of other aspects of the model. For example, Dornbusch (1976) introduced rational expectations into a dynamic version of the Mundell–Fleming model with sticky prices and perfect capital mobility, and found that the exchange rate may 'overshoot' its long-run equilibrium response to a previously unanticipated monetary policy initiative. This model specification and prediction are now well-known in the literature on exchange rate determination and are discussed further in other chapters of this volume. It is noteworthy, however, that the long-run predictions of the model are similar to those of the simple specification which is contained in Table 5.1. In particular, the 'twin deficits' prediction emerges intact insofar as fiscal policy continues to exert no influence over domestic output in a regime of market-determined exchange rates because its effects are transmitted abroad through the current account balance.

When stochastic disturbances are added to the *IS* and *LM* schedules of our simple Mundell–Fleming model, we can investigate the relative insulating properties of fixed versus flexible exchange rates to protect the domestic economy from aggregate demand or monetary disturbances. The resulting analysis constitutes a straight-forward generalisation of Poole's (1970) analysis for a closed economy. In the case of high capital mobility, the second conclusion of our Mundell–Fleming model about the enhanced effectiveness of fiscal policy under fixed exchange rates and of monetary policy under flexible rates can be transformed into conclusions about the relative insulating properties of alternative exchange rates. The result is that fixed exchange rates insulate the economy better when disturbances are predominantly monetary in nature because reserves rather than output will be affected. On the other hand, flexible exchange rates provide better insulation in the face of aggregate demand disturbances because the exchange rate rather than output will be affected in this case. As Marston (1985) points out, this ranking is maintained in extensions of the model to incorporate rational expectations as long as wages are fixed in the short term. Many generalisations of this model have appeared in the recent literature to investigate the optimal degree of exchange rate manage-ment in an economy which is faced by both temporary and perma-nent nominal and real disturbances of domestic and foreign origin. Daniel (1985) provides a concise summary of this literature which concludes that the optimal exchange rate policy will usually involve some degree of 'leaning against the wind' rather than completely fixed or market-determined rates.

We can summarise this section by noting that the results which have emerged from 'postulated' models of the open economy have demonstrated a considerable range of variation depending upon the precise model specification. An interesting study by Kawai (1985) which specifies a very general open economy macromodel finds that a wide range of responses to policy disturbances are possible. The more definite results which emerge from simpler models may well conceal important complexities which would explain why they are not readily supported by empirical evidence. It is with considerable interest therefore that we now turn to examine the more recent studies which derive the macroeconomic relationships from first principles of microeconomic optimisation.

RESULTS FROM OPTIMISING MACROMODELS

Macroeconomists since Keynes have become aware of the need to derive their behavioural relationships from the microeconomic first principles of optimising behaviour. A renewed sense of urgency has been injected into this endeavour since the realisation of Lucas (1976) that perceived changes in the policy regime may well cause economic agents to alter their maximising behaviour in ways which modify many previously 'postulated' macroeconomic relationships. The significance of this development for the present discussion lies in the fact that a number of recent contributions to the literature on open economy stabilisation policy have been based upon macroeconomic models which derive their important relationships from the microeconomic foundations of individual optimising behaviour. These models fall conspicuously into a twofold classification; namely, those which result in Walrasian market-clearing macroeconomic frameworks and those which allow for the existence of market disequilibrium. Obstfeld (1981), Kimbrough (1985) and Frenkel and Razin (1986b) have constructed the former type of model while Dixit (1978), Neary (1980), Persson (1982), van Wijnbergen (1984), Cuddington and Vinals (1986a, 1986b) and Moore (1989) have constructed models which allow for the existence of various types of market disequilibria.

In this section we present a summary description of the results which have emerged to date from the disequilibrium models which allow for the existence of unemployed resources with fixed prices. This facilitates comparison with the results which have emerged from the Mundell–Fleming vintage 'postulated' models which were discussed in the previous section. It is noteworthy that the early work on optimising disequilibrium models of the open economy by Dixit (1978) restricted the analysis to a fixed exchange rate economy which produces and consumes a single tradeable commodity. Neary (1980) extended this to examine an economy which produces and consumes a tradeable as well as a non-tradeable commodity. Further refinements by Helpman (1981), Persson (1982), Cuddington, Johansson and Lofgren (1984) and Cuddington and Vinals (1986a,b) permit the analysis of flexible as well as fixed exchange rate open economies utilising the 'cash-in-advance' view of money demand, while Moore (1989) further refines the model by incorporating the implications of allowing the goods to be invested for inventory purposes as well as being consumed.

Perhaps the most popular version of this approach is that which is provided by Cuddington, Johansson and Lofgren (1984). Table 5.2 presents a summary description of the basic components of this framework. The economy being modelled produces and consumes a traded (T) and a non-traded (N) good with the price of the former (P_T) being fixed in world markets. These goods are assumed to be perishable and are produced by firms which employ sectorally mobile labour and immobile capital. The wage rate is consequentially equalised across sectors and it is fixed in nominal terms while the role of the capital stock is not further considered. Unlike the simple Mundell–Fleming model which assumes that the supply of output is perfectly elastic at the prevailing price level, this models both the demand and the supply side of the macroeconomy. Households seek to maximise their welfare by supplying labour and demanding commodities while firms maximise their profits by demanding labour in order to supply commodities.

The optimisation behaviour of households is summarised by the utility-maximisation problem of equation (5.22):

$$MAX\ U(L^S,\ Y_T^D,\ Y_N^D,\ A^1)$$

$$s.t.\ P_T Y_T^D + P_N Y_N^D + (A^1 - A) = WL^S + \pi \tag{5.22}$$

where L denotes labour with money wage rate W and Y_i and P_i $(i = T,N)$ denote the sectoral outputs with their prices, π denotes profits which are distributed to households at the start of each period and A denotes wealth at the start of each period. In addition, superscripts D S and ^{1} denote respectively the demand for, the supply of and the end-period value of the relevant variable. Solving this optimisation problem in the usual manner yields the household labour supply, commodity demand and target saving equations (5.24)–(5.26) in Table 5.2. The optimisation behaviour of firms is likewise summarised by the profit maximisation problem of equation (5.23):

$$MAX \; P_i F(L_i) - WL_i \qquad\qquad i = T,N \qquad\qquad (5.23)$$

where $F(L_i) = Y_i^S$ are the sectoral production functions. Solving this problem as usual yields the labour demand functions (5.27) in Table 5.2 which, when substituted into the production functions, yield the sectoral output supply equations (5.28). National income, expenditure and the balance of trade are defined by the following three equations while the next equation (5.32) defines the demand for money in the economy. The specification of the latter reflects the cash-in-advance approach of Clower (1967) which has recently been employed by Helpman (1981) and Persson (1982) amongst others. This approach models the demand for money as a medium of exchange while insisting that all transactions must be made using money. The demand for money therefore equals real expenditure so that velocity is fixed at unity in this model.

Although various types of disequilibrium positions are possible in situations where there exists an inappropriate vector of relative prices, we shall confine ourselves here to situations of Keynesian unemployment where the demand for non-traded goods is deficient. The resulting sales constraint ($\bar{Y}_N$) will force producers of non-tradeables to curtail their *effective* demands (denoted by $\hat{\;}$) for labour according to equation (5.27^1):

$$\hat{L}_N^D = \hat{L}_N^D(\bar{Y}_N) \qquad\qquad (5.27^1)$$

which is obtained by inverting the production function and evaluating it at the point where the constraint is binding. As a result of this, households will face a labour supply constraint ($\bar{L}$) which will curtail their *effective* commodity demands according to equation (25^1):

$$\hat{Y}_T^D = \hat{Y}_T^D(P_T, \, P_N, \, A + \bar{Y}) \qquad\qquad \hat{Y}_N^D = \hat{Y}_N{}^D(P_T, \, P_N, \, A + \bar{Y})$$

$$(5.25^1)$$

where $\bar{Y} = \pi + W\bar{L}$.

The total supply of non-tradeables which firms will be able to sell ($\bar{Y}_N$) is thus given by the sum of the households' *effective* demands and that of the government.

$$\bar{Y}_N = \hat{Y}_N^D(P_T, \, P_N, \, A + \bar{Y}) + G_N \qquad\qquad (5.33)$$

Substituting this into equation (5.29) in Table 5.2 yields the equilibrium level of income in situations of Keynesian unemployment which is presented as equation (5.29^1) in Table 5.2.

TABLE 5.2   An optimising open economy macromodel

Households

$$L^S = L^S (P_T, P_N, W, A + \pi) \tag{5.24}$$

$$Y_T^D = Y_T^D (P_T, P_N, W, A + \pi) \qquad Y_N^D = Y_N^D (P_T, P_N, W, A + \pi) \tag{5.25}$$

$$S = A^1 (P, P, W, A + \pi) \qquad - A \tag{5.26}$$

Firms

$$L_T^D = L_T^D(P_T, W) \qquad L_N^D = L_N^D(P_N, W) \tag{5.27}$$

$$Y_T^S = Y_T^S(P_T, W) \qquad Y_N^S = Y_N^S(P_N, W) \tag{5.28}$$

Output, expenditure and the balance of trade

$$Y = P_T Y_T^S (P_T, W) + P_N Y_N^S (P_N, W) \tag{5.29}$$

$$Y_D = P_T Y_T^D (P_T, P_N, W, A + \pi) + P_N Y_N^D (P_T, P_N, W, A + \pi) + P_N G_N \tag{5.30}$$

$$BOT = P_T^* [Y_T^S (P_T, W) - Y_T^D (P_T, W, A + \pi)] \tag{5.31}$$

Money demand

$$M = M (P_T, P_N, Y + A, G_N) \tag{5.32}$$

Keynesian unemployment

$$\bar{Y} = P_T Y_T^S (P_T, W) + P_N \hat{Y}_N^D (P_T, P_N, A + Y) + P_N G_N \tag{5.29}[1]$$

Notes
1. The model as presented corresponds to the Keynesian unemployment version of Cuddington, Johansson and Lofgren (1984) with perfect capital mobility.
2. There is no domestic bond in the model so fiscal policy is implicitly financed by foreign debt.

When the monetary authorities operate a fixed exchange rate regime, they cannot also determine the supply of money, so monetary policy is ineffective. The level of income in this case is determined entirely by conditions in the product markets as described by equation (5.29[1]). Under floating rates, however, the money supply becomes an exogenous variable under the control of the authorities and the level of income is determined together with the exchange rate by conditions in both the goods and money markets.

We can analyse the operation of stabilisation policy in this optimising model in a diagrammatic fashion as we did with the 'postulated' model of the previous sections. The small country assumption together with the 'law of one price' ensures that the price of traded goods is fixed in units of foreign currency ($P_T = sP_T^*$) so that the P_T^* fixed at unity, P_T is the exchange rate. The analogues of the *IS* and *LM* schedules are obtained by plotting the equilibrium conditions (5.29¹) and (5.32) in (Y, P_T) space as the *GG* and *MM* schedules in Figure 5.2.

Consider first the effects of a bond-financed fiscal expansion in which the government raises its demand for non-traded goods. When the exchange rate is fixed, the output of tradeables will not be affected, because these goods are produced by unconstrained profit-maximising firms. The higher demand for non-tradeables will, however, alleviate the sales constraint which previously faced firms in this sector, the *GG* schedule shifts to G^1G^1 and the economy will move from point *A* towards *B*. This illustrates the workings of the usual multiplier process which raises aggregate demand for both

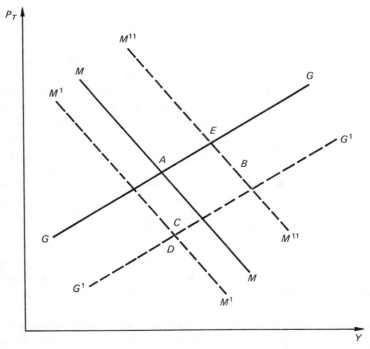

FIGURE 5.2 **Stabilisation policy in the optimising model with Keynesian unemployment and perfect capital mobility**

traded and non-traded goods and causes the balance of trade to turn into deficit. When the authorities operate a regime of floating exchange rates, the rightwards shift in the GG schedule to G^1G^1 is accompanied by a leftwards shift in the MM schedule to M^1M^1. This happens because the higher transactions demand for money necessitates an appreciation of the exchange rate (i.e. a fall in P_T) to restore equilibrium in the money market. The economy will consequently move from point A to C in this case. The output effects of this policy initiative will remain positive as long as the government expenditure multiplier with a fixed exchange rate exceeds the transactions demand for money. If it doesn't, the MM schedule will shift further than the GG schedule and the economy will end up with less output at some point left of D on the G^1G^1 schedule. It is interesting to note that while the output of non-traded goods will rise, the exchange rate appreciation induces firms to produce less traded goods. The balance of trade effects are consequently indeterminate – a deficit will emerge unless the overall aggregate demand effects of the fiscal expansion are sufficiently negative to outweigh the reduction in production of tradeables.

Consider next the effects of expansionary monetary policy in which the authorities engage in open market operations to shift the MM schedule rightwards to $M^{11}M^{11}$. When the exchange rate is fixed the resulting loss in foreign exchange reserves will result in a decline in the supply of money and the $M^{11}M^{11}$ schedule will return to its original position. This replicates the result obtained in the 'postulated' model that the authorities cannot simultaneously target on the money supply and the exchange rate. When the exchange rate is market-determined, however, the resulting depreciation will move the economy from A to E. The higher price of traded goods will lead to more production in this sector and the higher aggregate demand will impinge upon both sectors so that more non-traded goods will also be produced as firms in that sector experience a relaxation of their sales constraint. The balance of trade effects of this policy initiative are indeterminate insofar as they depend upon the relative increase in the supply and demand for traded goods.

Having now examined the operation of stabilisation policy in the context of both 'postulated' and optimising models of the open economy, it is opportune at this point to compare the results. Table 5.3 accomplishes this task for the case of perfect capital mobility. It is interesting to note that while the qualitative effects of fiscal policy under fixed exchange rates are similar in both models, the same does not apply to a regime of floating rates in which both the output and balance of trade effects are ambiguous in the optimising model. This result goes together with those which have emanated from the more recent 'postulated' model specifications discussed in the previous section and it demonstrates the extent to which the *fourth* conclusion of our simple Mundell–Fleming model about fiscal impotency and 'twin deficits' analysis constitutes a special case. When we turn to consider the potency of monetary policy in the 'postulated' and optimising models with perfect capital mobility, it is not surprising that the predictions are similar when the authorities operate a regime of fixed exchange rates. When the exchange rate is market-determined, however, monetary expansion turns the balance of trade into deficit in the 'postulated' model while the outcome is ambiguous in the optimising model.

We can summarise this section by noting that the qualitative results which emerge from the optimising model with Keynesian unemployment are similar to those which emerge from the Mundell–

TABLE 5.3 Stabilisation policy in 'postulated' and optimising open economy models with perfect capital mobility

Model specification	Total output	Output of non-traded goods	Output of traded goods	Exchange rate	Balance of trade
A 'Postulated' model					
Fiscal policy					
Fixed Exchange Rate	+			0	−
Flexible Exchange Rate	0			+	−
Monetary policy					
Fixed Exchange Rate	0			0	0
Flexible Exchange Rate	+			−	−
B Optimising model					
Fiscal policy					
Fixed Exchange Rate	+	+	0	0	−
Flexible Exchange Rate	?	+	−	+	?
Monetary policy					
Fixed Exchange Rate	0	0	0	0	0
Flexible Exchange Rate	+	+	+	−	?

Fleming vintage 'postulated' model when international capital movements are unrestricted across fixed exchange rates. This situation does not obtain when the authorities operate a floating exchange rate regime. It is worth noting that recent work by Cuddington and Vinals (1968b) and Moore (1989) demonstrates that a richer set of responses to stabilisation policy can emerge from the optimising models when different types of disequilibrium situations are investigated. This literature is, however, still in its infancy and much future research remains to be done.

INTERNATIONAL CAPITAL MOBILITY AND THE 'TWIN DEFICITS'

One of the enduring predictions which emerges from the 'postulated' macroeconomic models discussed in Section 1 concerns the importance of international capital mobility for assessing the effectiveness of stabilisation policy under alternative exchange rate regimes. We saw in Figure 5.1 how the *second* and *third* conclusions of the Mundell–Fleming model imply that fiscal policy will be more (less) effective in stabilising output in a floating exchange rate open economy with low (high) capital mobility, and that it will exert no influence on output with perfect capital mobility because the entire fiscal stimulus will be exported through the current account balance. It is not surprising, therefore, that much recent research has been concerned to investigate the extent to which capital has become increasingly mobile across political frontiers. The seminal work in this area has been reported by Feldstein and Horioka (1980) and Feldstein (1983). These researchers argued that if international movements of capital are unrestricted, there should be no relationship between domestic savings and investment because the former would be exported to the country with the highest available rate of return rather than being used to finance domestic investment. On the other hand, if international capital movements are severely restricted, we should expect to observe a close relationship between domestic savings and investment. It is intriguing to observe that in this case the $(I - S)$ term in equation (5.14) should approximate zero which would appear to imply the emergence of the 'twin deficits' case. In order to test which of these cases is the better description of the facts, Feldstein and Horioka (1980) estimated the following econometric relationship:

$$I = \alpha_0 + \alpha_1 S + u \qquad (5.34)$$

They calculated the average gross domestic saving and fixed investment rates for each of fifteen industrial countries over the period 1960–74 and regressed the cross-section average investment rates on a constant and the average saving rates. The results demonstrate conclusively that domestic savings and investment rates are highly correlated over the period of study. Feldstein (1983) extended this data period to include 1975–79 and obtained similar results. Subsequent research by Penati and Dooley (1984) confirmed these findings which seem to indicate that the development of the international financial system has not yet succeeded in creating perfectly mobile capital across political frontiers. It is interesting to note, however, that more recent research on this issue by Dooley, Frankel and Mathieson (1987) have questioned the interpretation of earlier studies by noting that observed correlations between domestic saving and investment rates does not necessarily imply that domestic residents are forced to accept lower rates of return on domestic investments. Rather, these variables are both determined endogenously and it is possible that the factors which generate high saving rates in a given country will also generate high rates of investment.

While the results of empirical research into the issue of international capital mobility remain unconvincing, a number of researchers have focused upon another aspect of equation (5.14) in order to examine the extent of empirical support for the existence of a close relationship between fiscal policy and current account imbalances. If $(I - S)$ is stable over time, we can test for the existence of a close 'twin deficits' relationship by estimating the following econometric relationship:

$$(M - X) = \beta_0 + \beta_1 (G - T) + u \qquad (5.35)$$

If the β_1 coefficient is statistically significant and close to unity, this would provide evidence which is favourable to the 'twin deficits' case. Laney (1984) estimated this equation on annual data from 59 countries over a period of 25–30 years to 1982 and found mixed evidence of a statistically significant β_1 coefficient. Subsequent work by Kearney and Fallick (1987) using both cross-section and time-series data for the OECD countries and by Darrat (1988) using time-series data for the US has, however, concluded that there is little evidence in favour of such a relationship. It is interesting to observe that the latter study found strong evidence of reverse causation in the US, which implies that current account imbalances determine fiscal policy stances as much as vice-versa. As with the work on capital mobility, the results from this investigation are not yet convincing although the bulk of available evidence is not very supportive of a close causal relationship between the stance of fiscal policy and current account performance.

CONCLUSIONS

The purpose of this chapter has been to explore a number of key issues in open economy stabilisation policy. Recent developments in modelling the open economy with macroeconomic relationships which are derived from the first principles of microeconomic optimisation suggests a dichotomisation of the literature into the more traditional 'postulated' models and their more recent optimising counterparts. Within these alternative frameworks, three key issues of current interest were examined: *first*, how do alternative exchange rate regimes affect the ability of policymakers to influence domestic economic activity through monetary and fiscal policy? *second*, to what extent has the international mobility of capital increased in recent times? and *third*, does there exist a close 'twin deficits' relationship between fiscal and current account imbalances?

We have seen how alternative exchange rate arrangements have important implications for the operation of monetary and fiscal policies in both 'postulated' and optimising models, and that optimal exchange rate policy for an economy which is faced by different kinds of disturbance will usually involve some degree of 'leaning against the wind'. We have also seen mixed evidence for the enhanced mobility of capital across political frontiers together with limited empirical support for the view that fiscal policy stance is an important determinant of a country's performance on current account of the balance of payments. The major conclusion which emerges from our investigation, however, concerns the extent to which the results from 'postulated' models have been shown to be highly sensitive to variations in model specification. This finding suggests that future research may best be focused upon improving the specification of optimising models of the open economy.

6 International Policy Coordination

DAVID CURRIE

INTRODUCTION

The focus of this chapter is on current issues of macroeconomic policymaking. In contrast to much of the academic literature, its purpose is to build bridges between the rather technical and abstract academic literature on the subject and the current process of policy discussion and coordination in policy circles.

The paper falls into three sections. The first sets out some theoretical concepts that are helpful for analysing issues of international policy coordination. The following section then considers whether and why policy coordination should be regarded as desirable in principle, addressing various arguments that suggest that coordination may be unhelpful and then moves on to consider certain obstacles. The final section then considers what form coordination should take if it is to be beneficial; and then moves on to consider how coordination might be achieved, addressing the very considerable difficulties that lie in the way of establishing coordinated policy amongst the key economies in the international system.

WHAT IS POLICY COORDINATION?

International economic policy coordination is the process whereby 'countries modify their economic policies in what is intended to be a mutually beneficial manner, taking account of international economic linkages' (Group of 30, 1988). This is a broad definition, encompassing a spectrum of forms of coordination from the rather limited to the ambitious. At the ambitious end is the Bonn economic summit of 1978, where the Group of Seven countries agreed to a full-blown package deal (see Putnam and Bayne, 1987). At the more limited end is the multilateral surveillance process carried out by the International Monetary Fund under the Bretton Woods fixed exchange rate system, and that more recently established by the Group of Seven countries: such surveillance may act to coordinate policies between countries, albeit in a partial and limited way.

The case in principle for the international coordination of macroeconomic policy is based on the presence of significant policy spillovers between countries, so that policy actions taken by one country impact on other countries and vice versa. In the presence of such spillovers, uncoordinated decision-making by governments may well result in an inefficient outcome. A better outcome for all countries can occur if governments agree between themselves a mutually acceptable coordinated policy, taking account of the interdependencies between them.

This basic point may be illustrated diagrammatically using the Hamada diagram (Hamada, 1985) in Figure 6.1. This illustrates the two country case, but the argument generalises in a straightforward way to many countries. On the horizontal axis, we represent the policy instrument, I_1, of country 1; on the vertical axis the policy instrument, I_2, of country 2. The objective function of country 1 defines a set of indifference curves, connecting points of equal welfare, as perceived by country 1. In the absence of spillovers, these indifference curves would be vertical lines, with the welfare level defined uniquely by the instrument setting I_1, of country 1. But with spillovers, the instrument setting I_2 of country 2 influences the welfare of country 1. As a consequence, the indifference curves become ellipses around the bliss point B_1 (or point of highest welfare) of country 1. Similar elliptical indifference curves map out points of equal welfare around the bliss point, B_2, of country 2.

Efficient policies are those for which the indifference maps of two countries are tangential. These are represented by the contract curve joining B_1 and B_2. These policies are Pareto-efficient, in the sense that one country's welfare can rise only if the other country's welfare falls.

Uncoordinated decision-making is not likely to lead to policies on the efficient contract curve. This may be seen as follows from Figure

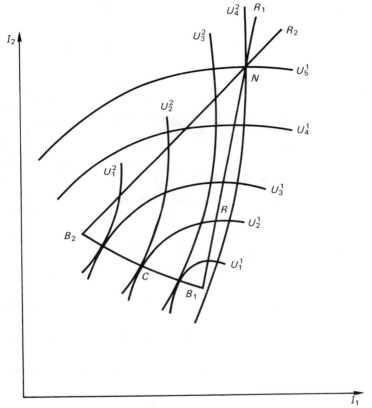

FIGURE 6.1 Hamada diagram

6.2. In the absence of coordination, country 1 will treat country 2's policy as given when deciding upon its own policy. For any setting, I_2, it will therefore choose I_1 to maximise its welfare. Thus it chooses I_1 to give the point of tangency between the indifference curve and the horizontal line corresponding to I_2. Varying I_2 then traces out the reaction function, R_1 of country 1, connecting the horizontal points on its indifference curves.

The reaction function R_2 of country 2 can be defined similarly depicting the optimal choice of I_2 for given I_1. R_2 connects the points where the indifference curves of country 1 are vertical.

The outcome of uncoordinated decision making is the Nash point,

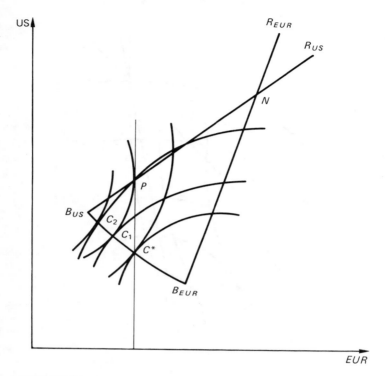

FIGURE 6.2   The consequences of European fiscal precommitment

given by the intersection of the two reaction functions. At this Nash outcome, both countries are doing the best they can, given the policies of the other country. But the outcome is inefficient. The Nash point is Pareto-inferior to at least a subset of coordinated policies lying on the contract curve.

This Hamada diagram illustrates neatly the potential inefficiency of uncoordinated decision making. By treating the other country's (or countries') policy actions as given, governments carry out policies that, in the aggregate, are undesirable. A more efficient outcome can be obtained by agreeing jointly on a policy in a cooperative manner.

Three points should be noted about this. First, this result depends on policy spillovers. In the absence of spillovers, the bliss point of each country becomes a line (vertical for country 1 and horizontal for country 2), so that the optimal policy setting for one country is independent of that for the other. In this case, both countries can obtain their optimal welfare setting, and uncoordinated policymaking is not inefficient. However, this is a special and rather unlikely case, since policy spillovers are prevalent.

Second, coordination of policy does not require agreement over objectives by governments. The objectives of governments can be quite different, and yet coordination of policy can be desirable. This is illustrated in Figure 6.1: the bliss points of the two countries differ, so there is an intrinsic policy conflict. None the less this conflict is best dealt with by cooperation, so that policies put the economy on the efficient contract curve B_1B_2. The precise point on B_1B_2 that is chosen will depend on the process of bargaining that arrives at the agreed coordinated policy.

Third, the coordinated outcome suffers from the problem of free-riding or reneging. If country 1 thinks that country 2 will continue with the agreed policy at, say, C, then it pays country 1 to renege to point R on its reaction function, R_1. This will be all the easier if it is difficult to monitor policy actions, so country 1 can argue with some plausibility that it is adhering to the agreed policy bargain while it is simultaneously reneging. Moreover, the incentive to renege may be stronger for coordinated policies between many countries, since the non-reneging countries may well have some incentive to continue with the agreed policy amongst themselves even though one of their number has reneged. Thus, for example, in the case of two countries, if each country states that it will revert to the Nash, non-coordinated policy if the other country reneges, this may well be sufficient to sustain the coordinated policy.

This last point focuses attention in the issue of the *sustainability* of coordinated policies. However, the question of sustainability has wider ramifications that touch on the issues of time inconsistency and reputation in policy. These issues arise because of the presence of an intelligent, forward-looking private sector, so that to be sustainable policies must carry credibility with the private sector.

To consider this point further, we start by noting that forward-looking behaviour by the private sector may enlarge the range of policies available to the government. To see this, consider the example of a government that wishes to lower inflation by tightening monetary policy (by raising short-term interest rates, for example). In the absence of forward-looking expectations, such a tightening will only begin to lower inflation when the policy is enacted (whether through its effect on aggregate demand or, in the context of an open economy, by inducing an appreciation of the exchange rate). But with forward-looking expectations, the announcement of a *future* tightening of monetary policy is sufficient to lower inflation if the announcement is believed (although the reduction may be smaller in magnitude). The expectation of a tighter monetary policy in the future will immediately raise longer-term real interest rates, thereby dampening aggregate demand. The interest rate increase will lead to an appreciation of the exchange rate, with consequences for the behaviour of domestic prices and wage behaviour. Thus the announcement of tight money in the future, if it is believed, will act to reduce inflationary pressures now. One example of such announcement effects is provided by the UK Medium Term Financial Strategy. In announcing a gradual phased reduction of monetary growth over a five-year horizon, the MTFS combined accouncements of future tightening of monetary policy with an immediate action policy.

The literature has directed considerable attention to whether such announcements of future policy action are generally credible. The standard answer has been in the negative. It is argued that there will be an incentive for government to renege on the announcement when the time comes to carry it out. Thus the policies are said to be *time-inconsistent*. (See Kydland and Prescott (1977)). In the above example, if the announcement of tight monetary policy in the future does indeed bring down the rate of inflation, then the incentive to tighten monetary policy in the future will no longer exist. The private sector, if it is sufficiently astute, can pursue this line of reasoning for itself and consequently the initial announcement will not be believed. Thus, it is argued, time-inconsistent policies which seek to exploit the power of policy announcements are not credible. Credible policies are those which are time-consistent; that is, those which incorporate no future incentive to renege. However, the costs of imposing time-consistency can be rather high, when measured in terms of the performance of stabilisation policy. The non-credibility of announcements is therefore costly.

It may be that governments can precommit their policy action, so sustaining the time-inconsistent policy. But in general there are other plausible circumstances in which announcements of future policy changes are generally credible. It is essential to view the policy problem as a repeated policy game, responding to continuing stochastic shocks to the economy, in contrast to the one-shot policy game implicitly assumed in the above argument. The presence of continuing stochastic disturbances affects governments' incentives to adhere to policy announcements. The temptation to renege on policy announcements made in response to past disturbances is tempered by the fear that credibility will be lost and that policy will be less able to cope with future disturbances. (See Currie and Levine, 1986.) If the rate of discount is not too high, this repeated nature of the policy problem may well eliminate any incentive to renege, rendering policy announcements both credible and sustainable. In terms of the above example, the government will not renege if it expects the economy to be subjected to continuing inflationary disturbances, to which policy must react. This argument will be strengthened if a government's reputation extends across a range of its activities, so that reneging in the sphere of macroeconomic policy has implications for its credibility in microeconomic policy, for example.

As we see in the following sections, this point has important implications for international policy coordination, both in theory and practice.

WHY COORDINATION?

In the previous section, we showed that the general case for coordination of international macropolicy rests on the presence of policy spillovers. Such spillovers are prevalent, as some examples may demonstrate.

- Governments may be reluctant unilaterally to expand, or to offset a deflationary tendency, because of the resulting balance of payments deficits and downward pressure on the exchange rate: the consequence may be a deflationary bias in the world economy.
- Governments may tend to tackle inflationary pressures by a combination of tight money and an appreciated exchange rate, coupled with expansionary fiscal policy to offset the output consequences of the resulting loss of competitiveness; the

consequence at the world level may be unduly high real interest rates and an inappropriate monetary-fiscal policy mix.

- Governments may reasonably treat commodity prices as determined in world markets, and neglect any effects of their own expansionary policy actions on commodity prices; but if generalised such demand expansion may prove over-inflationary because of the consequences for the commodity terms of trade.
- Governments may have inconsistent objectives concerning their desired current account position, and noncoordinated policy initiatives to try to secure these may well prove disruptive to the international economy.

These, and other, spillovers have been an important aspect of the experience of floating exchange rates over the past decade and a half. As the discussion suggests, certain of the spillovers are likely to exert opposite biases to the stance of macropolicy overall. But the different dynamics by which these effects will be governed are likely to be rather different, so that in a changing world these will not be offsetting in any helpful manner. The existence of these spillovers therefore suggests a *prima facie* case that the international coordination of macropolicy might well lead to appreciable benefits in terms of a more stable, better-functioning economy.

In spite of this, much of the literature on international policy cordination gives a somewhat negative view of the benefits to be expected. (For a recent survey, see Currie, Holtham and Hughes Hallett (1989).) The pioneering study by Oudiz and Sachs (1984) suggests rather minor gains, equivalent to less than one half a percent of GDP, from complete and perfect coordination of monetary and fiscal policy among the three G3 countries (US, Japan and Germany) for the period 1984–86. Such calculations give an upper bound for the realisable gains from the actual process of policy coordination, with its imperfections and delays, so these results give little support to the advocates of coordination. Some later work gives still less encouragement. Rogoff (1985) points out that international policy coordination may actually be welfare-decreasing, if the coordination process eases the constraints on governments to engage in inflationary monetary expansions. In his example, governments *without reputation* are deterred in part by the prospect of a depreciating exchange rate from springing monetary surprises on their private sectors with a view to raising output. Coordination to peg the exchange rate results in a greater incentive to spring monetary surprises, so that the equilibrum inflation rate rises, with an overall fall in output. Although the example is specific, it is a general point that coordination without reputation may be counter-productive (see Levine and Currie (1987a), Currie, Levine and Vidalis (1987)). Frankel and Rockett (1988) investigate the consequences of the plausible assumption that governments differ about their view of the world. Using six of the international models participating in the recent Brookings model comparison exercise (Bryant et al., 1988) as representing possible views of the world, they examine all the 216 possible combinations where the two governments (the United States and the rest of the world) can subscribe to any of the six models, and the true state of the world can in turn be any of the six models. Coordination gives benefits in just over 60 per cent of the combinations; in more than one-third of the combinations, coordination makes matters worse for at least one of the countries.

However, this rather pessimistic view of the benefits to be expected from international policy coordination has been questioned by more recent work. The Frankel/Rockett result that model uncertainty greatly reduces the benefits to be derived from international coordination depends crucially on the assumption that policy-makers stubbornly take no account of the presence of differences of views of the world in formulating their policies. Frankel (1987) shows that use of a compromise model in case of disagreement about the true structure of the world increases appreciably the probability of benefits from coordination. Holtham and Hughes Hallett (1987) show that ruling out 'weak' bargains, in which one party or the other expects the other party to be made worse off by the bargain, greatly improves the success rate of coordination when it occurs. They argue that governments would wish to rule out such bargains because they are likely to be reneged on and will jeopardise future coordination attempts. Ghosh and Masson (1988) show that the presence of model uncertainty may appreciably raise the benefits of coordination, provided that governments design coordinated policies with explicit regard to the presence of model uncertainty. It may be objected that policymakers are indeed stubborn in recognising only one view of the world, but this is hardly consistent with the significant exchange of views on such matters in international fora;

moreover, this would point to the need to educate policymakers on the dangers of this approach rather than to avoid international coordination.

Recent work has also placed in context the Rogoff (1985) result that, in the absence of reputation, coordination may be undesirable. Levine and Currie (1987b) and Currie, Levine and Vidalis (1987) show a related result, that in the absence of coordination, reputational policies may be undesirable. This is because the coordination failures, especially those with respect to the exchange rate, that arise with non-coordinated policies are increased when governments have reputation, so that they can more readily influence market expectations. Currie, Levine and Vidalis (1987) find that, using a two-bloc reduced version of the OECD Interlink model, the noncoordinated, non-reputational policy is very prone to instability, because governments are tempted to engage in self-defeating competitive appreciations of their exchange rates to combat inflation, coupled with fiscal expansion to avoid undue consequences on output. The non-reputational policies, by contrast, are prone to excessive inflation, for reasons analogous to those of the Barro/Gordon model. The resulting interest rate spiral can easily prove unstable. More recent work using Minimod, a reduced version of the Fed's Multi-Country Model, gives similar findings, suggesting that this result is not a quirk of one particular empirical model.

An implication of these findings is that the gains from reputation and the gains from coordination can be secured only jointly, at least in the international policymaking context. Currie, Levine and Vidalis (1987) use the reduced version of the OECD Interlink model to measure these gains empirically. The benefits of coordination with reputation are found to be rather small in the face of purely temporary disturbances to supply or demand. But the benefits are estimated to rise steeply as the persistence of the disturbance increases. Moreover, these benefits rise through time: noncoordinated, nonreputational policies are more likely to push undesirable adjustments into the discounted future, so that the long-run consequences of these policies are dismal. In the long run, the gains from cooperation in the face of permanent supply or demand shocks are very considerable indeed, amounting to some 15 per cent of GDP for 1 per cent disturbances. This provides an upper bound for the combination of shocks of different persistence. Holtham and Hughes Hallett (1987) use seven alternative models of the international economy drawn from a Brookings model comparison exercise to obtain estimates of the gains from cooperation of the order of 4–6 per cent of GDP. Interestingly, they find greater benefits from models with rational expectations, suggesting that the potential benefits from international policy coordination with reputation may be considerable, particularly if coordination focuses on how policy should adjust to persistent or permanent disturbances to the international economy.

Obstacles to policy coordination

In view of this recent work, it may be helpful to ask why the climate for effective policy coordination is not more favourable. Is it because these results are over-optimistic, or because of misperceptions by expert commentators? Several possible answers suggest themselves.

First, in all the academic work reviewed above, the policies being coordinated are fully optimal ones and therefore highly complex. (Optimality is defined with respect to an explicit objective function, but the existence of significant gains from coordination does not appear to be sensitive to the choice of objective function.) It is plausible to suggest that policies that are to be implemented in practice should be relatively simple in formulation (however complex the calculations that may be used in their design), though it is not straightforward to define simplicity. If this is so, then it applies with greater force to internationally agreed coordinated policies. This argument suggests the need to search for simple policy designs that might guide international policymaking. If such policies took the form of rules or guidelines, this may also provide a helpful way for policymakers to establish and maintain a reputation *vis-à-vis* the private sector. Of course, simplicity imposes certain costs in terms of policy performance, so that the realisable gains from policy coordination will be less than suggested above. We return to the question of simple rules and the gains from coordination in the next section.

Second, much of the practical debate on policy coordination has centred on internationally agreed exchange rate targets, with the coordination of underlying monetary and fiscal policy assuming a more subsidiary role. This may correspond to the practical experience of coordination over the years since the Plaza agreement in February 1985, where central bankers agreed to a coordinated intervention to manage a fall in the dollar from its peak, but it does not correspond to the academic literature which has largely focused on monetary and fiscal coordination. Whether exchange rate targets in some form or other can deliver a significant portion of the potential gains from coordination is an important issue that we return to in the next section; here we merely note that such targets without the supporting adjustment of monetary and fiscal policy are unlikely to be helpful. If exchange-rate targeting comes to mean attempting to fix nominal exchange rates at levels that are inconsistent with fundamentals, then the benefits are likely to be severely negative. The much publicised attack by Feldstein (1987a, 1987b) on international policy coordination is, in fact, a justified criticism of exchange rate agreements of this form, and is therefore not inconsistent with the argument of this essay.

Third, it may be that the quirks of policymaking in the early 1980s have shielded the international economy from some of the effects of uncoordinated policies. Standard analysis would suggest that uncoordinated action by the main economies to disinflate would lead to excessive contraction of policy, particularly on the monetary side, partly because each country would not take into account the consequences of other countries' policy actions on its own rate of inflation, and partly because each country might seek to manipulate its exchange rate at the expense of the others. In practice, although the world economy went through a period of slow growth in the first half of the 1980s, this was not as severe as this argument would suggest. This experience might be interpreted as suggesting that the coordination problems associated with Nash noncooperative behaviour in the international economy are not as severe as might be thought.

However, this would be a wrong inference. For the early 1980s were strongly influenced by differences of world view of the kind analysed by Frankel and Rockett (1988). Whereas Europe adopted a classically monetarist view of the world in tackling its inflation problem, the US took a supply-side view. Hence although monetary policy was generally tight, fiscal policy was relaxed in the US in contrast to Europe. (It is, of course, controversial as to whether US policy was quite as well formulated as this argument suggests, but it makes no difference to the argument if US policy was guided by other factors.) In consequence, fiscal policy was much less deflationary at a world level than would have been the case if a common view of the world had prevailed, though it generated the imbalances between the US and the rest of the world which now represent the focus of policy attention. Arguably, therefore, this accident of policymaking shielded the world economy from the effects of uncoordinated general disinflation.

Fourth, there are important questions to be asked about the available threat strategies to sustain coordinated reputational policies. One of the key policy spillovers is the ability of countries to engage in Reaganomics at the expense of the rest of the world: tight monetary policy can be used to maintain low inflation while a relaxation of fiscal policy boosts domestic expansion. In effect, the induced appreciation of the real exchange rate improves the inflation/output trade-off for the country, but at the expense of the rest of the world.

Such a policy has attractions, certainly in the short run, for economies that are not highly specialised in international trade, since export industries can avoid undue damage by switching supply to meet domestic demand. (This condition is satisfied for the US and Europe, considered as a whole but probably not for Japan.)

Now a credible threat by the rest of the world to match fiscal laxness may well serve to restrain US policy. But a feature of the recent past is that such a threat has not been credible. Japan's export industry would be damaged by a bout of Reaganomics: thus its principal threat has been that of refusing to open up its domestic market to trade, and this threat has been easily neutralised by reciprocal US threats of protection. In the case of Europe, this is not the case, though it may appear so from the perspective of the individual European economy. More relevant is the fact that Europe has no means of concerting its macroeconomic policies, particularly on the fiscal side. But there is a further reason why Europe cannot credibly threaten Reaganomics. This is because the EMS acts principally as a D-mark bloc, with other members committing their monetary and fiscal policy to maintaining an exchange rate link to the DM. Since German fiscal policy is tightly constrained by constitutional and other restraints, this arrangement rules out the possibility of major imbalances in the monetary/fiscal mix in Europe.

The absence of a credible response by the rest of the world to Reaganomics by the US has important consequences for the types of policies that are likely to be sustainable. Sustainability in this context has two aspects, as we have noted in the previous section.

Thus there is the question of whether either party will wish to withdraw from the agreed bargain at some future point in time; and there is the question of whether either government will wish to renege on its commitments *vis-à-vis* its private sector (i.e. the issue of time-inconsistency). If future reneging of either kind is anticipated, then the coordinated reputational policy will not be feasible, and the gains from coordination will not be reliable.

There are frequently strong incentives for one side or the other to renege on a coordinated agreement if it can do so without punishment. Thus some punishment strategy, explicit or implicit, is required to sustain the coordinated policy. The simplest way in which coordinated policies might be sustained is by each side threatening to revert to the Nash equilibrium in the event of reneging by the outer side. Thus in the Hamada diagram of Figure 6.2, the horizontal axis depicts the European fiscal/monetary mix (with a move along the axis representing a more relaxed fiscal policy relative to monetary policy), while the vertical axis depicts the US fiscal/monetary mix. B_{US} and B_{EUR} are the bliss points of the US and Europe respectively: each side benefits in the short run at least, from a more relaxed fiscal stance relative to the other since a loose fiscal/monetary mix appreciates the exchange rate and thereby helps to give a more favourable inflation/output tradeoff. R_{US} and R_{EUR} are the reaction functions. A coordinated equilibrium, C^*, on the locus of efficient bargains connecting B_{US} and B_{EUR} may be sustained by the threat on either side to revert to the noncooperative Nash equilibrium, N, for some punishment period. Similar considerations apply to the punishment, for a certain period of time, of reneging on the reputational aspects of policy, the Nash point being the nonreputational policy. As we have noted, under a fairly wide range of circumstances, the threat of reversion to the Nash point is sufficient to sustain a coordinated reputational equilibrium such as C^*.

Difficulties arise, however, if one party to the bargain is unwilling or unable to carry out the threat. Suppose, for reasons outlined above, that Europe is precommitted to maintain the monetary/fiscal mix at a level corresponding to C^*, given by the vertical line passing through C^* and P. Then the equilibrium will be at P, lying on the US reaction function. P represents a Pareto-inefficient point, being dominated by the set of efficient points on the arc connecting C_1 and C_2. The absence of a European threat enables the US to extract a higher level of welfare, but this is at the expense of a very much lower level of welfare for Europe. (Indeed, it is possible for Europe to be worse off than in the Nash equilibrium, if the European indifference curve passing through P intersects R_{EUR} beyond N.) Europe suffers much like the too well-behaved child who suffers chronic bullying at school. Perhaps part of the European vision of those who look to greater unity in Europe is that Europe might then respond more effectively to US initiatives, and that the world economy might then function better. (An analogy, perhaps worrying, with the arms race suggests itself.) The absence of a threat by Europe leads to a very much less efficient world equilibrium than would otherwise arise. Moreover, it is one characterised by appreciable world imbalances, arising from the more relaxed stance of fiscal policy (relative to monetary policy) in the US compared with Europe.

Of course, these considerations are only part of the explanation of events in the first half of the 1980s; the influence of the supply side view of the world, discussed earlier, also needs to be brought into the story. (In terms of Figure 6.1, if the US subscribes to a supply side view, the effect will be to shift B_{US} up vertically, accentuating the tendency towards expansionary fiscal policy in the US.) However, while the supply side view has faded in the US, the absence of a credible threat in Europe has continuing relevance. To see this, consider the current position of the world economy. A coordinated strategy for dealing with the imbalances in the world economy might well involve the type of adjustments outlined by the Institute for International Economics (1987). This involves fiscal retrenchment in the US, partially offsetting expansionary measures in the rest of the world, together with some further decline in the dollar and certain structural adjustments. A key question to be asked of such a package is whether the players have incentives to pursue it. The answer to this must be rather negative. If the political will were present in the US, a sharp cut in the fiscal deficit after the presidential election, with monetary policy maintaining the growth of nominal income, could well eliminate the major imbalances. In the absence of adjustment elsewhere, the cost of this strategy is likely to be a further sharp fall in the dollar, leading to a less favourable division between output and inflation. However, the major costs may well be felt in the rest of the world, as the fall in the dollar affects adversely non-US export industries, inducing recession in the rest of the world.

If European policy is largely precommitted, for reasons outlined above, this makes recession in Europe rather more likely on this scenario. But the lack of potential for a European policy threat is still more serious, for it may remove the pressure on the US to adjust fiscal policy. If, as the signs suggest, Europe is more worried than the US by a further fall in the dollar because of worries over profitability in export markets, then the pressure on the US to cut the fiscal deficit is much reduced. The absence of a threat strategy in Europe reduces the prospects of an efficient resolution of current world imbalances. In terms of Figure 6.2, the danger is that equilibrium will be at a point such as *P*, rather than at an efficient point such as *C**.

The formal analysis of these questions in the academic literature is rather limited and partial, but the rather heuristic analysis presented above suggests that it may merit further attention. The policy lesson from this is that precommitment may be helpful only if it is general, and not if only a subgroup of the key economies precommit: a complete absence of precommitment may well be preferable to partial precommitment by a subgroup of countries.

WHAT FORM OF COORDINATION?

We have argued in the previous section that there may well be appreciable potential gains from the coordination of macroeconomic policy among the main G7, or more particularly G3, economies. (The G7 countries are the US, Germany, Japan, UK, France, Italy and Canada, the first three being the G3.) In this section, we consider the form that this coordination might take. We start by examining some insights that the theoretical literature offers on this issue, and then move to consider coordination at a more concrete level.

At the outset, it is helpful to distinguish between rule-based forms of coordination and *ad hoc* or discretionary forms of coordination. Rule-based forms of coordination are exemplified by regimes such as the Gold Standard, the Bretton Woods system and the European Monetary System. In such regimes, coordination may take an implicit, rather than explicit, form, with the requirement that rules be observed replacing the need for overt consultation and agreement on the coordination of policy. By contrast, *ad hoc* forms of coordination take the form of one-off bargains negotiated explicitly between the parties to the agreement. The experience of coordination amongst the G3 countries since the breakdown of the Bretton Woods system has been of this type, with a series of summits, with Bonn in 1978 and the later Plaza and Louvre accords.

Although this distinction appears straightforward in practice, the recent theoretical literature might appear to have dissolved it. To be sure, the pioneering paper of Kydland and Prescott (1977) on time inconsistency drew the same sharp distinction between rules and discretion. However, the more recent literature emphasises that the time-consistent, discretionary policy can be expressed as a time-invariant feedback rule. (See, for example, Levine and Currie (1987b).) Thus it suggests that the relevant distinction is not between rules and discretion, but rather between those rules with, and those without, reputation. However, this argument rests on very specific assumptions. In particular, it assumes that policymakers have stable preferences, that these preferences are quadratic, and that they have a model of the world which is stable and linear in structure. Without these assumptions, the distinction between discretionary coordination and rule-based forms becomes a very real one. A rule book for the conduct of international macroeconomic policy way well act to limit the shifts in policy that might otherwise arise from changes in the preferences or views of the world of policymakers, unless these changes are large enough to lead to the rule book being torn up. Whether or not this limitation is advantageous is a question that we take up in a moment.

Rule-based forms of coordination

What advantages accrue from a rule-based approach to coordination? First, explicit well-designed rules may well provide the best means of harnessing the benefits of reputation in policymaking, which, as we argued in the previous section, may well be essential if international policy coordination is to be beneficial. (See Levine and Currie (1987a), Currie, Levine and Vidalis (1987).) This may be so even if the rules are rather simple and rigid in form, such as an exchange rate commitment to an adjustable peg arrangement, which as Giavazzi and Pagano (1986) demonstrate, may well be advantageous in establishing a reputation for resisting inflationary pressures.

Second, there is the point that the adoption of a rule-based system may encourage the parties to the agreement to consider the repeated aspects of the policy game. In the presence of continuing stochastic disturbances to the system, the scope for advantageous cooperative bargains becomes much greater, so that coordination is more likely (cf. the 'Folk Theorem' of game theory). This is because countries in different circumstances may find it hard to formulate coordinated policies, because of the difference in initial conditions. But such differences in initial conditions become less important in the presence of ongoing stochastic disturbances, because such disturbances create the prospect that at some future date positions will be reversed: this increases the willingness of both sides to agree to a set of rules that involve a sharing of the adjustment process. *Ad hoc* summitry that does not generate guidelines or rules for policy may well limit too greatly the scope for advantageous bargains.

Finally, there is the argument that an internationally agreed set of rules may helpfully act as an external discipline on the conduct of governments. This was clearly true of Bretton Woods, and is also true of the European Monetary System (cf. the Mitterrand experiment of 1982 and its aftermath where the incoming Socialist administration first embarked on expansionary fiscal policies and then reversed them in order to observe the constraints imposed by EMS membership). This constraint may act in at least two ways, that may be in large part observationally equivalent. It may constrain erratic shifts in the stance of government from affecting macroeconomic policy, thereby ensuring predictability of policy. It may also allow governments more readily to carry out policies by pointing to the obligations of pre-existing international agreements, reducing the necessity of arguing the domestic case for such policies.

Against this, there are a number of potential drawbacks of a rule-based system. A rule book must in large part be symmetrical in the obligations that it imposes on the parties that agree to it. (See Binmore (1989) for a discussion of the types of bargains likely to form the basis of a social contract of this form.) This does not exclude the possibility that the rule book may operate asymmetrically in its effects (as with the European Monetary System), or that it includes certain key asymmetries with respect to one key party (as with the US role within Bretton Woods). But it seems implausible that a rule book could incorporate wholly different rules for the different parties. By contrast, one-off summit agreements may readily incorporate asymmetries and, indeed, almost certainly will, since the chance of symmetrical obligations arising from a one-off bargain is rather remote. A related point is that a rule-based approach also makes it much harder to strike bargains over a range of policy areas. An example of such a bargain is provided by the 1978 Bonn summit. This involved the US agreeing to a change of energy policy, Japan agreeing to trade liberalisation, while Germany engaged in macroeconomic expansion. The macroeconomic aspects of the Bonn summit have since been criticised, perhaps unfairly, but the other aspects of the bargain were undoubtedly beneficial. It is hard to see how such a deal could have been struck within a rule-based approach.

Prospects for agreements

What, then, are the prospects for agreements, either of a rule-book kind or of a one-off agreement? It is worth noting at the outset that most examples of agreements on new rule books are the product of very particular historical circumstances: in the case of Bretton Woods and GATT springing from the special circumstances in the aftermath of the Second World War and the unusual influence of the United States; in the case of the European Monetary System, arising from the shared political objective to give renewed impetus to the European Community. Examples of a gradual transition to a new rule book are few and far between, though one might cite the transition towards a single market in 1991 in Europe and the growing influence of European law in European countries, together with the example of international cooperation in public health discussed by Cooper (1986).

If a transition towards a new rule book for international macro-economic policy is to occur, it seems that it will have to do so without the advantages either of a hegemonic influence or of a political consensus amongst the major powers. (In many respects, the political consensus between Europe and the US seems more fragile than for some time). It may well be that this rules out of court the possibility of any such agreement, and it certainly makes exceedingly remote the prospect of the rapid adoption of a new rule book. But it is possible to identify certain factors that might aid a more gradual transition.

First of all, it seems likely that the start of the process will be *ad hoc* bargains, in which the discretionary, non-rule based, element of the bargain dominates. This is partly because the world economy currently exhibits severe imbalances: the asymmetrical interests that this generates between countries makes it easier to strike *ad hoc* deals than to formulate a new rule book. (Moreover, such *ad hoc* deals are likely to include issues other than macroeconomic policy, including conceivably non-economic issues such as European defence). It is also because it will be necessary to build confidence and trust (both by the parties to the agreement and by the private sector) in the process of coordinated policy. As experience grows, so an increasing proportion of the bargain may take the form of operational rules to guide policy between summits. If the process of building confidence is successful, these operational rules may, over time, become increasingly crystallised as ground rules for subsequent negotiations, outside the domain of negotiation. At the same time, the monitoring of the observance of such rules may be delegated to the level of technical review by officials, without the normal intervention of ministers. This gradual process towards a rule book starting from a position of absence of trust is analagous to that analysed by Binmore (1989) in a more general setting.

An essential prerequisite for this process to come to fruition is that the agreements must be soundly based, free from misinterpretation, and devoid of wishful thinking. Stupid coordination of macroeconomic policies will be the surest way of discrediting the coordination process. In this respect, the Louvre Accord of February 1987, which may appear to fit in with the process described above, may well have set back appreciably the prospects for G3 coordination. Agreements on targets for exchange rates without an accompanying willingness to adjust underlying macroeconomic policies will simply fail, since sterilised intervention policy cannot bear the weight that is thereby thrust on it. The result will be to erode confidence in the ability of policymakers to deliver on their commitments. Recent experience bears this out.

All of this will require a higher level of technical input into the summit process than has been apparent in the last few years. Comparison of the detailed analysis and negotiation that took place prior to the 1978 Bonn summit with the sketchy and hasty preparations for the Plaza and Louvre Accords leads to the conclusion that it is unsurprising that the later agreements were less well-founded and subject to differences of interpretation by the participants. (See

Putnam and Bayne, 1987). A related issue is the rather weak level of technical support on international macroeconomic policy questions available to certain of the key G7 countries. One means of tackling these deficiencies would be a greater support role for the IMF or OECD in the summit process.

Alternative proposals for international cooperation

What guidance does the academic literature give as to the specific form that international cooperation may take? There are a variety of proposals on offer, ranging from Tobin's proposal for a tax on international financial transactions to proposals for a return to the gold standard. (For a recent review, see Dornbusch and Frankel (1987).)

However, the most detailed and developed proposal for international macropolicy coordination is the target zone proposal of Williamson (1983). In its early form, this was simply a proposal that policy should be directed to limiting the variation of real exchange rates to lie within a certain, rather wide, band around the equilibrium level, calculated so as to give medium- to longer-run current account equilibrium. This was open to the objection that it provided no anchor for domestic inflation, since a given real exchange rate is consistent, in principle, with any evolution of nominal variables. While the original proposal could be defended as an attempt to internalise a key policy externality (namely the ability of countries to engage in Reaganomics at the expense of others), rather than as a fully comprehensive set of rules for the conduct of international macropolicy, it was certainly vulnerable to the objection that it did little to encourage policymakers to focus on the links between exchange rate targets and adjustments of underlying fiscal and monetary policies. It is therefore helpful that the most recent statement by Williamson and Miller (1987) of the extended target zone proposal sets out a comprehensive set of rules for the conduct of monetary and fiscal policy in pursuit of real exchange rate targets and domestic nominal income targets (of a flexible type).

Thus Williamson and Miller propose the following elements to their scheme. First, interest differentials between countries should be varied to keep exchange rates within a given band around the agreed equilibrium level for the real exchange rate, chosen so as to give medium- to longer-run current account equilibrium. Second, domestic fiscal policy should be varied to take account of domestic targets for nominal demand growth; the targets being chosen to take account of the need to reduce inflation towards zero, to expand demand in the face of low capacity utilisation, and to adjust the current account towards equilibrium.

Stated in this way, the proposals put at least as much weight on the adjustment of monetary and fiscal policy in a way consistent with the achievements of exchange rate and other targets than on the achievement of the exchange rate targets themselves. Thus they bridge the gap between the academic literature on policy coordination reviewed briefly in the previous section of this chapter and the practice of policy coordination over the last few years since Plaza. It is also of interest that model-based appraisals of the proposals also place the emphasis on the rules for monetary and fiscal policy, rather than the exchange rate zone element. (See, for example, Edison, Miller and Williamson (1987), Currie and Wren-Lewis (1988a and 1989); for a theoretical appraisal, see Alogoskoufis (1989).) These appraisals suggest that the extended target zone proposal has merit, and is likely to have improved on historical performance had it been in force over the past decade. Currie and Wren-Lewis (1989) also find advantages in the implied assignment of monetary policy to the external objective and fiscal policy to the internal objective, relative to the alternative suggested by Boughton (1989) and implicit in much IMF discussion (IMF, 1987), that fiscal policy should be assigned to external balance, and monetary policy to the domestic objective.

We do not attempt here to assess the technical merits of the extended target zone proposal. We would merely note that certain modifications of the Williamson/Miller rules may be over-restrictive: for example Currie and Wren-Lewis (1988a) suggest that the rules may be over-restrictive in precluding a real exchange rate appreciation in response to a higher inflation relative to the rest of the world. We would also note that there is a need for further assessment of the scheme, particularly to see how far rules can be made robust in performance with respect to differences in model structure.

Here we merely conclude by noting certain features of the proposal that are helpful in thinking how the process of policy coordination can be taken further. These features are not specific to the Williamson/Miller proposal and might be incorporated in other rules for the coordination of policy.

First, the rules may be thought of as a concrete means of making sense of the 'indicators' debate initiated by G7 summit meetings. By incorporating a variety of relevant variables into the two key targets for the real exchange rate and the growth of domestic demand, and by proposing simple rules linking these targets to policy instruments, the proposal imposes a simple and helpful structure on an otherwise thoroughly muddled discussion. If the 'indicators' debate is to go forward, this surely represents the line of advance.

Second, the proposals in their latest form have the considerable merit of emphasising the necessity of adjustments of fiscal and monetary policy if exchange rate targets are to be pursued. This is a helpful antidote to the wishful thinking of recent policy initiatives. (For further discussion on this point, see Currie, Holtham and Hughes Hallett, 1989.)

Third, the proposals have sufficient flexibility to be consistent with the gradual evolution, described above, of the policy process from a one-off bargain towards a more complete rule book for the conduct of policy. This flexibility has several forms. First, the proposed permissible zones of variation for the exchange rate are wide, and therefore offer considerable flexibility. One can well imagine wide limits being set initially as a part of a more general one-off package, and these limits then becoming more stringent over time. Second, there is scope within the proposals for countries to set their domestic nominal demand objectives in individual ways, giving greater or lesser weight to the inflation objective relative to capacity utilisation. Thus the proposals do not seek to impose on countries how they should manage their domestic economies, but rather merely to seek to limit undesirable spillovers onto the rest of the world.

Finally, the proposals offer flexibility in whether the greater emphasis is placed on the underlying rules for the conduct of monetary and fiscal policy, or on the stabilisation of real exchange rates. Of course, a central aim of the rules is to limit exchange rate variation, but there is a choice as to whether to lead with the exchange rate objective or with the underlying policy adjustments. Recent experience may be taken to suggest that leading with the exchange rate objective will push fiscal and monetary policy into the background, with possibly unfortunate consequences for the viability of the coordination proposals. Against that, cooperation amongst the G7 central banks represents the practical basis for coordination on which to build; (See Group of 30, 1988). An increased emphasis on the rules for the conduct of monetary and fiscal policy within current arrangements for exchange rate management may well offer the most practical way forward in the evolution towards a new rule book for the conduct of international macroeconomic policy.

7 Domestic and International Financial Imbalances and Adjustment[1]

ANDREW DEAN

INTRODUCTION

International economic developments in the 1970s and 1980s have been dominated by large swings in exchange rates and in the balance of payments positions of the major countries and world zones. These swings have been closely related and strongly influenced by domestic developments in the individual countries. In turn these have been influenced by divergent policies, most notably in the 1980s, with the rise in the dollar in earlier years being associated with the growing Federal deficit, rapid growth and relatively high interest rates in the United States. The gross maladjustments in the domestic and international financial balances in recent years have placed unprecedented burdens on adjustment mechanisms. Because all of these factors are closely interrelated, untangling the various causal factors lying behind them is a difficult task.

The unifying theme of this chapter is the linkage between the domestic and external sectors, the current account of the balance of payments being the mirror image of the net domestic savings position of each economy. This link means that imbalances necessarily have both an international and a domestic aspect, even though the emphasis of this book is on the international dimension. The following sections first describe the nature of the link between internal and external imbalance. The issue of sustainability is then discussed and changing views of the way in which imbalances are corrected are reviewed. Alternative adjustment channels are examined and then three recent episodes of international imbalance are explored in order to investigate more concretely the ways in which imbalances can arise and the ways in which they are resolved.

THE NATURE OF IMBALANCES

Imbalances – in the sense of a mismatch of resources, financial or otherwise – occur all the time in economic systems. Indeed, in most cases it is desirable that they should occur. For they provide the signals that, when necessary, set off mechanisms that lead to the reallocation of resources as economic circumstances change. There is disagreement as to whether the adjustment mechanisms are automatic or not – indeed, this has always been one of the major disputed questions of economics. Most economists would probably agree that when market mechanisms are allowed to act, a process of adjustment will occur, but there is still much dispute about the timing of such changes and whether discretionary policy should be used to accelerate the process. In the specific case of external imbalances, there is also an important issue about whether the balance of pressure on surplus and deficit countries to adjust is too asymmetric, an issue that remains unresolved.

In certain circumstances imbalances can coexist with an equilibrium situation. For example, a country may be able to sustain a continuous deficit on its visible trade over a long period of time if it is also running an offsetting surplus on its invisibles account. In the nineteenth century Britain ran a fairly permanent trade and current-account surplus, offsetting this with the export of capital through its investment in its colonies. Developing countries, because of their generally higher rate of return on capital, have traditionally run current-account deficits which have been financed by capital inflows intended for direct investment (though such inflows have often ended up in other places). It is only in recent years that this situation has reversed itself and the flow has, in many cases, been in the other direction. This latter example indicates that a situation which had seemed sustainable over many years can change rather rapidly.

Knowing whether an imbalance is sustainable or not, is a difficult question, as is knowing at which point correction should be sought. Of course, if there are automatic self-equilibrating mechanisms, then it is perhaps not necessary to consider corrective actions. Yet it may be that letting the market lead correction will entail undesirable volatility and overshooting of certain key financial variables such as the exchange rate. It is therefore important to be able to understand the nature of financial imbalances and in particular to be able to assess whether the internal and external elements are mutually sustainable.

The link between internal and external imbalance

The link between domestic and international financial balances can be illustrated by going back to first principles and setting out a simple national accounts framework defining national income and private sector savings:

$$Y = C + I + G + [X - M] \tag{7.1}$$
$$\text{and} \quad S = Y - C - T \tag{7.2}$$

where
$Y =$	national income	
$C =$	private consumption	
$G =$	government expenditure	
$X - M =$	exports minus imports, or the current account of the balance of payments	
$S =$	gross private sector savings	
$T =$	government revenues.	

Combining 7.1 and 7.2 it can be seen that:

$$X - M = [S - I] + [T - G] \tag{7.3}$$

Thus the current account of the balance of payments $(X - M)$ is equal to the difference between private sector savings and investment $(S - I)$ plus the difference between government income and expenditure $(T - G)$ – i.e. equal to net domestic savings. Put another way, a current-account deficit implies the country absorbing more real resources than its own contribution to world output.

Given that changes in the current account are exactly offset by movements in the capital account, then:

$$X - M = K = [S - I] + [T - G] \tag{7.4}$$

where K is a capital inflow or outflow depending on the balance of X

and M. A capital outflow offsets a current-account surplus ($X > M$), with excess net domestic savings being placed abroad. A capital inflow offsets a current-account deficit ($X < M$), foreign savings flowing into the country to finance that deficit.

The interest in 7.4 is that it presents different ways of looking at the same phenomenon. A domestic imbalance, excess or deficient savings, has its exact counterpart in an international imbalance, represented either as a surplus or deficit on the balance of goods or services or as a capital outflow or inflow. The latter can also be represented as the net acquisition of external assets. This can be seen either by looking at the disposal of savings or by examining the balance of payments accounts. Net domestic savings must, by definition, have an asset counterpart and this can only be in the form of a rise in the holdings of net external assets. Similarly, a current-account surplus has as a counterpart either an autonomous net capital outflow or a rise in the central bank's foreign currency reserves; in either case net external assets are increased.

Consider a recent case of 'imbalance'. In 1986 Japan had a large surplus on the current account of her balance of payments. At the same time this payments surplus – more money coming into Japan as foreigners' payments for goods and services than leaving to pay for goods and services – was offset, by money being placed abroad in the net purchase of external assets (a capital outflow). Japan, therefore, had a current-account surplus, a capital outflow and an increase in net external assets (incidentally, making her the world's largest creditor). The net export of goods and services meant that Japan was producing more than she was consuming (in the broader sense of the three domestic expenditure components in 7.1 above, namely private consumption and investment and government expenditure). Hence, she had positive net domestic savings, representing the excess of private savings over investment plus the partial offset of a budget deficit or government dissaving. In the parallel case of the United States in 1986, government dissaving was not offset by net private sector savings, so that national expenditure exceeded national output, and there was thus a deficit on the current account of the balance of payments and an inflow of capital.

All the relationships described above are *ex post* national accounting identities which provide a convenient framework for analysing domestic and international financial imbalances. They indicate nothing about the causality involved in movements of national income and expenditure. It is important to stress that no causality is implied, because it is incorrect or dangerous to leap from an identity such as 7.3 above, to saying that the US current-account deficit $(X - M)$ is linked directly to the budget deficit $(T - G)$. This would be a likely reaction to a superficial look at the way in which the so-called 'twin deficits' of the United States have emerged at much the same time during the 1980s. There is clearly some relationship between the two, but a direct linking would be wrong because it would imply a knowledge of *ex ante* movements which could only be provided by additional information about the way the economic behaviour of private sector agents and government is determined and hence the main channels of influence. More specifically, the other elements of the equation are private sector savings and investment decisions, both being strongly influenced by monetary and tax policy. Closer inspection of the US flow of funds indicates that the growth of private sector savings was outstripped by the growth of private investment in the mid-1980s, at the same time as the general government's fiscal deficit expanded sharply. The rise in the US external deficit is therefore associated with increased dissaving by the government and a reduction in the net savings of the private sector. The situation in Japan, however, is rather different. There the external surplus was associated with a growing excess of savings over investment which more than covered the budget deficit; hence, private sector savings have been used to finance government dissaving and to purchase external assets. These contrasting examples caution against concluding that there is a mechanical statistical link between current-account and budget deficits.

In sum, the fact that the *ex post* identities hold reveals nothing about the *ex ante* pressures in the system. Exchange rates, interest rates, asset values and many other macroeconomic and microeconomic factors react and change in order that *ex ante* disequilibria are eliminated and behaviour is influenced in ways that mean that the identities are satisfied.

In discussing financial imbalances, it is possible to break into the problems at different points, reflecting different elements of the threefold identity outlined in 7.4 above. Some argue that, in the end, the heart of any problem of imbalance ultimately lies in the domestic economy; hence it is changes in net private savings behaviour and in the budget deficit which ultimately lie behind any external problem. Current-account developments merely reflect changes in domestic behaviour so that it is movements in domestic savings and invest-ment which need to be examined when imbalances are being adjusted. Others prefer to look at the counterpart issues on the external side, arguing that it is adjustments in trade or in capital flows that are the most important elements in the correction of imbalances. In reality they are just opposite sides of the same coin and the mechanisms of adjustment work through both domestic and international channels. However, for analytical purposes it is useful to focus on one aspect of the issue at a time.

There is one further complication. Beyond the national identities summarised in 7.4 above, there are also global constraints. In principle, all international flows of trade and capital must add to zero when measured in a consistent and uniform way. Every export must have a counterpart import – though in practice there is a 'black hole', the world current-account discrepancy, that arises because recorded imports in the world are about $50 billion greater than recorded exports (see International Monetary Fund, 1987). Thus, a country's external imbalance is not just the counterpart of an internal imbalance but also the counterpart of an external imbalance of the opposite sign in the rest of the world. This makes the causality even more difficult to establish. It also means that there are external constraints on corrective action by one country acting alone which are more important than may at first seem to be the case. To take a simple example, a country attempting to correct a current-account deficit may carry out policies to improve competitiveness and gain export market share. This is a viable policy so long as there is a willingness by others to accept the counterpart loss of competitive-ness, reduction in market share and deterioration in current-account position. In practice, if the country is small (and the rest of the world, by corollary, very large) such changes may not be resisted, except perhaps by the most seriously affected trading partners. But with a large country such as the United States, any attempts to reduce an external deficit will entail important counterpart adjust-ments that could well create tensions. One of the unresolved issues of the US deficit correction of the 1990s is where the counterpart adjustment will occur, given that a continuation of the deficit at well over $100 billion a year is regarded by many as unsustainable.

Sustainability

It is not necessary for the current account of a country, even over a long period of time, to be equal or close to zero. In the context of the analysis of savings/investment balances, the current account indicates only whether the country is a net saver or borrower from abroad. Because profitable investment opportunities are not spread around the globe in the same way as savings capacities, some countries are likely to be net savers, hence investing in (lending to) the rest of the world, while others are likely to be net investors, hence borrowing from the rest of the world. There is no problem with this so long as the money borrowed has been invested in ways that give a rate of return sufficient to service repayments. In principle, a current-account deficit is sustainable so long as the borrowing abroad is used for investment and the expected real rate of return on the capital is no less than the cost of borrowing. On the other hand, if the borrowing is for the purposes of current consumption, or is used on projects with an inadequate return, then it would be unsustainable for two reasons. Firstly, in such circumstances, the country will eventually encounter difficulties in servicing the continuous rise in external debt. Secondly, foreigners will not be prepared to continue financing such consumption, except at much higher rates of interest which would tend to lead to a reversal of the deficit. However, in practice, because of fungibility, there is no such direct link between the provision of funds and the return generated on those funds. For so long as overall investment in the economy is large enough and productive enough to generate the real income growth needed for debt service without a subsequent consumption squeeze then the foreign borrowing may be regarded as sustainable.

The issue is rarely so clear-cut because it is never easy to establish the exact use of funds in an economy and rarely possible to know whether present trends are permanent or temporary. While unsustainable imbalances are likely to be large, not all large imbalances are unsustainable. For they may be associated with factors that are temporary or likely to unwind, such as imbalances which are due to differences in cyclical positions that are likely to reverse, or imbalances associated with terms-of-trade shocks or major resource discoveries. The judgement on sustainability is ultimately made by the market since the sources for financing a deficit will dry up whenever it becomes clear that the current-account deficit has become unsustainable. Sustainability can therefore be defined in terms of both the current account and the capital account. A surplus on the latter will continue only so long as there are profitable investment opportunities (Salop and Spitäller, 1980). The market's appraisal of such opportunities would normally be expected to take into account any risk factors involved in the investment.

The period over which an imbalance may be sustainable may also have changed because liberalisation of financial markets has allowed easier access to funds. Financial markets have become more integrated, with domestic markets having been opened up and controls on capital flows having been progressively removed. The gross volume of financial flows has also increased enormously. This has facilitated the finance of current-account deficits, but it has also given the markets the ability to impose their judgements on the sustainability issue. Furthermore market judgements can be erratic, changing rather suddenly. The flow of commercial bank lending to the developing countries came to a rather abrupt end in the 1980s with the realisation that interest payments as well as eventual repayment were under threat. Ultimately, therefore, financial imbalances become unsustainable because accumulating debt requires financing. Debt service payments rise as the amount of external debt increases, thus exacerbating the current-account deficit. Concern at the stock position then constrains the capital inflow required to finance the current account, resulting in pressure for balance of payments adjustment. Hence, adjustment becomes necessary as financing constraints emerge.

The point at which adjustment occurs may depend significantly on the characteristics of the country in question. Countries with, for whatever reason, a low credit rating will find external finance dries up much more rapidly than for more creditworthy countries. Furthermore, the access to an availability of different types of finance may also be country-specific. Capital markets, for example, are less available to developing countries than industrial countries. It was the developing countries' dependence on bank finance which became a problem when external conditions changed and the banks were no longer able or willing to provide the level of financial intermediation services that they had provided prior to the debt crisis.

The amount and type of finance are also influenced by global trends which can affect the availability of finance for a country through time independent of the particular circumstances of the country. Thus, in the 1970s, partly as a consequence of the oil price shocks, the absolute size of international imbalances rose and there was a shift in the structure of finance, the private sector displacing the official sector. The asset-growth objectives of banks coincided with a period when oil funds were being deposited with the banking system and developing countries were demanding finance. The availability of finance facilitated by the intermediation of the banks enabled external imbalances to be sustained but also allowed the domestic savings/investment imbalances to intensify. The causality is not clear; what is clear, however, is that neither of these imbalances could have arisen without the financial intermediation mechanisms that then existed. As the economic environment deteriorated – interest rates rising sharply and world output and trade slowing – some of the developing countries, with their burden of previous debt accumulation, were unable to meet their obligations. This would probably have been the case under any financing regime, although conditions in the 1970s seem to have been particularly conducive to the accommodation of the imbalances. There were further structural changes in the 1980s with the location of external surpluses and deficits changing and a parallel shift in the structure of financing from banks to the capital market. Such changes are examined below in the analysis of recent episodes of international imbalances.

CHANGING VIEWS OF THE ADJUSTMENT PROCESS

The way in which the adjustment of domestic and international financial imbalances is viewed has changed through time as economic conditions have changed and with changing fashions in economic doctrine. The switch from fixed to flexible exchange rates, for example, had been quite widely expected to lead to the end of balance of payments problems, since market-induced changes in exchange rates were expected to take care of any imbalances. But the switch heralded an era when international imbalances and their domestic counterparts became more pronounced.

At one time there was a general belief in the correction of imbalances by automatic mechanisms. There were differences of view as to how the correction might occur. Some argued that the principal channel was via price adjustments, others that volume adjustments played a key role, but with most acknowledging that the two channels of adjustment operated together. The polar cases of automatic adjustment were non-sterilisation with fixed exchange rates and cleanly floating exchange rates; both cases assumed that market forces operated relatively unhindered, thus delivering a new equilibrium position without disruptive changes.

In general, economists now believe that the adjustment mechanisms are probably more complicated than previously envisaged. As Tobin (1987) has pointed out, there is also now some scepticism as to whether there are any reliable mechanisms for the correction of imbalances. This scepticism has to a large extent been fostered by the relative inefficacy of flexible exchange rates, compared with earlier expectations, to self-correct imbalances, especially in the 1980s. The development of unprecedented and persisting imbalances between the major industrialised countries – in particular the United States and Japan – despite very large changes in exchange rates, has led to some rethinking of adjustment mechanisms.

There have also been switches in focus as between different elements of the balance of payments. In a period when capital accounts were strongly controlled, and systems of international financial transactions were less sophisticated than today, it was natural that the emphasis of theories of adjustment should be on the current account, in particular on the trade account. This remained true until the end of the 1950s. The arguments in Meade (1951) and other models of balance of payments adjustment of that era revolved around changes in traded goods; capital movements sometimes featured, but not as the driving force of adjustment. The emphasis changed in the 1960s. The models of Fleming (1962) and Mundell (1962) incorporated capital movements which changed in line with monetary policy under both fixed and floating regimes. Until that time capital movements had not figured importantly in theories of balance of payments adjustment; from the 1960s onwards they assumed a more important, sometimes even an overwhelming role in models of adjustment. The monetary approach took the current and capital account together and assumed that changes in reserves were the balancing mechanism which equilibrated the demand for and supply of money, with domestic adjustments occurring as a consequence of monetary tightening or easing (Johnson, 1977).

The first analyses of adjustment mechanisms examined the way in which relative prices internationally might change under a gold standard system. For a country in external deficit, gold would flow out to the country in surplus. In line with the quantity theory of money, absolute prices would fall in the deficit country and rise in the surplus country. This would involve a change in relative prices which would be the equilibrating mechanism to correct the trade imbalances.

The same type of mechanism was supposed to apply in the fixed exchange rate system set up at Bretton Woods, though with links that were much less direct. Here international money (gold) was supplemented by national money supplies. The link between locally-created money and gold or foreign exchange reserves was looser, so that both the degree and the timing of adjustment, depended also on domestic monetary policies and the link with domestic prices. It was the failure of this system to work as automatically as it might in theory that led to occasional changes in parities and finally to collapse.

The move to floating exchange rates in the early 1970s supposedly brought into effect equilibration of current-account balances via the market determination of exchange rates. Any imbalance would be reflected in an excess demand or supply of the currency, whose price would adjust in a direction that would automatically lead towards balance. One great difficulty, however, was the dynamic path that might be taken to reach equilibrium. Not only would the reaction of trade volumes take time but there was also the possibility of overshooting of the currency, a process that was modelled at a later stage by Dornbusch (1976) who assumed differential speeds of adjustment in goods and asset markets (domestic prices adjusting less rapidly than exchange rates). His model was characteristic of the asset market approach which developed in the mid-1970s, the salient feature being the potential importance of capital flows arising from portfolio adjustments which could dwarf current-account flows.

With floating exchange rates, the price adjustment mechanism is also central. Changes in relative prices internationally are brought about by changes in the value of a currency with monetary conditions and expectations playing a key role in the determination of both the exchange rate and domestic prices. The way in which relative prices change then depends on the pricing behaviour of importers and exporters. And the degree to which changes in the price of traded goods flow through to the level of prices generally is determined in particular by the reaction of wage behaviour. One advantage claimed for floating rates was that, given some inertia in wages and prices, they allow a rapid change in relative prices. But in practice adjustments have not proven to be made in a smooth, troublefree way. Exchange rates have tended to move in very volatile ways and not necessarily in the direction that would be indicated by the imbalance (Williamson, 1985). Capital flows have tended to have a much more important role in determining exchange rate movements than was envisaged, with the demand and supply of currency being determined not only by the demand and supply for traded goods but also by portfolio considerations concerned with expected movements of asset prices and exchange rates.

ALTERNATIVE CHANNELS OF ADJUSTMENT

Adjustment mechanisms can be viewed from either the domestic or international side. Focusing on the domestic side entails looking at the difference between national savings and investment, or the gap between domestic demand and output. Using this focus, current-account adjustment can then be analysed in terms of the determinants of savings and investment behaviour as has been done by Turner (1986). A focus on the international side leads to an analysis of the determinants of current-account transactions, specifically incomes and relative prices, or the capital account. The growth of domestic demand influences imports while the growth of foreign demand influences exports. Relative competitive positions, which are affected both by the exchange rate and by domestic wages, prices and productivity, influence the gains and losses of market shares. The effects on trade are summarised by income and price elasticities for exports and imports – the traditional absorption and elasticities approaches which are usually important ingredients in international models. Different schools of thought tend to emphasise either the international or domestic aspect, though recognising that adjustment will come through both sides of the account. There need be no conflict between the elasticities, the absorption and the monetary approaches, although the different emphases may well be due to differences of view as to the causality and hence the driving forces lying behind adjustment. Kindleberger (1987) has argued that all three approaches are needed, since no one model of the balance of payments is likely to be good for all occasions. While in the short run one model may drive the adjustment process, in the long run the three models will converge.

An illustration of this can be provided by tracing through the way in which changes in exchange rates are assumed to influence imbalances (as is done in Dean and Koromzay, 1987). A real depreciation, when analysed from the trade side, is assumed to lead to a change in relative prices which leads to a switch in expenditure. Some part of the total level of expenditure on domestic and foreign goods is switched (at least in relative terms) from foreign to domestic output. In terms of relative price movements, the depreciation is normally expected to lead to a less-than-proportionate rise in export prices measured in the home currency, which means a fall in the foreign currency price, and hence a rise in the volume of exports. Similarly, the price of imports in domestic currency tends to rise, leading to a lowering of import volumes. Real net exports thus increase. So long as the volume responses are sufficiently large to outweigh the negative terms-of-trade shift that arises because export prices rise less than import prices, the trade balance improves. In general, this will happen so long as the sum of the price elasticities is greater than one – the so-called Marshall–Lerner condition. However, because the terms-of-trade shift occurs a lot more rapidly than the volume adjustment (it is, after all, the reason for the adjustment), the trade balance tends to deteriorate in the short run before improving – the so-called J-curve.

In terms of a domestic, savings/investment framework, the way in which a depreciation works is more complicated, since it is necessary to trace through the behavioural reactions throughout the whole economy. So long as there is spare capacity – which is, of course, also a consideration when expenditure switching is traced through the trade side – then depreciation will lead to an increase in profitability in both export and import-competing sectors. This will entail a rise in output and, so long as policies are geared to maintaining domestic demand on a roughly unchanged path, an increase in total output relative to demand. Put another way, and recalling the identities set out earlier, there will be an increase in domestic savings relative to investment. On the other hand, if the economy is already at full capacity, then depreciation would only be dissipated in inflationary pressure, with the initial change in relative prices being reversed and a real depreciation failing to take place. In such circumstances domestic demand needs to be reduced if the necessary switch of resources is to take place, a combination of expenditure-switching and expenditure-reducing policies being required. A key factor to stress is therefore the way in which monetary and fiscal policies hinder or encourage the adjustment of domestic behaviour in reaction to the external changes.

Some would claim that the preceding analysis is essentially short-term or static in nature. A more dynamic approach is needed which focuses on income elasticities of demand for a country's imports and exports and on relative growth rates (Thirlwall, 1988). Furthermore, with such elasticities and growth potential being determined by the structural characteristics of an economy, adjustment policies of a structural rather than macroeconomic kind may need to be pursued to correct imbalances. No doubt both are required, the argument being over the respective weights to be placed on each.

IMBALANCES IN THE 1970s AND 1980s

In the period up to 1973, under the Bretton Woods system, external imbalances could and did build up. But in general adjustment mechanisms began the process of correction before imbalances built up to substantial proportions. There were basically two methods of correction; domestic adjustment (deflation in deficit countries) or realignment of the exchange rate, which was in principle counte-nanced only when it was necessary to correct a 'fundamental disequilibrium'. The latter action was regarded as a last resort – there were still memories of counterproductive competitive devalua-tions in the interwar period – and was often resisted on political grounds. For the exchange rate came to be seen as a sort of virility symbol. Governments therefore tended to resist what was seen as an admission of weakness; this was particularly pronounced in the case of sterling in the mid-sixties when the British economy laboured under what many regarded as an uncompetitive exchange rate for three years before eventual devaluation in November 1967. The final decision to devalue was adopted because the only alternative in the face of continued external imbalance was substantial domestic deflation. This was a common dilemma for deficit countries – the constraints on surplus countries have always been less clear – and one which led to periodic questioning of the system. The system was criticised by many as being too rigid, with professional economists increasingly coming to the view that a flexible exchange rate system would be more rational, removing balance of payments constraints and allowing a more independent domestic policy. Others believed the failings of the system arose from the unwillingness of governments to make the necessary domestic adjustments. In the end, it was the US concern not to have its policies dictated by the needs of exchange rate stability which led the Nixon administration to cease convertibility of gold at a fixed price. This led fairly quickly to the end of the era of fixed exchange rates.

It is ironic that it was in the first years of flexible exchange rates, with their promise of an end to balance of payments crises, that one of the largest external dislocations of the postwar period took place. This was the oil shock, which destroyed the rather delicate balance between the surpluses of the industrialised countries and the deficits of the developing countries which had hitherto seemed likely to be sustained. Table 7.1 is a summary table which indicates the evolution of current-account balances for the major industrialised countries and non-OECD zones over the period since floating. It indicates the rise and fall of the OPEC surplus in the mid-1970s, which is the first of the three imbalance episodes analysed below. The other two episodes, the developing country debt crisis of the early 1980s and the imbalances among the major industrialised countries since the mid-1980s, can also be seen in the global patterns indicated in Table 7.1.

The rise and fall of the OPEC surpluses

There have been two peaks to the OPEC surplus since the early 1970s. The first came in 1974, following the initial sharp rise in the price of oil, with the peak surplus of $67 billion falling off relatively quickly and then passing into deficit in 1978. The second peak came in 1980, with the further sharp oil price rise which occurred following the start of the Iran–Iraq war. On that occasion the peak surplus of $103 billion disappeared within two years. The aggregate OPEC figures of course conceal diverse positions and behaviour. At one extreme there are countries like Saudi Arabia or the United Arab Emirates with massive reserves of oil, hence enormous potential production and income, yet relatively small populations. They

TABLE 7.1 The evolution of current-account imbalances

	1975	1976	1977	1978	1979	1980	1981	1982	1983	1984	1985	1986	1987	1988	1989	1990	1991
Current balances ($ billion)																	
United States	18.1	4.2	−14.5	−15.4	−1.0	1.5	8.2	−7.0	−44.3	−104.2	−112.7	−133.3	−143.7	−126.6	−121.5	−118.1	−123.8
Japan	−0.7	3.7	10.9	16.5	−8.8	−10.8	4.8	6.8	20.8	35.0	49.2	85.8	87.0	79.6	60.8	61.1	68.6
Germany	4.3	3.7	4.0	8.9	−5.4	−13.8	−3.6	5.1	5.3	9.8	16.4	39.2	45.2	48.5	60.9	70.8	75.7
OECD	5.7	−15.5	−21.0	12.1	−27.4	−67.0	−22.5	−24.9	−21.8	−60.8	−52.0	−15.6	−38.0	−50.2	−85.3	−72.3	−71.4
OPEC	19.9	20.9	5.3	−22.5	27.0	85.1	48.2	−7.2	−20.7	−5.6	2.2	−28.5	−6.2	−14.8	−1.8	−0.7	−0.1
Non-oil LDCs	−33.9	−19.0	−13.4	−23.0	−37.4	−64.8	−85.1	−69.1	−35.0	−21.8	−23.9	−10.3	10.9	4.5	−8.6	−12.1	−12.6
Eastern European countries	−9.6	−8.3	−3.2	−4.7	−2.4	−3.1	0.8	9.6	13.6	14.6	8.0	11.0	18.7	14.0	11.5	7.2	5.1
World discrepancy	−17.9	−21.9	−32.3	−38.1	−40.2	−49.8	−58.6	−91.6	−63.9	−73.6	−65.7	−43.4	−14.6	−46.4	−84.2	−77.9	−79.1
Current balances (% GNP)																	
United States	1.1	0.2	−0.7	−0.7	−0.0	0.1	0.3	−0.2	−1.3	−2.8	−2.8	−3.1	−3.2	−2.6	−2.3	−2.1	−2.1
Japan	−0.1	0.7	1.6	1.7	−0.9	−1.0	0.4	0.6	1.8	2.8	3.7	4.4	3.6	2.8	2.2	2.1	2.2
Germany	1.0	0.8	0.8	1.4	−0.7	−1.7	−0.5	0.8	0.8	1.6	2.6	4.4	4.0	4.0	5.1	5.4	5.4
Net Investment income ($ billion)																	
United States	12.8	16.0	18.0	20.6	31.2	30.4	34.1	28.7	24.9	18.5	25.9	21.6	22.3	2.2	−13.4	−14.7	−22.3
Japan	−0.3	−0.2	0.1	0.9	2.0	0.9	−0.8	1.7	3.1	4.2	6.8	9.5	16.7	21.0	21.0	28.3	34.1
Germany	0.6	0.8	−0.6	2.0	1.1	2.0	0.5	−1.2	1.6	3.6	3.2	4.0	3.9	4.6	10.9	12.2	15.4

Source: OECD Economic Outlook 46, December 1989; estimates for 1989, projections for 1990 and 1991.

tended to spend their enhanced oil revenues relatively slowly, even though the Saudis in absolute terms have become very large spenders, and so were classed among a group of 'low absorbers'. In fact even the Saudis have managed to create certain problems for themselves by cutting back production significantly in recent years in order, as 'swing producer', to keep the oil price up. At the other extreme, there have been other countries with much larger populations, 'high-absorbing' countries, that have generally used oil revenues to the full in the purchase of consumer or investment goods from abroad. Some of those countries, such as Nigeria, Venezuela and Mexico (which is outside OPEC) have, despite their oil resources, become problem debtors, in the sense of having had to reschedule debt in recent years.

The way in which the OPEC current-account surpluses have on two occasions risen and then disappeared does not correspond exactly to the way in which adjustment has been described above although the relevant elements are there. In the wake of the first oil shock, as some of the industrialised countries retrenched and cut back their oil demand, the oil producers stepped up their domestic expenditure with unprecedented speed. With the expansion of domestic absorption in the oil-producing countries, import volumes increased extremely rapidly – by 75 per cent in 1974 alone, albeit from a low base – leading to a halving of the OPEC surplus within a year and its elimination within four years. But while Saudi Arabia retained a large surplus, some of the other OPEC countries moved into deficit rather sooner. An element of this same change in domestic absorption occurred in the years following the second oil-price shock, though then the surplus of over $100 billion was dissipated even more quickly. But there was an element of price adjustment also – and hence expenditure switching – since, over time, the effect of the rise in oil prices was to alter the demand and supply of energy. New sources of supply began to be exploited at the new prices and energy efficiency increased enormously so as to substantially reduce the demand for OPEC oil. The combination of the increased absorption and reduced demand for oil, which led to both a lower production and price of oil, soon resulted in the need for current-account adjustment. There was a large reduction in the import volumes of the oil producers, initially in 1983 and then more markedly in 1985–87; in total, OPEC's import volumes were more than halved between 1983 and 1987.

For some of the countries, of course, there has been a cushion to such expenditure-reduction, because of the external assets previously accumulated. For the initial current-account surpluses were offset by capital outflows, a large part of which ended up in the banking system, often being used indirectly to finance those deficits that had arisen from the rise in oil prices. Capital flows between countries began to build up to a significant extent, with the banks providing the financial intermediation necessary to lubricate the system.

The industrialised countries had been put in an unaccustomed position by the quadrupling of oil prices. Current-account surpluses had come to be regarded as normal by OECD countries, with capital flows being made to the developing countries to take advantage of the scope for development there. In the years 1965 to 1972 the OECD on average had an annual surplus of $10 billion. The additional cost of oil imports by OECD countries, measured at 1973 volumes and 1974 prices, was about $65 billion (Solomon, 1975). Although OPEC imports rose by about $16 billion in 1974, it was clear that these countries would not be able to immediately absorb their additional revenues and that their surpluses would be redistributed around the system through the banking system. The non-oil developing countries, whose oil import bill increased by an estimated $9 billion – roughly equivalent to the official development assistance paid by OECD countries – received some of the OPEC surplus funds at the other end of the chain. With the capital and money markets effectively concentrated in OECD countries, OPEC countries had little option but to invest their surpluses there, some of this money then passing to the non-oil developing countries as private capital flows and as official and multilateral assistance. Of course, this process happened twice round, for the OPEC surplus built up on two occasions, with capital flowing from OPEC and through the financial system to the non-oil developing countries (Table 7.1).

The availability of finance, and the need for it to find an outlet, was one factor which contributed to the debt crisis described below. For the counterpart to the sudden emergence of the large OPEC surpluses was the financing of deficits elsewhere. The role of the banks was central to this process. The banking system was able and willing to provide the international financial intermediation role. And if such intermediation had not been available, deficits would not have been financed (and surpluses disposed of) in the way that occurred. Imbalances could not have been sustained for as long as they were and adjustment would have taken place sooner. But it was necessary not only to have the intermediation mechanisms but also for the portfolio preferences of the suppliers of finance (and the intermediaries) to be consistent with the international imbalances that generated the need for and the wherewithal for the financing.

In terms of savings/investment balances the development of the OPEC surplus represented a massive increase in OPEC savings, which could be interpreted as an outward shift in the world savings schedule (Crockett and Ripley, 1975). Although there would be likely to be some offset to this increase in savings as real incomes in oil-importing countries fell and as government dissaving increased, the likely result, at least until OPEC spending rose substantially, would be a rise in global savings and investment, the two necessarily, being equal for the world. Another offset, which may have further limited the deflationary bias associated with the rise in the world propensity to save, was the role of finance in sustaining expenditure in oil-importing countries. Sachs (1981) has argued that the pattern of post-oil shock current-account flows reflected an interaction between OPEC saving and shifting worldwide investment patterns. Athough there was a significant worsening in investment opportunities in the developed economies, which led to a reduction in world real interest rates, there was a sharp rise in the interest of developing countries, reflecting both favourable domestic developments and a readiness by banks and official bodies to increase their lending and assistance programmes.

The developing countries' deficits and the debt crisis

The counterpart to the OPEC surpluses of the 1970s and early 1980s occurred in the OECD and the non-oil developing countries, with the largest part occurring in the latter. It was only briefly, in 1977 and 1980, that the current-account deficit for the OECD area in aggregate was larger than that for the non-oil developing countries. Until recently it was unusual for large current-account imbalances in OECD countries to be sustained for long. International and domestic pressures usually forced adjustment, either through adverse capital flows and a fall in the exchange rate or through domestic policy adjustments. The developing countries, on the other hand, have traditionally been capital importers; they have run current-account deficits which have been financed by capital inflows, provided mainly by banks and aid agencies. The effect of the oil price shocks was both to increase the import bill for those developing countries without oil but also, through recycling of surplus funds, to increase the potential supply of finance. The position for these countries, though it had deteriorated, was at least tolerable since they were able (though not in all cases, of course) to increase their foreign borrowing and continue to run external deficits on current account. This was a situation that could continue only so long as there were: (i) surplus countries willing to transfer excess savings to other countries, (ii) the financial intermediation necessary to transfer the funds, and (iii) the willingness of investors to continue to lend to developing countries. The latter depended on the rate of return available and the risk attached to the investment. In practice the risk factor meant that bank finance was increasingly restricted to those countries considered to be creditworthy by the banks, emphasising once again the link between adjustment and the availability of finance as determined by the portfolio preferences of the suppliers.

In the early 1980s several factors combined to worsen the prospects for the non-oil developing countries (World Bank, 1985). The rise in the oil price, the recession in the industrialised world, the fall in real non-oil commodity prices, high real interest rates and then the rise of the dollar, were all unfavourable factors which both increased their existing debt burden and led to a reassessment by the banks of the financial situation of these countries. Until then, the situation had been what one might describe as 'permissive' of continued developing-country current-account deficits. The financial markets had expanded enormously and had been encouraged to do so by the fact that capital controls had been eased in many countries. These factors were reflected in the large rise in the ratio of private to official capital flows to these countries. By 1981 the non-oil developing countries were running current-account deficits of $70 billion and accumulating debt at an accelerating rate. With external conditions having turned against them and with real interest rates at unprecedented levels, it became clear that debt repayment was now in jeopardy.

The debt crisis originally came to a head in 1982 when Mexico was unable to continue its payments. It led to a re-examination of the debt situation of the developing countries, led to a spreading of repayments but a drying-up of new money and started an adjustment process that continued throughout the 1980s. With capital inflows being greatly reduced, the debtor countries had little option but to reduce their domestic absorption relative to income, the only dependable means of doing so in the short term being to cut back on import volumes. A group of seven major, mainly Latin American 'problem' debtors cut their import volumes by 40 per cent between 1981 and 1983 and continued cutting in the following two years (Saunders and Dean, 1986). This was expenditure reduction in a massive way but there was also expenditure switching, resources being transferred into the export sector where export volumes for these problem debtors, having fallen sharply in 1982, rose by a total of over 20 per cent in 1983 and 1984. The combined trade balance of this group moved from a surplus of $10 billion in 1982 to one of $42 billion in 1984, the current-account balance (including net investment income payments) moving from a deficit of $39 billion to a surplus of $3 billion over the same period.

For a broader group of non-oil developing countries the deficit moved up rapidly in the period 1979–81, peaking at $72 billion in 1981, before moving back close to zero in 1986–87. The extreme compression of import volumes was also reflected in significant domestic adjustments. The import intensity of output fell markedly for all groups of developing countries with output growth itself being affected most (outside the Middle East) in those countries where debt problems required the greatest cuts in imports (Mirakhor and Montiel, 1987). For the fifteen heavily-indebted (Baker Plan) countries, the rate of growth fell to virtually zero in the period 1982–85, compared with growth rates averaging 5 per cent annually in the previous 15 years, with import volumes falling by an average of 10 per cent per annum through these years of adjustment. The retrenchment in these countries fell most heavily on imports of consumer goods and capital goods. Most significantly, the import of capital goods fell by 50 per cent in the period 1982–84, the counterpart of substantially reduced investment, thus contributing to the rebalancing of the domestic savings/investment balances. For a group of 34 'market borrowers' (an IMF classification) gross capital formation fell from 26 per cent of GDP in 1981 to 20 per cent in 1984, foreign capital inflows having fallen from roughly 4 per cent of GDP to ½ per cent of GDP over the same period (Watson et al., 1986). The adjustment to the loss of external finance thus fell more heavily on domestic investment than on domestic savings, which changed little in this period. The reduction in imports affected the growth of productive potential, also affected exports (Khan and Knight, 1986) and hence severely affected growth prospects in the developing countries. The adjustment process for developing country debtors can also be analysed in terms of transfer theory as in Reisen and van Trotsenburg (1988), which relates the theory to the budgetary and transfer problems of seven problem debtors.

Imbalances in the industrialised countries

The international financial imbalances of the 1970s and early 1980s largely reflected the movements in the OPEC surplus and the large current-account deficits incurred by the developing countries. The banks acted as financial intermediaries to recycle funds between the two. This is not to discount balance of payments problems in the industrialised countries, the most serious of which was the crisis in the United States in 1977–78, one of several case studies examined in OECD (1988). But the intermittent problems of individual OECD countries were not of the systemic global kind that seemed to characterise the problems associated with the non-industrialised world. Nevertheless, the pattern of financial imbalances did change in a significant way in the 1980s, the new factor being the emergence of persistent imbalances in the major industrial countries.

It has been unusual in the postwar period for a major industrialised country to run a systematic and relatively high external imbalance for anything longer than a few years, though smaller countries have often done so. Until 1986, no major country had recorded a string of current-account deficits of at least $2\frac{1}{2}$ per cent of GNP for as long as three years (OECD, 1986a). Table 7 shows that the three largest industrialised countries – the United States, Japan and Germany – will each have run current-account imbalances of more than $2\frac{1}{2}$ per cent of GNP for a period of at least five years from 1984 onwards. This unprecedented situation has led to doubts about the self-equilibrating nature of international and domestic imbalances.

The counterpart of these imbalances has been an increase in capital flows between the industrial countries which has led to a large net accumulation of international assets and liabilities, together with profound changes to net creditor/debtor positions.

Since 1981 the United States has run down a substantial net external asset position and become the world's largest debtor country. On present rates of increase it could soon have a larger net external debt position than the combined total of all the developing-country debtors. Meanwhile, Japan has become the world's largest creditor, with about $300 billion net external assets at the end of 1988 compared with virtually zero net assets at the start of the decade. Germany, relative to her size, has had an equally impressive expansion in her traditional creditor status. Those net positions are nevertheless not especially large as a proportion of GNP, relative to the experience of the nineteenth century, for example. But they have arisen in developed industrialised countries in financing intra-OECD imbalances, rather than the more traditional flows from the rich developed to the poor developing countries. The imbalances emerged extremely quickly and, as of 1988, though showing signs of attenuation with substantial volume adjustment already occurring, they did not look likely to readily disappear. One factor which makes correction more difficult, as the developing countries have found, is that changes in external asset and liability positions feed on themselves, since the changing net investment income flows which derive from these net stock positions exacerbate the current-account imbalances.

The developing country debt situation continues to be an import-ant influence on world capital flows and is likely to remain a problem for many years to come. But its significance as regards financial flows has been supplanted more recently by the enormous financing requirements associated with the imbalances within the OECD, in particular the cumulative US external deficit. Financial intermediation has thus switched towards the finance of the US deficit, with non-residents purchasing assets in the United States, while additional finance to developing countries has dried up.

The origins of the international imbalances are not straightfor-ward and clear. From the trade side, two factors stand out: (i) over the period 1983–84 US domestic demand grew some 10 per cent more than demand in the rest of the OECD, a gap that had not been reversed by 1988; and (ii) the earlier rise of the dollar had a detrimental effect on US competitiveness which, even if it has largely been reversed subsequently, is a factor which has not yet led to an unwinding of the effects on trade patterns and the location of industry. There are also specific factors concerning the US geographical pattern of trade, in particular the previous importance of Latin America as a market for US exports and the rise of the newly-industrialising countries in Asia as a major competitor, that may make the process of trade adjustment more difficult (OECD, 1986b).

This trade perspective, though it provides important insights on the imbalances, hides some perhaps more fundamental factors that lie behind the adjustment process. One needs to look further than the immediate trade mechanisms signified by an examination of the relevant trade elasticities and the relative income and relative price movements and ask a set of matching questions: (i) why did US demand grow faster than elsewhere? and (ii) what explains the rise and fall of the dollar? These are, of course, more difficult questions, in that they involve a consideration of the full mechanics of how the domestic economy works as well as a consideration of how economies interact internationally. Looking at this issue in a more global way, domestic demand and output, savings/investment balances, exchange rates and trade flows are all endogenous elements in a larger macroeconomic system with no simple causality running between the variables. Nevertheless it is possible to use such theories to suggest ways in which imbalances have arisen and ways in which adjustment might occur.

There is a further major area of contention that should also be mentioned. This is the issue of whether it is the current or capital account of the balance of payments which is in the driving seat. Returning to the case of the US imbalance, and to put the issue at its starkest; did the current-account deficit require a capital inflow and therefore lead to the need for high interest rates or did high interest rates and an expanding economy arising from the fiscal deficit lead to a high dollar and an external deficit? Even this is putting the issue too simply, missing several arguments in the chain of causality. There was a complex interaction that went on. However, most economists would probably now subscribe to a view that saw a relation between the particular policy mix in the United States – tight monetary and loose fiscal – with economic expansion, high real interest rates, the rise in the dollar, strong capital inflows and a deterioration in the current account. The period 1980–85 saw a growing US current-account deficit and a rising exchange rate. This was possible because the *ex ante* increasing demand for the dollar as an asset exceeded the contemporaneous current-account deficit. Viewed in this way the causality runs from the capital account via the exchange rate to the current account, which is the reverse of the way in which the causality had traditionally been viewed.

In terms of the domestic situation, one result of the increase in the US budget deficit, taken together with the fact that this was not matched by an increase in excess private savings, was that expenditure ran ahead of output, implying net borrowing from abroad (the capital inflow/current-account deficit). The situation was different in Japan and Germany where large surpluses built up. In both of those countries, the authorities were engaged in a process of budget consolidation from about 1983 onwards. But government dissaving was in both cases offset by an excess of private savings over private investment. This underlines the importance of the interconnections between the private sector, the government and the external sector and also helps to explain why the causality is not always clear.

CONCLUSIONS

The key issue is whether the recent imbalances of the sort described above really matter. If, at its simplest, Americans wish to spend more than they earn and Japanese and Germans are willing to lend them the means to do so, why should we worry? If Japanese and US households, in making decisions about their desired ratios of income to wealth, tend respectively to be high and low savers, and if government dissavings are also regarded as having been made through some sort of free societal decision, then why should there be concern if in aggregate the Japanese have excess savings which they are willing, at an equilibrating interest rate, to lend to the Americans?

Such a situation has been characterised by Corden (1985) as one where there has been an increased exchange of financial assets for goods; as with any free exchange, there is assumed to be a gain from trade, the trade here including financial assets. Not surprisingly, there are various reservations, mentioned by Corden, about such a view, mostly reflecting concerns about policy. In the first place, fiscal and monetary policy may distort savings and investment decisions. In the case in point, savings have generally been discouraged in the United States and may have been encouraged elsewhere. Policy in the area of investment may also have led to distortions which will have led to non-optimal trade. Secondly, government budget deficits

– one part of the supply of financial assets – may not be optimal from the national point of view.

Perhaps more important than these considerations, however, is the fact that, to come back to the earlier discussion, the situation may be unsustainable. Continued US external deficits, and the parallel accumulation of net external liabilities by the United States may be explicable in terms of portfolio adjustments or differential monetary policies, but the dynamics of debt accumulation mean that lenders will eventually be unwilling to continue to provide finance, at which point the whole edifice can unravel in rather sudden and undesirable ways. Since it is known that eventual correction is likely to involve a depreciation of the dollar, this generates expectations of exchange-rate changes and uncertainty. The problem with the major imbalances of the mid-1980s is that they have been widely viewed as unsustainable and have thus generated such uncertainty. This uncertainty was not dissipated by the attempt by the major industrialised countries in 1987 to stabilise their exchange rates; uncertainty and volatility were merely transferred to interest rates and eventually stockmarket prices. The subsequent adjustment occurred in ways that were probably more costly than had policies been changed so as to instigate the process of adjustment at an earlier stage.

The lessons from this are that, given divergent policy mixes, it is impossible to avoid volatility in financial markets. If one attempts to stabilise exchange rates it is likely that there will be greater volatility in interest rates and vice-versa. In these circumstances, it is important that there is policy consistency between the major countries. The experience of the 1980s indicates that inconsistency only leads to pressures in markets that necessitate disruptive adjustments over the longer run. This argues for a greater coordination and consistency of policy than has been evident in recent years.

8 The Analysis of International Debt

NICK SNOWDEN

INTRODUCTION

By the end of 1985 the total stock of foreign debt owed or guaranteed by governments of developing countries amounted to $628 billion, or almost one-third of their combined GNPs (IBRD, 1987, Table 19). Two questions concerning this debt are addressed here:

(1) What caused the international borrowing which led to its accumulation?
(2) Was the international debt 'crisis' of 1982 the consequence of 'excessive' borrowing and lending, or of the *terms* on which the loans were initially extended?

These terms increasingly involved floating interest rates as commercial banks came to dominate international lending in the 1970s. The second question therefore highlights the appropriateness, or otherwise, of bank involvement, and the chapter will focus on these institutions and the loans they extended.

After a brief review of the facts of international lending, the next two sections outline respectively a neo-classical analysis of the demand for, and supply of, country loans. Governments are here assumed to be 'rational actors' maximising *national* economic welfare. Assuming lenders are also 'rational' a major theoretical conclusion is that country lending would tend to fall short of the optimum rather than to exceed it. In this framework, the 1982 debt crisis would be the outcome of *unforeseen* changes in the world economy, rather than a reaction to a spasm of unwise lending. The subsequent section develops this argument, emphasising the importance of floating interest rate debt in precipitating the crisis, and analyses *post* crisis debt rescheduling negotiations using the neo-classical framework.

More institutionally orientated literature, however, suggests that overlending was a characteristic of this market and was to contribute to the later crisis. The remaining sections assess these arguments. On the demand side political factors apparently impelled 'excessive' foreign borrowing by governments. On the supply side, aggressive lending strategies by banks are investigated. Finally, a conclusion summarises lessons for policy.

CURRENT ACCOUNT DEVELOPMENTS AND LDC BORROWING: 1970–82

Accumulation of external debt arises when countries borrow to finance deficits on the current account of the balance of payments. Current account balances, displayed as a fraction of GNP in Table 8.1, are therefore a useful starting point for the analysis of country debt.

The dramatic increases in the surpluses of the Arab OPEC countries in 1974–6, and to a lesser extent in 1980–81, are perhaps the most outstanding features. These 'autonomous' surpluses were necessarily reflected in deficits elsewhere (see Chapter 7). The recessionary impact of the OPEC action on industrial economies was accompanied by a cyclical downturn in 1974 and government disinclination to stimulate demand in view of growing inflationary pressure (Argy, 1981, Ch. 18). As industrial countries therefore returned rapidly to external balance, Table 8.1 shows that the counterpart of OPEC surpluses was to be found in LDC deficits. However, Sachs (1981), and Khan and Knight (1983) show that the distribution of deficits was not closely related to oil-dependence at the country-level. The transient current account surpluses of the 'middle income oil exporters' (a group including Mexico, Nigeria, and Venezuela), emphasise this point in Table 8.1.

The external deficits, however caused, changed both the quantity and nature of foreign borrowing and debt accumulation as indicated in Table 8.2. In *real terms*, the flow of borrowing in 1982 was 92 per cent higher than in 1970, and its composition had changed dramatically. While the 60–40 per cent division in 1982 between official (government) and private sector sources was little changed, the aid

TABLE 8.1 Current account balances as a percentage of GNP in selected groups of countries, 1970–82

Country grouping	1970	1971	1972	1973	1974	1975	1976	1977	1978	1979	1980	1981	1982
High-income oil exporters	15.7	26.2	22.5	21.2	51.5	40.2	35.0	26.3	15.5	21.2	31.4	32.2	20.1
Industrial countries	0.8	1.0	0.9	0.7	-0.2	0.6	0.1	0.1	0.7	0.0	-0.5	0.0	0.0
All developng countries	-2.3	-2.7	-1.4	-0.9	-1.9	-3.9	-2.2	-2.2	-2.6	-2.0	-2.3	-3.9	-3.7
Middle-income oil exporters	-3.0	-3.0	-2.4	-1.1	3.3	-3.4	-2.4	-3.6	-5.1	-0.2	0.8	-3.8	-4.4

Source: IBRD (1985), Table 2.1, p. 17

TABLE 8.2   LDC net resource inflow by source and stock of outstanding debt 1970 and 1982 ($ billions in current values)

	1970	1982
Official Development Assistance (Aid)	8.1	34.7
Grants by private voluntary agencies	0.9	2.3
Non-concessional flows	10.9	60.4
1. Official	3.9	22.0
2. Private	7.0	38.4
(i) Direct investment	3.7	11.9
(ii) Bank lending	3.0	26.0
(iii) Bond issues	0.3	0.5
TOTAL	19.9	97.4
Stock of outstanding debt	68.0	546.0

Percentage of public debt at floating interest rates

	1974	1982
All LDCs	16.2	38.7
'Major borrowers'*	18.4	46.7

* Comprising Argentina, Brazil, Chile, Egypt, India, Indonesia, Israel, South Korea, Mexico, Turkey, Venezuela and Yugoslavia.
Source: Compiled from Tables 2.3, 2.4 and 2.6 of *World Development Report 1985* (IBRD 1985). This Report provides valuable material in connection with the subject matter of the present chapter.

component of official finance had fallen. In the private sector, the real flow of foreign direct investment was 40 per cent higher in 1982 than in 1970, but capital market finance was 188 per cent higher largely reflecting the contribution of the banks. By 1982, banks were supplying 27 per cent of total inflows to LDCs compared with the (approximate) 12 per cent share represented by direct investment; a reversal of the proportions typical of earlier years (OECD 1983 and 1985).

Banks therefore contributed disproportionately to financing the enhanced current account deficits of the 1970s. This financing helped to sustain the demand of borrowing countries for imports and thereby softened the deflationary global impact of the oil price increases. World Bank data in Table 8.2 highlight the parallel debt accumulation and a major corollary of the trend towards bank finance; the growing proportion of floating interest rate debt. More detailed figures make clear the concentration of this type of finance. Around 87 per cent of LDC debt owed to banks was accounted for by twenty countries in 1982 (OECD, 1983, Table H.6.). It is further estimated that 75 per cent of net floating rate debt in 1982 was owed by Mexico, Brazil, Argentina and South Korea alone (Bank of England, 1983). Relative to other forms of foreign finance, notably relative to foreign direct investment, these countries were increasingly exposed to interest charges which would vary in line with the cost of underlying bank deposits; a critical element in the 1982 crisis. From $23 billion in 1982, new long-term loan commitments by banks to Latin America fell to $2 billion in 1983 marking the end of voluntary bank lending to that previously favoured continent (Watson et al., 1986, Table 8). Having softened the impact of the oil 'shock' in the 1970s, this credit contraction was to force drastic borrower adjustment in the 1980s. How is the sequence to be explained?

THE DEMAND FOR INTERNATIONAL LOANS

Current account deficits reflect two components; the domestic saving–investment balance and the government's budget deficit (see equation 7.4). Neo-classical analysis emphasises the possible motives for borrowing which would, *ex post*, be reflected in the observed investment-saving, and budget balances. It has been suggested that these motives may be divided, primarily, into three components; 'consumption', 'adjustment' and 'investment' (Eaton and Gersovitz, 1981a).[1]

The consumption motive could be important for countries facing sharp swings in their income around a trend; a pattern typical of primary commodity exporters. Borrowing would permit a smooth pattern of consumption to be maintained. Under the adjustment motive, a country may borrow to support the gradual introduction of policy changes forced on it by deteriorating external circumstances or competitiveness. In the case of an oil price rise, the increased import bill might otherwise require quick and painful adjustments in order to cut import demand. Finally, the investment motive lies behind the theoretical presumption that capital should flow from developed to developing economies. Provided the marginal product of capital in the capital poor economy exceeds the real rate of interest on world capital markets, such borrowing should be self-financing, with revenues being generated by the new projects.

The oil price increases were a shock experienced *simultaneously* by oil-importing countries. The financing of the resulting current-account deficits required capital-account inflows ultimately deriving from the oil producers. How might the adjustment motive for borrowing be applied given this global dimension? Appropriate adjustment would probably involve investment spending, since the oil price increases had an appreciable impact on the global supply of saving. It has been estimated that the net saving (current account) surpluses of the industrial countries in 1974–78 declined by not less than half a percentage point of their combined GNPs (OECD, 1985, p.159). Similarly, the oil 'tax' increased the net saving (current account) deficit of the LDCs by at least one percentage point of their GNPs. At their peak, however, the current account surpluses of the Gulf oil producers amounted to over 2 per cent of the combined OECD GNPs (ibid.). Taken together these estimates imply a significant positive shift in the global supply of saving, suggesting thereby a simple explanation for the worldwide decline in real interest rates at this time (Sachs, 1981). To this 'loanable funds' view of interest rate determination, however, may have to be added a lag in adjustment of inflation expectations, since real rates actually turned negative.

With this inducement to increased investment spending, it has been suggested that the natural location was increasingly to be found in some of the more dynamic developing economies (ibid.). Declining productivity growth, wage push, and other indications of economic difficulty in the OECD economies are contrasted with the 'outward-looking', trade-orientated, policies that had been adopted by the 'newly-industrialised countries' (NICs). In terms of equation 7.1, therefore, the deficits would reflect an investment–saving gap justified by projects capable of earning a competitive rate of return. It is worth remarking that the consumption and adjustment motives for borrowing would tend also to be manifested in budget deficits (as falling income reduced tax revenues).

In reality, however, budget deficits may derive from other influences. The assumption that governments carry out policies reflecting the interests of the representative citizen implies that public and private motives are always consistent. Equally stringent is the assumption that domestic income transfers can be costlessly effected through the tax mechanism (Eaton and Taylor, 1986). Recent US fiscal deficits, in contrast, together with the attendant foreign borrowing, appear to have been the outcome of domestic policy conflicts. For the present, however, the assumption that governments seek to maximise national welfare in their approach to international borrowing will be retained.

LOAN SUPPLY, BANK ASCENDANCY, AND THE 1982 CRISIS

Turning to the supply-side of the market, two questions arise. Firstly, what factors in theory would influence the supply schedule for loans? Secondly, what explanations are there for the increasingly dominant position of the banks in this supply? In answering the first question it is necessary to recognise that loan markets are inescapably influenced by uncertainty. The lender is hostage to the intentions of the borrower and must assess the probability of the loan being repaid; a probability likely to be influenced by the interest rate charged on the loan. Two reasons have been stressed; the adverse selection and incentive (or moral hazard) effects (Stiglitz and Weiss, 1981).

If two potential borrowers are likely to obtain the same mean return on funds borrowed, but the variance of these possible returns is higher in one case than the other, adverse selection suggests that a rise in interest rates will tend to exclude the 'safe' borrower, leaving the lender with the riskier loan. The moral hazard, or incentive, problem arises when the individual borrower is induced by a rise in loan interest rates to undertake projects with a higher probability of the loan not being repaid. In each case, the distribution of potential returns to the 'safe' borrower or project will be less likely to involve the possible non-repayment of the loan. The mean of these distributions, therefore, will be more severely affected by a rise in interest rates than in those where default is more likely. In those adverse outcomes, the interest rate has no effect and the mean expected return to the *borrower* falls by a smaller amount.

From the lender's perspective, a positive association between default risk and loan interest rates implies that a rise in the latter will not lead to a proportionate increase in expected returns. In consequence, and as displayed in Figure 8.1 below, the loan supply schedule becomes backward bending at high interest rates. A further implication of default risk (to be discussed in the context of Figure 8.1), is that market *equilibrium* may be characterised by *credit rationing*. In these circumstances, both loan volume and interest rates charged are lower than the intersection of the demand and supply curves would suggest.

In the domestic environment, failure to repay a loan usually implies insolvency on the part of the borrowing enterprise. Bankruptcy proceedings allow lenders to seize control of assets thereby ensuring that default is only worthwhile if indebtedness exceeds net worth (e.g. Cooper and Sachs, 1985). The added complication internationally, however, is the lack of a legal framework to provide this degree of lender protection. There are usually few assets to be seized within the jurisdiction of the creditor's courts, and the debtor's courts are unlikely to be of assistance, *especially if the borrower is the government of the country concerned*! (Eaton and Taylor, 1986). Despite this legal weakness, most bank lending has been to governments, or has been publicly guaranteed, and the default risk therefore becomes 'sovereign' risk. The offsetting advantage in lending to governments is that they can appropriate foreign exchange with which to make loan service payments. A loan to a foreign citizen, on the other hand, is prone to a 'transfer risk' if the borrower is unable to obtain foreign exchange with domestic currency. In this form, then, the major added complication of international lending is that governments might *choose* to default well before becoming insolvent. This *endogenous* default decision has been called 'debt repudiation' (Eaton and Gersovitz, 1983).

Potential debt repudiation represents an additional dimension of moral hazard in international lending. Higher loan interest rates augment debt service obligations and, by increasing the probability of repudiation in future years, further support the assumption of a backward-bending supply schedule for country loans. Indeed, in the absence of legal redress for lenders, it is clear that *some* sanction must exist for international lending to take place at all. At least for some time, debt repudiation would probably exclude the delinquent country from further borrowing and Eaton and Gersovitz (1981b) emphasise the resulting loss of access to future consumption 'smoothing' as the major sanction available to lenders. The loss of short-term credits necessary for the easy conduct of international trade would be a further significant penalty (Gersovitz, 1985). Without such access, transactions would be restricted to a cash, or 'brown paper bag', basis at considerable cost (Krugman, 1985).

The above argument suggests that a country will default whenever the discounted present value of its loan service obligations is in excess of the present value of the costs imposed by sanctions. Credit rationing might, in principle, be used by lenders to prevent this situation from being reached. Unfortunately for the lender, this calculation is surrounded by uncertainty, not least because of the difficulty of arranging legally enforceable restraints on the future behaviour of the borrower. A large number of possible actions, *after the loan has been granted*, could make eventual repudiation more likely. For instance, a long-term loan may be jeopardised by further high levels of borrowing from other lenders (Sachs, 1984). The inability of countries credibly to forswear such actions tends further to tighten credit constraints.

These moral hazard elements in international lending, it has been suggested, also help to explain the predominant role of banks in the business. Given the large size of the typical country loan, banks joined together in 'syndicates', thus spreading loan risks across a number of institutions in different financial centres. Default on any one loan, (through the cross-default clause in syndicated loan agreements), meant that the country would be declared in default by all such lenders, and access to capital markets would end. Further, banks could agree to terminate the supply of international trade credit (which they dominate), and they may be in a better position to check the extent of overall country borrowing (Gersovitz, 1985, and Kletzer, 1984 rspectively).

Neo-classical analysis therefore suggests that bank intermediation supported by loan syndication and the cross-default clause, may have been encouraged by the moral hazard complications prevalent in country lending. It is not clear, however, why this explanation of bank dominance should have become so important in the 1970s. Lending in the nineteenth century, for instance, was dominated by bond issues (Arndt and Drake, 1985). Other explanations of bank preeminence will be discussed below in the context of possible over-lending. Retaining the neo-classical perspective for the present, a key point in the credit-rationing literature should be emphasised. Credit rationing implies lower international lending than would be expected on 'textbook' grounds. In the simplest case of complete predictability of the costs and benefits of default, for instance, lenders would provide funds at risk-free interest rates until debt reached the critical credit limit. Default would not actually occur but, compared with the textbook case where lending would be limited only by opportunities for productive investment, the threat of default lowers welfare (Sachs, 1984).

When uncertainty about the future is introduced, risk premia added to interest rates will produce the upward-sloping supply schedule, rather than the discontinuous one just described. Moreover, defaults *will* now occur but only as a result of factors which were not perfectly predictable at the time the loan was made. Such an unanticipated event would be the experiment with unorthodox economic policies in the USA after 1979. Restrictive monetary policy in the early 1980s, contributed both to high world interest rates and to the recession in the major economies. How might credit markets be expected to respond to these disturbances? An earlier response had been that the average maturity of bank loans tended to shorten as indebtedness increased in the 1970s (Wionczec, 1979). This 'short leash' allowed more regular review of borrower behaviour as loans were renewed, but also left borrowers vulnerable to the changes in market sentiment which were shortly to follow.

EXTERNAL SHOCKS AND THE DEMAND FOR RESCHEDULING

The impact of the above-mentioned shocks on countries with high stocks of floating interest rate (r) debt (D) can be derived from the following expression, (using the assumption that any trade deficit must be financed by borrowing):

$$\Delta D = rD - (X - M) \tag{8.1}$$

If the country has a zero trade balance ($X - M$), debt has to rise by the amount of new borrowing required to finance interest payments on the existing debt (rD); the first term on the right. A trade deficit would add further to borrowing whereas a large enough trade surplus could reduce the debt outstanding. In growth rate terms:

$$\Delta D/D = \mathring{D} = r - (X - M)/D \tag{8.2}$$

where $\mathring{D}$ is the annual proportionate change of the debt.

Since debt must be serviced in foreign currency, a popular indicator of creditworthiness was the debt–export ratio, $d = D/X$. The proportionate change in this ratio depends on the relative rate of growth of the components:

$$\mathring{d} = \mathring{D} - \mathring{X} \tag{8.3}$$

Substituting from (8.2) in (8.3), and re-arranging, a key relation in the debt literature emerges (e.g. Bergsten, Cline and Williamson, 1985; Dornbusch, 1985a):

$$\mathring{d} = (r - \mathring{X}) - (X - M)/D \tag{8.4}$$

This states that the debt–export ratio grows if nominal interest rates are higher than the growth rate of nominal dollar export earnings, unless offset by a sufficiently large trade surplus. This formula serves to emphasise the sudden increase in perceived risk in LDC lending after 1979. Between 1980 and 1984, the London inter-bank offer rate (LIBOR), to which loan interest rates were linked, averaged 12.9 per cent. Growth of export earnings, in contrast, averaged only 2.3 per cent reflecting both recession and declining inflation in major export markets.

In terms of the loan market theory outlined above, this sudden change in world conditions could be enough to explain the debt crisis of 1982. Trade surpluses were now needed to prevent a continuing rise in the debt–export ratio thus imposing a substantial transfer burden on the borrower. Lenders may well have perceived an increased probability of default, especially in view of uncertainty surrounding the future prospects for world interest rates and economic growth. Krugman (1985) uses a credit rationing framework to explain the emergence of loan rescheduling and involuntary lending when such disturbances arise. In his two-period model, a country with 'inherited' debt seeks to maximise its utility from running a first-period trade deficit financed by foreign borrowing. The loan is repaid with interest in the second period unless, at the start of that period, the country chooses to default. Sanctions would then be imposed by lenders although the cost of these sanctions is not certain to either side before the loan is made.

Figure 8.1 below shows an initial equilibrium in the supply of loans to the country. The backward-bending supply schedule S_1 reflects the competitive (default) risk premium added to the cost of funds r^* by suppliers. An indifference map for the borrower is depicted, with utility (U) increasing for lower interest rates and higher loans (i.e. $U_3 > U_2 > U_1$).The slope of the curves reflects the assumed utility function. Higher interest rates can be offset by a larger loan, which finances the first period trade deficit. In the absence of default, however, repayment of this loan in the second period will require a trade surplus and lower domestic absorption. The concave slopes of the indifference curves reflect this trade-off, and suggest a credit rationed equilibrium at A. This credit rationing is relative to the intersection of the unconstrained demand curve for loans (D), and the supply curve (S_1). With defaults here raising the anticipated cost of lending, a competitive loan market would offer the rationed quantity at A where the gains from lower default incidence accrue to the borrower in lower interest charges.[2]

In this framework, the economic shocks discussed above would be likely to swivel the supply schedule to the left (e.g. S_2), as default probabilities increased. This threatens to be self-fulfilling, however, since the reduced loan supply and smaller trade deficit in the first period tend to raise the relative attractiveness of default at the beginning of the second. Once default is threatened on existing debt (repudiation), Krugman shows that lenders acting in concert would prefer involuntary new lending at, say, B in exchange for non-default by the borrower. Since it lies to the right of the new competitive supply curve, (which is based on *future* default probabilities), a loss on this individual loan is anticipated. The reward is receipt of first-period debt service and a positive probability of such receipts in the second. If default occurs, both of these will be lost. Although this benefit must be assessed against the cost of the extra new loans, heavy initial debt will make sure of the profitability of this action (Cline, 1983).

Two important points may be noted from this analysis. Firstly, involuntary lending is only worthwhile if it does not exceed the debt service payments due. It is never in the country's interest to default otherwise, given the positive costs imposed by sanctions. Some net repayment to creditors is a *quid pro quo* for avoiding these costs. It is the case that the net flow of funds has been towards lenders following the Latin American reschedulings in the early 1980s (Sachs, 1986). Secondly, the arrangement needs the concerted action of lenders since any individual lender would be unwilling to supply at a loss; there is a public good aspect to continued lending. As with such cases generally, the problem of 'free-riding' arises since some

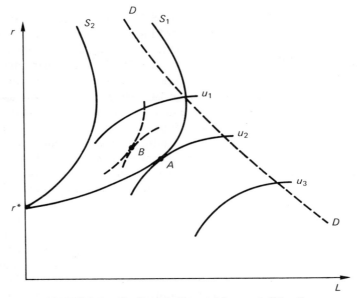

FIGURE 8.1   Credit rationing and 'concerted' lending

banks might avoid participating in the new lending while enjoying the benefit of the increased value of their outstanding loans.

This reasoning supports the recent intervention of the IMF both in ensuring the participation of banks roughly in line with their 'exposure', and in making possible more extended agreements between countries and their creditors. Much new lending is advanced in the form of rescheduling (postponing) principal repayments due on existing debt. Since negotiations are costly, there is an interest in lenders agreeing to reschedule payments coming due over a number of years. These multi-year reschedulings, however, require lender-confidence that the borrower will adopt policies which offer the hope of an eventual return to voluntary lending. Enhanced surveillance by the IMF in recent agreements with (for instance) Mexico is clearly relevant in this context (Watson *et al.*, 1986).

The analysis so far suggests that the debt crisis has been one of borrower illiquidity in the face of external shocks and associated loan market rationing. However, although this is probably the most popular interpretation of the crisis in international financial circles

(Mathieson, 1985, and Krueger, 1985), its completeness can be questioned. Firstly, our discussion of the determinants of the debt–export ratio suggests that the basis for credit rationing *before* 1979 was not at all clear. Between 1970 and 1979, the export earnings of non-oil LDCs advanced by an average of 20.2 per cent per annum compared with a LIBOR average of 10.3 per cent (Dornbusch, 1985a). In these circumstances, equation 8.4 shows that the debt–export ratio could be held constant ($d=0$) even if the trade balance was constantly negative! Equivalently, a country could borrow enough to cover annual interest payments *and* provide for a net resource inflow while maintaining constant this index of credit worthiness (Simonsen, 1985). If countries did not have to make net repayments, they had little reason to default, and credit rationing prior to the crisis is not readily explained (Eaton & Taylor, 1986). *How*, in any case, would rationing before the crisis be effected? The mechanism suggested by Stiglitz and Weiss is not obviously applicable to country borrowers from many lenders and, in this context, the mechanism has tended to be assumed rather than explained (e.g. Eaton and Gersovitz, 1981b). Certainly, 'country limits' which were set for their own prudential reasons by individual banks could not translate into overall credit limits for the borrower when the number of lenders was increasing. It may be the case that systematic credit rationing only emerged with anxiety over the existing level of country debt in the early 1980s, and it was this rationing which triggered the spate of rescheduling negotiations at that time (Cline, 1984).

With these complications in mind, the next two sections investigate the possibility that the credit rationing process *before the crisis* was unable to prevent borrowing which would have proved 'excessive' even in the absence of the global shocks of the early 1980s. Factors on the demand side and the supply side which may have impelled excessive borrowing and lending are considered in turn.

DOMESTIC FINANCIAL INSTABILITY AND EXTERNAL BORROWING

The recent revival of structuralist analyses of the inflation process in Latin America offers an interesting contrast to the view of governments as singlemindedly maximising national welfare so far adopted here. The alternative view emphasises the conflicting demands made on governments by differing domestic constituencies, and sees inflation as reflecting a 'struggle for shares' in national product between these interest groups within the economy (Baer, 1987). The consequence of their demands is that the pressure for public spending is strong whereas the ability to raise tax revenues is weak. Inflation, acting as a 'tax' on holders of money balances, operates as a residual form of finance to 'close' the resulting public sector deficits. Unless this inflation is matched by a continuous 'crawling peg' depreciation of the exchange rate, however, exporters will also suffer as *real* appreciation erodes the purchasing power of their earnings. The Brazilian response to the oil price increases of 1974 suggests that foreign borrowing was influenced by such processes.

Political calculations led the authorities to subsidise domestic oil consumption at the expense of a widening budget deficit (Baer, 1987). A sixfold rise in the real-world price of oil between 1963 and 1982 thereby produced less than a doubling of the Brazilian domestic price (Dornbusch, 1985b), and external borrowing absorbed the terms of trade loss to the economy. Despite Brazil's policy of maintaining purchasing power parity for the Cruzeiro against the dollar, which should have prevented inflation-induced over-valuation, the government did not devalue the currency in response to the oil price increase. Nor did they adjust the rate for the growing overvaluation of the dollar against other major trading currencies (ibid.). The resulting current-account deterioration was financed by further foreign borrowing. A 'maxi' devaluation in 1979 simply produced further inflation, (roughly 77–110 per cent in 1979–82), as a 'struggle for shares' wage–price spiral ensued (Baer, 1987). External borrowing became the 'slack' variable for the authorities given these difficulties.

Despite other differences, overvaluation of the nation's currency appears to have been a common theme for country debtors. As noted for Brazil, currency devaluation can contribute to the inflation process, and may be resisted for this reason when the need to control price rises becomes a political imperative. In the case of Argentina, for instance, governments have tended to oscillate between 'populist' and military regimes, and both have appealed to constituencies made up of differing groups. When inflation threatens to get 'out of control', friction is introduced within these constituencies, and the government is required to respond (Epstein, 1987).

This pressure was particularly strong on the military regime of 1976–81, and produced an unconventional response. Deliberate overvaluation of the exchange rate helped to stabilise inflation by strengthening the resistance of domestic producers to wage demands, (Dornbusch, 1985b). Combined with a reduction of tariff barriers, the exchange rate was set by a pre-announced 'tablita', (after December 1978), which implied gradual real appreciation. Unfortunately, this programme was combined with a failure to control public sector financial deficits, and these in turn contributed to a growing external deficit which had to be financed by foreign borrowing (Epstein, 1987).

Through permitting the imbalances associated with accidental or deliberate exchange rate overvaluation to be financed, these cases suggest that external borrowing constitutes a partial alternative to domestic inflation. Although the inflation tax is ameliorated, this policy choice imposes an alternative distribution of costs on the domestic economy which has the paradoxical effect of reducing the country's ability to service external debt. In the above cases (and more recently in the USA), exchange-rate overvaluation leads to a decline in the competitiveness of the traded goods sector, on which foreign exchange earnings depend. This inherent contradiction cannot continue indefinitely, and the Argentine case illustrates the eventual outcome. When domestic asset holders recognise the threat of an eventual devaluation towards a more realistic exchange rate, massive capital exports are induced. It is estimated by Morgan Guaranty that Argentina's gross external debt increased by $42 billion between 1976 and 1985. In contrast, 'capital flight' between 1976 and 1982 was $27 billion! For ten Latin American countries capital flight of $123 billion, representing almost one-half of the change in their gross external debt, is estimated to have occurred between 1976 and 1985 (Morgan Guaranty, 1986).

There was, of course, considerable variation in country experience. Chile, for instance, experienced little capital flight or large public deficits (Scheetz, 1987). Nevertheless, anti-inflationary currency overvaluation was used with the resulting external deficits financed by foreign borrowing. Public sector deficits, capital flight, and exchange rate overvaluation were, however, all central to the experiences of Mexico and Venezuela. In addition to damaging the very sector on which future debt service must depend, there is a further paradox in external borrowing as a response to an acute constraint on raising tax revenues. In such circumstances the maximum debt that can be incurred, while assuming future repayment, is governed not by the productive wealth of the economy but by the government's ability to tax it (Sachs, 1984). This point may be made simply by assuming that government saving, net of current expenditures, are at the rate t, of national output Q. If the population saves at the rate s, out of the output remaining, $(1 - t)Q$, the following expression links outstanding debt *next* year with this year's national saving–investment balance:

$$D_2 = (1 + r)D_1 + I_1 - tQ_1 - s(1 - t)Q_1 \qquad (8.5)$$

That is, debt grows by the interest rate on the outstanding amount (rD_1) plus the fraction of investment (I_1) not financed from domestic surpluses, and which therefore requires new borrowing. Adding one to each subscript, (denoting periods), provides an equivalent expression for debt in the third year. Substitution of the first expression for D_2 in the second, yields the following on rearrangement:

$$(1 + r)D_1 = \{s(1 - t) + t\}[Q_1 + Q_2/(1 + r)] - [I_1 + I_2/(1 + r)] + \bar{D}_3/(1 + r) \qquad (8.6)$$

If debt is to be limited by the third period, $(\bar{D}_3)$, this year's debt (plus the interest on it), is constrained by that limit, and the discounted present value of public and private saving out of future output (the first product term on the right-hand side of equation (8.6)), less that of the investment spending needed to generate it. The government saving rate, t, can be negative, given current transfer payments, and it is this rate which determines how much debt can be sustained if recourse to external borrowing is to be limited.

Defining national wealth as the discounted value of future national output (Q), less that of the investment outlays (I) needed to secure it, equation (8.6) shows that this would be the limit on external debt only if $t = 1$. This, however, would in turn suggest that consumption could be depressed to zero, and it becomes clear that taxable capacity rather than national wealth is the yardstick against which to measure whether or not outstanding debt is 'excessive' (Sachs, 1984).

When external borrowing is used to accommodate competing domestic claims, a sudden reduction in its supply will impose difficult political choices involving losses for some groups. Following the 1982 crisis, Mexico resorted to an over-devaluation of the

peso which stimulated the inflation tax on money balances. Moreover, as the peso began to appreciate, capital flight into dollar assets
became less attractive and this permitted a massive reduction in the
interest burden on domestic bonds. In 1982 30 per cent of the
government's budget deficit was covered by the inflation tax, and the
rest by negative real interest rates engineered in this way (Ize and
Ortiz, 1987).

IMPRUDENT LENDING?

If, as the previous section suggests, much borrowing was imprudent,
why did lenders not prevent it through credit rationing? Were the
lenders themselves imprudent?

While an earlier section has noted that technical developments
such as loan syndication helped to encourage international lending
by banks, it is clear that other forces were propelling them in this
direction. The removal of controls on capital exports by the US
government in January 1974 allowed major banks there to attract
and on-lend to Latin America the OPEC deposits initially placed
with banks in the Eurocurrency markets (Stanyer & Whitley, 1981).
With the necessary infrastructure thus in place, banks actively
sought to expand their international lending as a means to promot-
ing balance-sheet growth and profitability. This strategic choice was
partly a response to the new 'recycling' opportunities but also to a
severe downturn in domestic loan demand following the recession of
1974–75. Sovereign lending appeared both to offer a means of
diversifying away from domestic business and to have a superior
loan loss record (IBRD, 1985, pp.113–15).

By 1982, however, the strategy had led the nine largest American
banks to have loans outstanding to Latin American borrowers
representing 176 per cent of their combined capital and reserves
(Sachs, 1986). Guttentag and Herring (1986) have argued that
'disaster myopia' helped to produce this outcome. Work in experi-
mental psychology suggests that subjective probabilities of an event
are reduced by a long time-lapse since the last occurrence. Moreover, when the probability is thought very small, there is a tendency
to disregard it altogether. Rising generations in bank management
may simply have ignored the possibility of 'disaster' with country
lending despite its potential implications for the banks.

Although plausible, it has been asked how far the thesis applies to the accumulation of 'country specific', as opposed to 'systemic' risks (Sargen, 1985). The banks expended considerable effort designing econometric models intended to 'predict' country risk in the form of the occurrence of difficulties with debt service payments. These had mixed success, which suggests that default probabilities (the basis of the loan supply curves discussed earlier), were not well estimated in practice (Cline, 1984, p. 206). Given the difficulties of prediction, the banks sought refuge in diversified holdings of country loans (Sargen, 1985). As Guttentag and Herring emphasise, the problem was that the banks were faced with *uncertainty*, as distinct from quantifiable *risk*, in this relatively new business.[3] Similarly, the means to predict the systemic risks of rising world interest rates and recession were even less to be found in the past.

Even if bank managements suffered from disaster myopia, the banks depended on wholesale deposits whose owners might have been expected to react to excessive risk-taking by demanding higher interest rates. This would have constituted a market constraint on imprudence (Snowden, 1987). The hypothesis therefore needs to be supplemented by explanations of why deposit costs did not reflect these risks in practice. A key consideration may have been the perception that large banks would not be allowed to fail (Guttentag and Herring, 1985a; Swoboda, 1982, 1985). Similarly conducive to disaster myopia may have been a belief that the largest debtors would receive official support if they were to approach default (ibid.). In this may lie an explanation for the country concentration of loans, although it has been suggested that the syndication process may have contributed to this result by creating a false sense of diversification on the part of banks (Lewis and Davis, 1987).

Finally, in the context of the above institutional factors, the importance of the competitive process in generating the observed levels of country debt may be noted. Over the decade of the 1970s there was an intensifying pressure on lending rate 'spreads' as new competitors entered the market (Guttentag and Herring, 1986; IBRD, 1985, pp. 110–12). Since existing lenders were using 'country limits', (which linked the growth of their lending to individual countries to the growth of their own capital and reserves), it was these new entrants which prevented the effective emergence of credit rationing in the market for country loans. Did these banks display disaster myopia as claimed?

An alternative interpretation is that the risks of lending to any country would actually appear to be lower for a new entrant to the market. If this loan offered a way of diversifying a portfolio of (say) domestic loans, a competitive bid would be *rationally justified for the individual bank*. Unfortunately, for the more heavily committed existing lenders, such action by new entrants would reduce the apparent security of existing loans. Prudent behaviour would then dictate that the 'old' lenders reduce their exposure to the country concerned. Limits were placed on this adjustment, however, by recession in the major industrial markets and by the implications for reported profits of a decision to purchase low yielding though safe assets (Snowden, 1985).

CONCLUSIONS

If neo-classical analysis suggests that credit rationing would hold international lending below the optimum, global macroeconomic conditions probably must be invoked to explain why countries following questionable policies were able to borrow as much as they did. Indeed, this macroeconomic environment affected market incentives in important ways.

The industrial countries, facing 'stagflation' after 1974, offered poor prospects for bank lending. In contrast, monetary conditions had left banks with abundant liquidity and provided them with an inducement to 'beat the bushes' to flush out extra loan demand (Davidson, 1972, p. 330). Given the configuration of low interest rates and dollar export earnings growth which world inflation was helping to generate, LDC borrowers were an attractive opportunity with which to support balance-sheet growth and reported earnings. If world inflation had been a 'monetary phenomenon', it therefore not only boosted bank liquidity but had a major influence on the apparent creditworthiness of new country borrowers (Kindleberger, 1986). The diversification demands of a growing number of banks could be satisfied through this route at the cost of a progressive weakening of any existing credit rationing. The emergence of floating interest rate loans also reflected the influence of inflation, and this was to prove a key weakness of bank intermediation as the interest rate risk was passed on to borrowing countries.

If inflation was to have these pervasive effects, the lurch towards global monetary contraction in the 1980s might have been expected to induce developments of similar moment. Unfortunately, a collapse in LDC export markets and an unprecedented increase in the interest rates to which they were exposed, were to be part of this adjustment. The result was to generate a net external claim on the chronically weak public finances of borrower governments. The belief that 'debt does not get paid, debt gets rolled' was to prove unfounded as markets responded to the new circumstances with severe credit rationing (Dornbusch, 1985).

For lenders, these changes were to be reflected by a substantial discount on the face-value of country loans outstanding in an emerging secondary market. The passing-on of interest rate risk had simply heightened the 'transfer' risk that countries may not always be able to generate the foreign exchange needed to maintain loan service payments. *After the event* both lenders and borrowers have had to absorb losses, suggesting that *contractual* risk sharing will be a vital element in the rebuilding of voluntary capital market finance for LDCs (Lessard and Williamson, 1985). Such sharing is a feature of debt-equity 'swap' schemes whereby investors are able to exchange discounted country debt for an amount nearer its original value in *local* currency at the official exchange rate. These funds may then be used for *equity* investment in local enterprises. While such investment implies a commitment to permit future dividend payments to foreign investors, these should reflect the performance of the investment financed and thus establish a link between outflows and income generation. Ultimately, however, the success of these schemes, as well as the return to 'voluntary' bank lending, will depend on governments following policies consistent with such commitments being met.

9 Exchange Rate Arrangements

ROBERT Z. ALIBER

INTRODUCTION

The history of the international monetary arrangements of the last one hundred years begins with the gold standard and continues with the gold exchange standard of the period between the two world wars, and then with the Bretton Woods system of the 1950s and the 1960s.[1] Each of these three periods when currencies were pegged has been followed by a period when many of the curriencies of the larger countries were not pegged. The first period of floating exchange rates began when the British authorities stopped pegging the pound to the US dollar in March 1919 and ended when the French franc was again pegged to gold in December 1926.[2,3] The second period of floating exchange rates began in September 1931 when the British authorities stopped pegging the British pound to gold and ended with the beginning of Second World War; in the early 1930s a number of countries followed Great Britain either at the same time, or in the next few months.[4] The third period of floating exchange rates began in February 1973, when the German authorities stopped pegging the mark to the US dollar; within a few days, the authorities in most other industrial countries also stopped pegging their currencies.

Individual countries have suspended convertibility of their currencies into gold or some other external asset at a time when most other currencies were pegged; Canada soon after the beginning of the Korean war; the British pound during the Napoleonic wars (1803–

196

25); the US dollar during and after the Civil War (1863–79) (Muhleman, 1895); the Swedish daler in 1745.[5] A few countries have ceased pegging their currencies for brief intervals in the belief that market forces might move their currencies to the values at which they might again be pegged; Germany stopped pegging the mark for several weeks in September 1967.[6] And some industrial countries stopped pegging their currencies in May 1971 and others in August 1971, before again pegging their currencies to the US dollar or gold in the Smithsonian Agreement of December 1971. No large country has since pegged its currency to gold or to the US dollar, although a number of European countries have pegged their currencies to those of other European countries.

This chapter examines the impact of structural shocks and of monetary shocks on the foreign exchange value of the British pound, the US dollar, and a number of other currencies. These monetary shocks involve an intended or an unintended change in the rate of money supply growth – or a change in the demand for money and for near-monies denominated in a particular national currency. The structural shocks include commodity-specific price changes, productivity shocks, and large changes in the relationship between the rate of economic growth in one country and the rates of economic growth in its large trading partners. The two oil price increases of the 1970s and the oil price decrease of 1982 are an example of a commodity-specific structural shock. Changes in the scope of credit rationing or of the availability of external loans, highlighted by the external debt crises of the developing countries of the early 1980s, are a structural shock, as was post-First World War reparations (Schuker, 1988). While the distinction between monetary and structural shocks is conceptually clear (monetary shocks affect the *general* level of commodity prices, and structural shocks affect, the *relative* prices of individual commodities), in practice structural shocks have both direct and indirect monetary consequences while monetary shocks may have structural implications.[7] The central question for this chapter involves the significance of structural shocks and of monetary shocks on the ability of the authorities in each country to maintain a parity for their currency; a variant of this question is whether the suspension of convertibility of national currencies into gold or some other external asset or the move away from parities primarily reflects structural shocks or monetary shocks. These observations also relate to the continuing debate between the proponents of floating exchange rates and the proponents of pegged exchange rates.

The first section in this essay relates different exchange rate arrangements to changes in the inflation rates and to changes in national rates of growth of income. The second section summarises the process of exchange rate determination. Changes in real exchange rates are considered in the next section. This is followed by a section which evaluates the impacts of structural and of monetary shocks. Finally the re-entry problem is discussed.

EXCHANGE RATE ARRANGEMENTS AND INFLATION

The currencies of many large countries have been pegged to an external asset for extended periods. The US dollar was pegged to gold for 170 of the last 200 years. Similarly the British pound was pegged to gold or to the US dollar for more than 150 of the last 200 years. The authorities in virtually every country have pegged their national currency to gold or some other external asset for many years. Few countries allowed their currencies to remain unpegged for an extended period – at least until the early 1970s.

There is a strong association between periods when national rates of inflation are high and variable and when currencies are not pegged, and between periods when national rates of inflation are low and stable and when currencies are pegged. The authorities in one country can maintain a parity for their currency in terms of an external asset only if they have a rate of inflation comparable to that in their major trading partners; otherwise the changes in demand for assets denominated in their currency will be volatile, and attainment of domestic financial stability difficult or unlikely unless they rely extensively on exchange controls.[8] The British decisions to suspend convertibility of sterling during the Napolenonic Wars and again in the First World War illustrate this (Laughlin, 1918). So does the US experience in the Civil War, and again in the 1970s and the 1980s (Friedman and Schwartz, 1963).

Two of the periods identified with pegged exchange rates were periods of rapid growth in the world economy. The 1880–1913 period was one of exceptional economic growth, sometimes referred to as the heyday of the Gold Standard. The 1950–70 period also was one of rapid economic growth, comparable to the earlier period;

rapid growth has been attributed to the stability provided by the International Monetary Fund (Roosa, 1984). In contrast the periods identified with floating exchange rates are associated with less rapid growth – one of these periods was the Great Depression (Nurkse, 1944).

Periods of inflation frequently are associated with wars. Governments stop pegging their currencies to relax the constraint on their ability to finance military expenditures. During the First World War commodity price levels increased sharply in every country as a result of rapid expansion of credit. Inflation rates also increased during the Second World War, but less so than during the First, in part because price controls and rationing were more extensive – national bureaucracies had grown between the two wars. During both world wars, the authorities intervened extensively in the foreign exchange market, and relied on comprehensive exchange controls.

The uniqueness of the 1970s and the 1980s monetary experience is that inflation has been rapid in the United States and most other industrial countries, and yet these countries have not been at war, nor have they been subject to an unusual increase in military expenditures. The surge in oil prices in 1973/74, which is sometimes cited – incorrectly – as the cause of the 1970s increase in price levels, occurred after inflation rates had reached double-digit levels; each of the oil price increases may have added two or three percentage points to an inflation rate that was near or above 10 per cent. While the US inflation rate increased in the late 1960s as US military activities in Vietnam excalated, the US inflation rate declined from 8 per cent in 1970 to 3 per cent in 1971. Changes in the foreign exchange value of the US dollar in the 1970s and the 1980s are inordinately large relative to the variations in the US inflation rate, and to the changes in the relationship between the US inflation rate and the inflation rates in most of the large US trading partners (Aliber, 1980).

The countries that continue to peg their currencies during inflationary periods are generally smaller than those that stop pegging their currencies; these smaller countries implicitly accept the inflation rates of the larger trading partners to which they peg their currencies. The Netherlands and, to a lesser extent, Belgium link the foreign exchange value of their currencies to that of the German mark. In the 1970s and 1980s, more than fifty countries continue to peg their currencies, either to the currency of another country (usually their former metropole) or to a synthetic market-basket of currencies (like the SDR).

Once countries have stopped pegging their currencies as a way to avoid or to reduce their sensitivity to imported shocks, they may seek to peg them to some other asset as a way to reduce uncertainty about exchange rates. In the early 1920s virtually every country except the losing belligerents sought to restore convertibility of its national currency into gold, and almost always at the prewar parity. Keynes accepted that the British pound should again be pegged in terms of gold, but criticised the choice of the value of the parity (*The Economic Consequence of Mr. Churchill*). In 1931 Sweden, Norway, and Denmark pegged their currencies to the British pound, after the British authorities had stopped pegging the pound to gold; a significant part of the foreign trade of these countries was with Great Britain. A dominant rationale for the requirement that member countries of the International Monetary Fund peg their currencies was the belief that the volatility of exchange rates was a major cause of economic turmoil; one of the legacies of the 1930s was the term 'begger-thy-neighbour'. The European Monetary System was established to reduce uncertainty about exchange rates on intra-European transactions, at a time of substantial uncertainty about the price of the US dollar in terms of the German mark, the French franc, and the currencies of other European countries.

THE PROCESS OF EXCHANGE RATE DETERMINATION

Market efficiency

Foreign exchange markets are in general efficient; day-to-day and period-to-period changes in exchange rates are not serially correlated, and the returns from holding assets denominated in one currency are not significantly higher than the returns in other currencies when an appropriate adjustment is made for the premium that investors demand for acquiring cross-border currency risks (Aliber, 1987; Wasserfallen, 1988). Occasionally there are brief episodes when period-to-period movements in exchange rates appear serially correlated, as in France in late 1923 and the first half of 1926, and in the United States in 1979. These episodes occur in the context of acceleration of inflation. Money is the ultimate storable asset; hence the dominant consideration in determining the currency denomination of assets in investors' portfolios is consistency among the anticipated spot exchange rates, the interest rates on comparable assets denominated in domestic currency and in foreign currency, and the current spot exchange rate; investors alter the currency denomination of the assets in their portfolios when the current spot exchange rate is inconsistent with the value inferred from the other three terms in the equation. The major source of inconsistency is that particular shocks have a larger impact on the anticipated spot exchange rate than on the interest rate differential. The maintenance of a parity for a currency for an extended period almost always requires that the anticipated spot exchange rate does not differ significantly from the parity and that when such differences develop, the investors believe that the anticipated spot exchange rate returns toward the parity. In the early 1920s, investors believed that many of the countries in Western Europe, including Germany, would be successful in pegging their currencies to gold at their prewar parities; as a result the foreign exchange value of these countries' currencies was significantly higher than the inference based on the changes in price levels. As investors became disillusioned with the likelihood that these currencies would again be pegged to gold at their prewar parities, the foreign exchange value of their currencies declined significantly toward the parity.

The role of official intervention

The exchange market may not satisfy the tests of market efficiency when official intervention is extensive, either in support of a misaligned parity, or when the authorities 'lean against the wind'. For brief episodes there are 'runs' in the movements in the spot exchange rate; the change in the price of foreign exchange from today to tomorrow is a function of the change in the same price from yesterday to today. And 'speculation' has been 'destabilising' for brief periods, almost always when the authorities appear to be unable – or unwilling – to convince investors that their anti-inflationary policies will prove effective (Aliber, 1962). This process leads to one of two outcomes; either the authorities adopt a set of policies that convinces investors that the inflation will be checked, or the reduction in the demand for money continues until the economy moves into a hyperinflation.

The necessary condition for the maintenance of a parity for a currency is that investors believe that the authorities are committed to the parity, and will incur the necessary costs in terms of their domestic employment and price level objectives so the parity can be maintained. Some investors always are sceptical of official statements that the parity will be maintained, because the authorities frequently have changed it after making such statements. The lower the credibility of the statements that the parity will be maintained, the higher the domestic cost of maintaining it. As the credibility of these statements about the commitment to the parity decline, investors shift more funds across national borders, for in the short run the anticipated return from the change in relative prices of different national currencies is large relative to the excess of interest rates on assets denominated in domestic currency relative to interest rates on comparable assets denominated in a foreign currency. This speculative 'one-way option' is relevant when currencies are pegged, as in the early 1930s or the late 1960s (and especially with narrow support limits around the parity); the devaluation of the British pound in November 1967 increased the cost to the authorities in France of maintaining their parity. Similarly the French devaluation of 1968 increased the cost to the German and Canadian authorities of maintaining the parities for their currencies. A somewhat similar one-way option appears relevant when currencies are not pegged, for currencies appreciate or depreciate for extended periods (even though no 'runs' have been detected in the time-series of exchange rate movements). In the late 1970s, the depreciation of the US dollar was associated with an increase in the anticipated US inflation rate and the decline in the real interest rate on US dollar assets. In contrast, in the early 1980s, the appreciation of the US dollar was associated with a decrease in the anticipated US inflation rate, and an increase in the real interest rate on US dollar assets. The change in the anticipated spot exchange rate appears four or five times more powerful than the change in the interest rate in explaining the movement in the current spot exchange rate.

When currencies are pegged, goods market competitiveness is the dominant factor in determining whether a parity for a country's currency can be maintained. The maintenance of parity requires that the interest rate differential be sufficient to induce investors to hold assets denominated in a currency that they believe is weak and subject to a possible devaluation. The cliché is that the increase in the discount rate of the Bank of England would attract funds 'from the moon', in the meantime, adjustment in the goods market would occur to restore trade balance equilibrium. When currencies are not pegged, the necessary condition for maintaining the spot exchange rate at or near its prevailing level is that domestic and foreign inflation rates are similar; the sufficient condition is that the changes in the domestic real interest rates are not significantly different from the change in the foreign real interest rates. The change in the interest rate differential required to avoid a large change in the current spot exchange rate is larger when currencies are not pegged than when currencies are pegged, because the change in the anticipated spot exchange rate is substantially larger when currencies are not pegged than when they are pegged.

The large more-or-less continuous movements in the spot exchange rate – that is, the 'runs' in the spot exchange rate, appear to occur primarily or solely in an inflationary context – indeed in the context of accelerating inflation. Speculation may in these circumstances be 'destabilising'.

CHANGES IN REAL EXCHANGE RATES

Purchasing power parity

The price level and exchange rate data provide empirical support for Purchasing Power Parity (PPP) as a long-run proposition – that nominal changes in exchange rates correspond with differences in the national inflation rates over intervals longer than three or four years. (Gailliot, 1970). In shorter intervals, however, there are substantial deviations from PPP; the reasons differ, depending on whether currencies are or are not pegged (Aliber, 1987; Officer, 1976). When currencies are pegged, the deviations reflect inflation rate differentials. This change in the price level differential may reflect an autonomous monetary shock which is likely to lead to a trade balance disequilibrium, or, less frequently, a monetary shock induced to offset or neutralise a structural shock – and hence to attain or re-attain a trade balance equilibrium. In contrast, when currencies are not pegged, the deviations from PPP almost always reflect the fact that the change in the current spot exchange rate is large relative to the contemporary change in the differential in national inflation rates.

The range of movement in real exchange rates has been substantially larger when currencies are not pegged than when they are pegged (Dornbusch, 1976). Similarly the deviation between the nominal exchange rate and the real exchange rate has been many times larger when currencies are not pegged than when they are pegged (except when pegged currencies are maintained behind an extensive array of foreign exchange controls). And these large changes in the real exchange rates reflect the fact that the change in the nominal exchange rate is significantly larger than the contemporary change in differential inflation rates. In the late 1970s, the US dollar depreciated much more extensively than the differential in inflation rates suggested. In the early 1980s – from 1979 to spring 1985 – the US dollar appreciated extensively, even though the US inflation rate was higher than those in Germany and in Japan. In the first half of 1926, the depreciation of the French franc was much more rapid than the contemporary differential in inflation rates suggested; in the second half of 1926, the French franc appreciated extensively, even though the price level in France was continuing to increase. The terms used to describe the phenomena of the deviation of the nominal exchange rate from the real exchange rate have changed over time; in the interwar period, the term was destabilising speculation, and subsequently 'vicious and virtuous circle' and 'exchange rate overshooting' have been used.

That PPP is valid in the long-run reflects the fact that when currencies are pegged, and inflation rates differ, the parity is likely to be changed to reflect changes in the relationship between national price levels. In contrast, when currencies are not pegged, the long-run validity of PPP reflects the fact that the movement in the spot exchange rate away from the equilibrium values inferred from price-level differentials is reversed, almost always in response to a change in monetary policy or fiscal policy. The change in policy leads to a change in the value for the anticipated spot exchange rate. In France in 1926, Poincaré became Prime Minister; inflationary anticipations changed because his promises to reduce the fiscal deficits had greater credibility than those of his predecessors; as a result, the French franc appreciated sharply. In 1976, the Labour Government in Great Britain was able to negotiate a 'wages compact' with the unions, and again inflationary anticipations were reversed; as a result the British pound appreciated sharply.

STRUCTURAL SHOCKS AND MONETARY SHOCKS

The oil shocks

The OPEC-sponsored oil price increase of 1973/74 and again in 1979/80 is the most striking example of a commodity-specific structural shock. This shock – like most commodity-specific structural shocks – had a less powerful impact on the oil-importing countries than on the oil-exporting countries, because the imports of the first group of countries are both much larger and more diversified than the exports of the second group. Moreover this shock had a smaller impact on the national income and the government revenues in the oil-importing countries than on the national income in the oil-exporting countries. The increase in the oil price led to an increase in the creditworthiness of the oil-exporting countries, and greatly increased their ability to attract foreign capital. Whether the several oil-shocks of the 1970s were sufficiently powerful to have induced the oil-importing countries to stop pegging their currencies is necessarily academic, since these countries had stopped pegging them in the early 1970s. Many of the oil-importing countries financed part or all of the increase in their oil import bills by borrowing. Few if any commodity-specific structural shocks appear to have had anywhere near the impact of the oil shock. The implication is that few commodity-specific structural shocks are so large that the authorities stop pegging their parities at the established values.

The oil price shock of the 1970s was associated with the 'Dutch disease' – the surge in export earnings from sales of natural gas and petroleum. If the currencies of these countries were pegged, the increase in oil export earnings was associated with an increase in nominal wage rates, and profits on exports of manufactures were squeezed between the world price of these products and higher production costs. If the currencies of these energy-exporting countries were not pegged, they tended to appreciate in the foreign exchange market; as a result the exports of manufactures of these countries tended to decline. Despite the coincidence in the 1970s of both large increases in petroleum output and the substantial increase in the price of oil, the only oil-exporting country whose currency appreciated measurably in real terms was the British pound; the real value of the Norwegian krona, the Dutch guilder, and the Danish kronor remained unchanged (Abuaf, 1985; Edison, 1981). The real appreciation of the British pound reflected the impact of capital flows to Great Britain in a period of rising oil prices, rather than the direct impact of the oil on the volume of exports (Aliber, 1984). The British pound had become a 'petro-currency' – and oil-importers would hedge their exposure to petroleum shocks by owning financial assets denominated in the British pound.

Productivity shocks

As a result of a productivity shock in the form of a rapid increase in output per worker especially in tradable goods, the price of these goods decline relative to the price of similar goods produced in other countries (Balassa, 1964). The Japanese experience in the 1910s and the 1920s and again in the 1960s illustrates this development (Hekman, 1977). So does the Korean experience in the 1970s and the 1980s. As prices fell, exports surged, and the increase in exports permitted further expansion in production and continued price-declines. These productivity shocks by themselves do not appear inconsistent with the maintenance of a parity, since rapid growth of exports is associated with the rapid growth of income and of imports. The German and the Japanese experience in the 1950s and the 1960s suggests that parities can be maintained as long as productivity continues to grow rapidly; in both cases adjustment to the growth in export earnings involved liberalisation of imports. The parities of both countries had been established in the late 1940s, when each country was still occupied; their currencies simultaneously were undervalued on the basis of cost and overvalued on the basis of availability of goods, since their ability to produce was constrained because of destruction of physical plant and trading relationships (Cooper, 1971).

Productivity shocks may have significant impacts on the real exchange rate through their impacts on changes in the pattern and scope of capital flows. Rapid growth countries are associated with high rates of return and are likely to attract capital from slow-growth countries. The decline in the rate of growth of a country may be associated with a shift from the country's role as a capital-importer to a capital-exporter; the United States went through this transformation about the time of the First World War and Japan in the late 1960s. The evidence on the exchange rate implications of this shift is mixed; Great Britain remained on the gold standard even as there was a surge in the capital outflow in response to a decline in its own rate of economic growth (Cairncross, 1913). In the late 1960s and the early 1970s, the decline in the growth rates of Germany and of Japan was associated with an increase in capital flows from these countries, and the decisions to stop pegging their currencies – although these decisions occurred as the US inflation rate was accelerating (Aliber, 1988a).

Asset price shocks

Asset price shocks reflect changes in the scope of credit rationing. The hyperinflation in Germany in the early 1920s reflected the inability or the unwillingness of the government to adjust to its reparations burden. Many debtor countries in Latin America were subject to a debt shock in the early 1980s, when the bank lenders suddenly became convinced that their loans to these countries were excessively large relative to their own capital and to the potential rate of growth of these countries. The adjustment to a credit rationing shock frequently involves significant monetary consequences; thus the reduction in the availability of external loans to the developing countries in the early 1980s was associated with an inflationary spurt in most of these countries because they were unable to reduce the fiscal deficit anywhere near as rapidly as they were obliged to reduce their current-account deficits.

The extent of the change in the foreign exchange value of a currency associated with a particular shock depends on whether goods markets are better characterised by excess demand or excess supply. The greater the excess supply, the larger the change in the real exchange rate necessary to effect the desired change in the trade balance. The 1930s elasticity-pessimism view of exchange rate determination reflects two factors – one was the ratchet-like sequence of devaluations beginning in 1929 and continuing for most of the decade; the second was that producers in each country were reluctant to give up market share in response to the devaluation of a foreign currency, because demand in most national goods markets was less than potential supply. In contrast, in the late 1940s goods markets were characterised by excess demand, and so the change in relationship among national price levels effected by the change in currency parities was effective in restoring trade balance equilibrium

– or would have been effective with appropriate domestic financial policies to absorb excess demand (Bernstein, 1956).

Monetary shocks

Financial capital flows across national borders from countries with low real interest rates to countries with high real interest rates. When currencies are pegged, capital flows are responsive primarily to differentials in interest rates that reflect national differences in savings and investment levels. In contrast when currencies are not pegged, capital flows are driven by disequilibrium in the international money market. Changes in real interest rates and hence in real interest rate differentials may reflect either structural factors, such as changes in time preference and productivity, or changes in inflationary anticipations. Large changes in real interest rates – including the transition to negative real interest rates – reflect monetary shocks. Monetary shocks affect real interest rates because changes in the nominal interest rates lag – or lead – the changes in the anticipated inflation rates.[9] Monetary shocks affect the nominal exchange rate through their impacts on both the anticipated spot exchange rate and the real interest rate; the large movement in the spot exchange rate occurs to obtain consistency between the anticipated spot exchange rate and the interest rate differential. The movement in the spot exchange rate is large because the change in the anticipated spot exchange rate is large. These large movements are independent of whether goods market prices are sticky, and instead reflect the fact that a particular monetary shock has a more powerful impact on the anticipated spot exchange rate than on the domestic interest rate.

The large changes in the nominal exchange rates and real exchange rates that occur when the currencies are not pegged reflect either monetary shocks, or an induced monetary response to a structural shock. These changes occur primarily because of large changes in the anticipated spot exchange rate, which are associated with large changes in the differential between the domestic inflation rate and the inflation rate abroad – or alternatively with large changes in the anticipated spot exchange rate. A reduction in the demand for money will be associated with a decline in real interest rates, and an increase in the anticipated rate of depreciation of the domestic currency. The frequent result of the reduction in the demand for money is that the increase in the price level is unusually large relative to the increase in the money supply. In the 1925 and 1926 French episode, the surge in the inflation rate came after the substantial decline in the foreign exchange value of the French franc; in 1979, the surge in the US inflation rate occurred after a briefer, and much less extensive increase in the US inflation rate.

Virtuous and vicious circles

One feature of the floating exchange rate system of the 1920s and again of the 1970s and the 1980s is the 'vicious and virtuous circles'. The currencies of the countries that experience higher-than-average inflation rates depreciate more rapidly than the contemporary inflation differentials suggest, and conversely. The rapid depreciation reflects the fact that investors extrapolate current or recent changes in inflation rates in projecting the anticipated spot exchange rate; moreover real interest rates may be declining. The rapid depreciation of the national currency complicates the ability of the authorities to achieve financial stability, and increases the cost to the authorities of achieving this objectives.

That the change in the real exchange rate may be smaller in the long run than in the short run reflects the change or reversal in the value of the anticipated spot exchange rate as a result of policy changes. Thus the French franc depreciated extensively in 1925 and the first seven months of 1926, much more rapidly than would been predicted on the basis of the contemporary change in inflation rate differentials. Similarly, the US dollar depreciated extensively in 1978 and the first ten months of 1979, much more extensively than would have been predicted on the basis of the contemporary change in differential inflation rates. In France in 1925 policy changes associated with a new government led to a downward revision in the anticipated inflation rate and to a revision in the anticipated spot exchange rate; investors shifted funds into the French franc, and the franc appreciated rapidly. Similarly the change in US monetary policy in October 1979 soon led to a sharp decline in the anticipated US inflation rate and hence in the anticipated foreign exchange value of the US dollar; investors shifted funds into US dollar assets, and the US dollar appreciated sharply.

Changes in real exchange rates induce changes in trade balances by altering the international competitive position of domestic plants and foreign plants. These changes in real exchange rates when currencies are not pegged occur as investors shift funds to profit from an apparent disequilibrium in the international money market. Thus changes (or anticipated changes) in the anticipated spot exchange rate have significant structural impacts. These disturbances when the currency is not pegged appear to have no good counterpart when currencies are pegged.

Changes in real exchange rates induced by changes in the anticipated spot exchange rate induce changes in the pattern of long-run capital flows (Aliber, 1988b). The movement in the spot exchange rate that occurs to achieve equilibrium in the international money market induces a disequilibrium in the international capital market.

The range of movements in real exchange rates in the 1970s and 1980s was larger than that of the 1920s, although the monetary shocks that led the authorities to stop pegging their currencies were significantly larger in the earlier periods. The commitments of national authorities in the 1920s to return to their pre-First World War parities limited the range of movement in the anticipated spot exchange rate. Even after this objective began to appear unrealistic for France and some other countries, the authorities were committed to a new parity for their currency. And the movements of floating exchange rates in the 1930s differed from the 1920s and the 1970s because the period was one of substantial deflation. Hence the changes in the anticipated spot exchange rates were smaller in the 1930s than in the mid-1920s and the 1970s and 1980s. A related difference is that various countries stopped pegging their currencies over an extended period – Great Britain in September 1931, and the United States in March 1933.

National differences in real interest rates appear to be larger when currencies are not pegged. Investors require a smaller premium for bearing the risks associated with cross-border flows of funds than when currencies are pegged.

THE ANCHOR AND THE RE-ENTRY PROBLEM

The anchor for pegging the national currency frequently is the currency of the monetary hegemon – and the currency of the monetary hegemon is attractive, both because the monetary hegemon is an important exporter of financial capital and because a substantial part of world trade may be invoiced and financed in its currency. Great Britain was a monetary hegemon for more than fifty years prior to the First World War. The United States and the other countries pegged their currencies to gold as a way to facilitate import of capital from Great Britain. The United States was a monetary hegemon in the 1940s, the 1950s and the 1960s.

Countries will peg their currencies to the currency of the monetary hegemon as long as the hegemon is able to maintain a low rate of inflation. If its inflation rate begins to increase, then some countries may cease pegging their currencies as a way to reduce importing inflationary impulses; for these countries the trade-off involves the advantages of international trade and investment of maintaining a fixed value for their currency, as opposed to the costs associated with importing inflation. The Canadian decision to stop pegging the Canadian dollar to the US dollar in 1950 and 1970 illustrates one aspect of this decision. In contrast, the decision of Mexico to continue to peg its currency to the US dollar during the same two years illustrates the second aspect of this decision.

The monetary hegemon receives a seigniorage payment from other countries in return for providing monetary stability. The payment varies with the willingness of individual countries to acquire financial assets denominated in the currency of the hegemon. The decline in the demand for the assets denominated in the currency of the hegemon may complicate its ability to achieve financial stability.

Periods when currencies are not pegged may be considered as interludes while countries seek to determine whether the monetary hegemon will pursue a set of policies that will lead to stability.

CONCLUSION

This chapter has evaluated the impact of structural shocks and of monetary shocks on exchange rate arrangements and on the relationship between the nominal exchange rate and the real exchange rate. Periods of price-level stability are periods when currencies have been pegged to an external asset, either a commodity money like gold or the currency of a major trading and financial country, like the British pound or the US dollar. Periods of inflation and deflation are periods when currencies are not likely to be pegged to external assets.

The decisions of individual countries to stop pegging their currencies reflect the fact that the perceived costs of maintaining the parity are too high in terms of the constraints on domestic policy choices; in part these costs may be those associated with attempting to neutralise imported inflationary shocks. The major shocks to the maintenance of parties are monetary, and frequently associated with wars. Structural shocks vary in terms of their impacts on the ability of the authorities to maintain their parities; few if any commodity-specific structural shocks have been so large that the importing countries ceased maintaining a parity for their currencies. Productivity shocks may have a major impact on the exchange rate arrangements because of their impact on the magnitude of international capital flows; indeed the induced impact of the capital flows on the level of the exchange rate appears more powerful than the impact on the change in trade flows.

The changes in real exchange rates when currencies are not pegged are substantially larger than when currencies are pegged. These large changes in real exchange rates are all monetary, and reflect the fact that a particular change in inflationary anticipations has a larger impact on the anticipated spot exchange rate than on the current interest rate. The asymmetric reaction is evident in the changes in the real interest rate. Because of asymmetric reactions, these monetary shocks have powerful structural impacts.

10 The International Monetary System

DAVID T. LLEWELLYN

INTRODUCTION

The focus of this concluding chapter is broader and is on the 'international monetary system' as a whole which encompasses *inter alia* arrangements with respect to specific issues discussed in preceding chapters. An attempt is made to show how the evolution of the system *as a whole* has implications for those issues, and to indicate some of the interrelations between the component parts of the system.

The international system has been subject to major structural change under the simultaneous impact of several pressures: (1) changes in the market and financial environment, most especially with respect to the volume of capital flows; (2) the size, location and forms of intermediation of international financial imbalances focused upon current account surpluses and deficits; (3) changes in the portfolio preferences of surplus and deficit countries with respect to financing and the disposal of surpluses; (4) changes in official regulation (most especially exchange control); (5) changes in the role and efficiency of official and private sector institutions in the international financial system, and (6) changes, or failures, in the management of the system as, for instance, argued by Scammell (1987) with respect to the 1930s.

Scammell emphasises the notion of predictability in international monetary arrangements and at times the international monetary system has been based upon regimes (e.g. the gold standard and, to a lesser extent, Bretton Woods) where there has been a high degree of predictability largely because the regime was based upon a fairly clear-cut and generally accepted set of rules. The absence of any clearly defined rules since the mid-1970s casts doubt on the concept of an international monetary 'system' as such; a set of 'international monetary arrangements' is a more appropriate description.

It is not proposed to offer either a detailed theoretical analysis of the major issues in international monetary arrangements nor to offer a detailed historical account of how the system has evolved. A succinct consideration of the former is to be found in Milner and Greenaway (1979), and the latter is well covered in Tew (1985 and 1988). Various aspects of both approaches are also discussed in Tsoukalis (1985b), Posner (1986) and Dorrance and Black (1984). The object is rather to consider the nature and significance of international monetary arrangements in the context of interdependence of countries; to identify the nature and causes of the underlying changes in the evolution of international monetary arrangements; and how these pressures change both the structure of the international monetary system and the issues which are judged to be significant.

FRAMEWORK AND ISSUES

Within a closed economy the sum of internal surpluses and deficits are equal. However, while this is by definition true, three immediate problems can emerge; (i) while equality is true *ex post* this may conceal considerable imbalances *ex ante*; there is no presumption that the sum of planned surpluses and deficits are equal; (ii) this may imply that counterpart imbalances are unwillingly held, which in turn induces subsequent changes in behaviour, and (iii) imbalances require financial intermediation mechanisms (financial institutions or the capital market) willing and able to absorb the surpluses and finance the deficits on terms which are acceptable to all counterparties. To the extent that financial intermediation services are not available, surpluses and deficits must be adjusted.

Similar considerations arise between countries and within the international monetary system as surpluses and deficits must be either financed or adjusted (see Chapter 7). By definition a country has a current-account deficit when the sum of internal deficits exceeds the sum of internal surpluses and this requires *net* international financial intermediation flows of this amount. However *gross* international financial flows always exceed this amount for two reasons: firstly, although changes in the magnitude of a country's net external assets are determined by the current-account surplus or deficit (abstracting from valuation changes due to asset price and exchange rate movements) wealth-holders change the *composition* of their external portfolios (i.e. the form in which they hold external assets and liabilities), which implies gross financial transactions over and above those necessary to finance a deficit. Secondly, to the extent that external markets and institutions can provide financial intermediation services more efficiently than domestic mechanisms, some of the gross internal surplus and deficits will be intermediated externally in a way that implies gross international financial flows independent of a current account deficit (Llewellyn, 1988). In a different context Meershwam (1989) also links domestic and international financial systems.

Although there are similarities, issues arise in international monetary relations that are absent within a country because key characteristics of national financial systems are absent globally. It is instructive to consider the characteristics that define a national financial system: the total absence of any form of exchange control between different parts of the system; a system-wide banking and capital market; a common currency with no internal exchange rate; a common monetary policy and monetary authority; a common macro-economic environment; a common payments system; and a common central government (although there may be regional governments within a country). This means that, in contrast to relations between countries, there are no identified internal balance of payments surpluses and deficits and hence the issue of internal balance of payments adjustment and financing does not arise, though a lack of competitiveness in a region within a country (which would be manifest as a current-account deficit of a country) may surface in the form of regional unemployment which cannot be adjusted by an internal exchange rate depreciation. It also means that any internal surpluses and deficits are automatically financed through the common monetary system, and there is no exchange rate risk involved in any transactions within the system. These characteristics also imply a very high degree of financial integration between different parts of the system (demonstrated by a common level of interest rates) and that the geographical location of investment is independent of the location of savings as the national capital market and banking system centralise the allocation of capital.

The special and unique issues and problems that emerge in the monetary relations between countries arise precisely because the characteristics of national financial systems are not found in the world system which comprises subsets of different national financial systems. However, although countries are synonomous with monetary unions, in practice this need not necessarily be the case, and the literature on optimum currency areas (see Ishiyama (1975) for an excellent survey of the issues involved) considers the criteria for effective monetary unions which may be larger or smaller than nation-states. A different approach with respect to a common currency is given in Cooper (1984). At a regional level, the debate over European Monetary Union and the creation of a common currency within the EEC raises similar issues (Delors, 1989; Llewellyn, 1988/89).

In a global flow of funds framework, international financial imbalances on current account necessarily have domestic counterparts. Just as within a national financial system, international (current-account) deficits have to be financed (by liquidating external assets or incurring external liabilities) and external surpluses have to be disposed of: current-account imbalances require international financial intermediation. However, when considering the size and geographical location of imbalances, together with the financing mechanisms involved, a central issue is the nature of causality: whether financial intermediation flows respond to autonomous current account imbalances, or whether changes in the supply of financial intermediation services or portfolio adjustments (such as through deregulation, changes in portfolio preferences, strategic decisions made, for instance, by banks) have an independent role in creating the imbalances. This issue, and the changing structure of imbalances and finance, is returned to in a later section.

Implications of interdependence

The special characteristics of the international monetary system derive from the economic and financial interdependence of countries and national financial systems: national economies are not closed though the international system is. This means that constraints that necessarily apply to the world system do not apply to the components. Thus for a country national absorption of real resources can exceed output and income, and a country can influence its competitive position, real wages, and the real value of financial assets via exchange-rate changes. Williamson (1982) also notes that credit-creation need not equal monetary expansion in a single country though it does for the system as a whole. This means that, while excessive credit-creation in a single country may leak out through a payments deficit, if there is excessive credit-creation in the system as a whole it will generate global inflation though, in the short run, the geographical incidence is indeterminate.

The implications of interdependence are that policy measures and autonomous economic and financial developments in one country have impacts of various magnitudes on other countries, and upon the closed system as a whole. It also means that the impact of domestic policy in any one country may be weakened to the extent that its effect is dissipated internationally. This raises the additional and central issue of the consistency of national targets. Inconsistent *ex ante* targets for current account imbalances (and the implied distribution of absorption relative to output) imply that some national targets are necessarily not met. A similar conflict may also arise with respect to inflation rates, most especially in a regime of fixed exchange rates. This means that each country, in varying degrees dependent upon its size and degree of openness, has the ability to impose costs (in terms of the non-satisfaction of domestic and external targets) on other countries and the system as a whole. Similarly, each can have costs imposed upon it. The power of countries to impose costs varies considerably and Panic (1988) describes the current international monetary system as essentially oligopolistic and dominated by the objectives and policies of a small number of countries but with no one country powerful enough to impose an economic order. This leads Williamson (1982) to conclude: 'A major test of a set of international monetary arrangements must surely be their success in ensuring that the policies chosen by the several nations add up to a total result that is appropriate in the light of the constraints that cannot be sidestepped in that closed economy, the world.' In a similar vein Crockett (1988) analyses the impetus to economic cooperation in terms of the recognition of the implications of interdependence: the spillover effects already noted, and 'public goods' (such as stability) at the international level.

A major dimension of potential conflict relates to what Llewellyn

(1980) describes as the 'incompatible trinity'. Both theory and the evidence of the Bretton Woods regime, and the experience of 'managed floating' rates since the mid-1970s, indicate that fixed exchange rates, freedom of international capital flows and precise control over the domestic money supply are incompatible. Thus, policy-induced changes in the money supply create profitable arbitrage opportunities through the effect upon interest rates and, if exchange rates are fixed, the resultant capital flows induce changes in domestic money supplies due to the domestic financial counterpart to central bank intervention in the foreign exchange market. Put another way, in a generalised regime of fixed exchange rates the growth of a country's domestic money stock is ultimately governed by the domestic counterpart of the growth of its external reserves in turn induced by its central bank's intervention in the exchange market. This is because ultimately fixed exchange rates are not compatible with permanent sterilisation. Towards the end of the 1960s an attempt was made to resolve this fundamental conflict by imposing controls on capital movements. As these were circumvented, and introduced their own unintended distortions, the conflict was later resolved by adopting floating exchange rates. Floating exchange rates mean that although in principle the money supply is domestically determined, the monetary authorities lose control over the exchange rate.

The central issues

Bringing the strands together, the arrangements within the international monetary system cover eight main areas. Central to any system or set of arrangements are exchange rates and the extent to which, either because of agreed rules of behaviour or because *ad hoc* decisions are made, central banks intervene in the foreign exchange market to influence their level. Coupled with this is a second issue related to settlement obligations when a deficit country's currency is purchased by other central banks. This links with a third issue known as the *confidence problem* associated with multi-denominated external reserves and refers to the instability that can arise when a loss of confidence in a reserve asset creates a general desire of holders to shift out of the suspect asset which in turn further weakens that asset. When related to a reserve currency this can have the effect of reducing the total volume of international reserves. This was the problem identified by Triffin (1960) when he highlighted an internal contradiction of the gold exchange standard (1944–71) based upon gold and the dollar. World reserves were held in the form of gold and dollar balances. The supply of gold at a fixed price ($35 per ounce) could not keep pace with the demand for reserves and hence there was a permanent requirement for a US balance of payments deficit as the only source of dollar reserves for the system. However, this presupposes total confidence in the ability of the US to stand ready to redeem dollars by exchanging them on demand for its own gold holdings at a fixed price. This was the nature of a confidence problem in that the persistent US deficit and counterpart rise in external liabilities on the basis of a fixed holding of gold reserves (the emergence of what came to be known as the 'dollar overhang') undermined confidence that the US would be able to honour its obligation. To the extent that countries exchanged dollars for gold with the US, total *world* reserves would fall as the gold holdings of the US declined while the other countries only changed the composition of their reserves (dollars exchanged for gold).

A fourth element in the monetary relations between countries relates to the linked issue of the balance of pressures that exist as between balance of payments financing and adjustment, and the extent to which the pressure for adjustment is symmetrical between surplus and deficit countries. The way in which balance of payments financing is conducted is a fifth significant issue for international monetary arrangements. In particular, whether financing is undertaken by transferring reserve assets or by borrowing, has implications for the growth of international debt and confidence in the international monetary system.

The arrangements for satisfying the requirements of central banks to hold international liquidity is a sixth major issue. Central in this is the form in which international liquidity is held (and in particular whether certain national currencies are held for this purpose) and the extent to which there are arrangements for the conscious control of the volume of international liquidity as against conditions where it is largely demand-determined.

The seventh issue is the $(n-1)$ problem. In a closed world of n countries and currencies only $(n-1)$ are able to secure their balance of payments and exchange rate targets unless the sum of n plans satisfies the identity constraint that the sum of surpluses and deficits is zero. In the absence of this condition, there is ultimately only one degree of freedom and a central issue is how *ex ante* plans are to be made consistent (e.g. via policy coordination), or how the single degree of freedom is to be disposed of. Under the Bretton Woods regime the $(n-1)$th country was the US which pegged its currency to a fixed price of gold while all other currencies were pegged against the US dollar. In this regime the deficit of the reserve currency centre is determined by the sum of the *ex ante* surpluses of other countries. In contrast, in a regime of completely floating exchange rates the problem is in principle solved by having no targets but allowing the market to reconcile any potential *ex ante* inconsistencies.

Finally, and pervading all of the issues identified, there is the question of the management of the international monetary system and the extent to which it is based upon the acceptance by governments and central banks of agreed rules of behaviour. The 'management' role of supranational organisations (such as the International Monetary Fund) is subject to considerable controversy given its potential implications for the perceptions of national sovereignty.

Types of systems

Most of the significant issues of concern in the international monetary system relate ultimately to the consistency of policy targets between countries. International interdependence necessarily implies that in one way or another *ex post* compatibility is secured between countries with respect notably to the balance of payments, the exchange rate and the rate of growth of the money supply. However, these may be secured at the expense of some *ex ante* plans not being achieved. This is obvious with respect to the balance of payments, as the sum of separate targets might imply an aggregate world surplus or deficit. In various ways, *ex post* these inconsistencies are eliminated. The degree of conflict and potential instability in the international monetary system is likely to increase: (i) the less consistent are *ex ante* plans; (ii) the greater is the degree of international economic and financial integration, and (iii) the more governments resist the mechanisms through which *ex post* compatibility is secured. De Grauwe (1973), for instance, suggests that the Bretton Woods arrangements became unstable largely because monetary policies between countries were inconsistent, and automatic equilibrating mechanisms were impeded by incompatible sterilisation strategies.

It is of interest, therefore, to consider how conflict and potential instability within the global monetary system might be minimised through various arrangements for either ensuring *ex ante* consistency or minimising the resistance to equilibrating mechanisms. Ultimately, five broad mechanisms for structuring the international monetary system may be identified: (i) automatic market mechanisms such as floating exchange rates or non-sterilisation of balance of payments induced changes in the money supply; (ii) the $(n-1)$ approach, whereby one country in the system agrees not to have an external target; (iii) *ex ante* policy coordination designed to ensure consistent targets and compatible means of securing them; (iv) an agreement to a precise set of policy rules which indicate what is required of policymakers in specified circumstances; (v) a multilateral approach, whereby some supranational authority indicates (and enforces?) policy measures which have been calculated to ensure consistency and stability in the system. In practice, actual arrangements in the international monetary system are likely to be a hybrid of the above mechanisms.

The Bretton Woods system as it developed was based essentially upon the $(n-1)$ principle (with the passive role played by the United States) but with a high degree of international cooperation; that is, it combined structures (ii) and (iv) with elements of (v). A comparable option is also available within regional arrangements, and to some extent Germany performed a similar role in the mini-snake and does so now in the European Monetary System (EMS). Since different organising structures may be applied to different parts of the global system, the issue arises whether there is an advantage in creating a dual structure whereby different solutions are adopted for countries within and between regional blocs. The case for a regional approach might be made in terms of there being less formidable problems of *ex ante* coordination among countries with a comparatively high degree of integration, and where other general political objectives might also be served by policy coordination.

During the 1970s, a series of attempts culminating in the EMS were made within Europe to create a regional subsector of the global monetary system and a different organising structure with respect to the five central issues outlined. In this and other respects the evolution of the international monetary system since the early 1970s has produced a hybrid structure which, in turn, has become one of the central characteristics of the system. There has been a much greater variety of arrangements than under Bretton Woods and the system has become less coherent.

BRETTON WOODS AND ITS DEMISE

Bretton Woods: a planned system

Although in practice over its close-on thirty years of operation it did not operate as originally intended, the Bretton Woods system is unique historically in that it was a consciously designed and widely-agreed system for the conduct of international monetary arrangements. It had clearly defined rules with respect to exchange rates and, in principle, with respect to the balance of pressures on balance of payments financing and adjustment. The Scarce Currency Clause (never invoked) also recognised the need for adjustment pressures to be reasonably symmetrical on deficit and surplus countries. It was designed as a compromise to avoid both the instabilities of the 'non-system' of the 1930s (sometimes volatile exchange rates, competitive depreciations, aggressive protectionism, and a general lack of international monetary cooperation) and the rigidities of the shortlived gold standard of the 1920s. It also reflected the more interventionist philosophy of the time and the notion that the international monetary system should be subject to more collective management than had been the case in the interwar years (see Cooper, 1988 and Tsoukalis 1985a).

The most formal aspect of the system was with respect to exchange rates where the rules were precisely stated: fixed but adjustable par-values (in practice against the US dollar) were set for each currency and central banks were required to intervene without limit when market rates moved to the outer limits of the small allowable margin of fluctuation. The anchor to the whole regime was to be fixed exchange rates and everything else followed from that. Recognising the potential danger of unfettered freedom for governments to change exchange rates (most especially after the competitive depreciations of the 1930s), and that such decisions had systemic implications of interest to all countries, the mechanisms for changing par values (only in cases of 'fundamental disequilibrium') required IMF approval; there was therefore in principle an element of collective decision-making on exchange rates.

The 1944 agreement established the IMF which was to have two main roles: to provide short-term financing facilities to countries in temporary balance of payments deficit, and to ensure that the 'rules of the game' were implemented. In the former role it had a powerful impact on the conduct of economic policy as the IMF invariably sets policy conditions as part of its financing facilities. Although this contributed to international liquidity arrangements there was no mechanism in the system for consciously creating international reserves, the need for which came to be supplied by the US as the system developed into a gold-exchange and ultimately a dollar standard.

The third main feature was that controls were to be eliminated on trade though they were allowed on capital transactions.

Why it broke down

The Bretton Woods system did not in practice work as envisaged: exchange rates became more rigid than intended; there was no systematic planned creation of international liquidity, and the balance of adjustment pressure was asymmetrically biased towards deficit countries. Above all, the system became a *de facto* dollar standard in several dimensions: the dollar was the anchor for exchange rates, the almost exclusive intervention currency, and the major source of reserves. The US became the $(n-1)$th country in the system and unable to change its exchange rate.

The proximate end of the system was in 1971 when the US announced that it would no longer supply gold to central banks in return for dollars; the dollar became inconvertible. More fundamentally the major contributing factors were the problems of maintaining fixed exchange rates and an independent monetary policy in a world of substantial international capital movements; the confidence problem associated with the inexorable rise in US external dollar liabilities against a fixed gold stock, and problems associated with the $(n-1)$ role. In particular, towards the end of the 1960s, the US pursued a more expansionary monetary policy than countries of Western Europe which, given the automatic sterilisation policies of the US and the requirement of central banks to intervene in the foreign exchange markets in order to maintain fixed exchange rates, meant that European monetary conditions came to be dominated by US monetary policy (Llewellyn, 1980; De Grauwe, 1973). This focuses the key problem of the $(n-1)$ approach to international monetary arrangements which requires for its stability the acceptance of the effective hegemony of the $(n-1)$th country and its policies.

After a series of attempts at securing a new and durable pattern of exchange rates (e.g. the 1971 Smithsonian Agreement), and attempts at moderating the volume of international capital movements, the regime of fixed exchange rates (the key element in the Bretton Woods system) was effectively abandoned in spring 1973. A major official international committee (Committee of Twenty) was established in 1972 to consider all aspects of reform of the international monetary system. It attempted to create another 'grand design' approach to a new international monetary system and one that would address the weaknesses of the old system. The Report (Committee of Twenty, 1974) surveyed these weaknesses though in the end no grand-design reform was made. The procedures, conclusions, and disputes within the Committee are discussed in Williamson (1977) who also discusses the weakness of the Bretton Woods regime.

Features of the post-Bretton Woods regime

The period since the demise of the Bretton Woods system has been one of structural change, market adaptation, and unprecedented financial innovation in the international financial system. The structure, operation, and institutions of the international system have since then evolved in a largely unplanned manner and without a clearly defined and agreed official framework. This evolution of international monetary arrangements may be captured by four dominant and related themes:

- Market-related adaptation to major shifts in the economic and financial environment, given the absence of officially agreed and clearly defined 'rules of the game'.
- Structural change in the relative roles of the private and official sectors (a 'privatisation' of international monetary arrangements).
- Increased international financial integration and the increasingly dominant influence of international capital movements.

– Financial innovation, both in the structure of the system and the particular role and operation of the private sector. Banks especially responded to a substantially increased demand for international financial intermediation, and to changes in their own portfolio preferences and strategies with respect to international business (see Chapter 7).

Without clearly defined ground-rules (perhaps because of their absence), there were major changes in the economic and international environment in the world economy to which the international financial system had to respond: increases in the size of international payments imbalances (see Stanyer and Whitley, 1981), structural changes in the pattern of world payments, a combination of inflation and recession, the structural aspects of two sharp rises in the price of oil, increased international capital mobility, sometimes volatile exchange rates and interest rates, and substantial changes in the conduct of financial policy in major countries. Since the early 1970s the system has evolved in a market-driven fashion rather than a conscious plan. These changes developed within a basically oligopolistic world political structure with power more diffused than in the period immediately after 1945 when the last 'grand design' was established.

In effect, a decision was made to live with a 'non-system' and a set of more or less informal monetary arrangements. Throughout the 1970s and 1980s, there has been no common exchange rate system, no clearly defined set of rules for official intervention (though various attempts have at times been made to design and implement guidelines), no effective control over the growth of international liquidity, and no clearly specified obligations with respect to balance of payments adjustment. Above all there have been no clearly defined rights and obligations of governments in their international monetary relations. The potential scope for conflict has therefore been substantial, particularly in the oligopolistic structure of the world monetary system that emerged. In effect, countries have been free to choose their own strategies, though in practice the degree of autonomy has been limited. Since the early 1970s, therefore, there has been no clearly defined monetary system. It has been a period of substantial structural change and financial innovation as the international monetary system has become 'privatised' and arrangements have become more avowedly market orientated and pragmatic. This implies a move towards the first of the alternative organising structures outlined earlier – an automatic market system was most obviously manifest in exchange-rate determination and the role of banks in balance of payments financing.

A view emerged that a decentralised system based more upon market mechanisms might be more feasible in the environment of greater financial integration in general and international capital mobility in particular. The enormous growth of international capital movements has in itself become a major feature of the international monetary system and means that in practice the system has to be flexible. An alternative collective system proved difficult to devise and none was agreed. This had both a negative and positive aspect. On the one hand, there was no agreement over many of the key issues. On the other hand, there was a positive belief that market mechanisms would cope with the adjustments of the time. The reform programme of the Committee of Twenty, based as it was upon 'stable but adjustable par values', proved infeasible. It misjudged the emerging trends towards a more decentralised approach to international monetary arrangements.

THE 1970s AND 1980s ENVIRONMENT

Having outlined the broad thrust of the post Bretton-Woods evolution of the international monetary system we turn to a consideration of the key aspects of international monetary arrangements over this period.

International imbalances

A major feature of the world economy since the early 1970s has been the persistent and large international financial imbalances on current account. There have been several significant structural changes in the size, location and financing of imbalances since the early 1970s. For most of the 1970s the major imbalances were the large surpluses of oil-exporting countries and the corresponding deficits of developing countries. The financial intermediation was conducted by banks: OPEC deposited surpluses at banks and some developing countries borrowed heavily from the private international banking sector. In the early 1980s the credit-standing of developing countries deteriorated sharply and banks ceased to lend, which in turn forced debtor countries to adjust their payments deficits.

Two major and related structural changes occurred during the 1980s: in the geographical location of financial imbalances (Table 10.1) and in the form of financial intermediation: away from banks towards the capital market. Table 10.1 shows that between 1978/81 and 1982/85 the fuel exporters' surplus was eliminated and turned into a deficit, there was a sharp cut in the developing countries deficit, and the US moved into substantial deficit while Germany and Japan moved into surplus. The trends were more powerful between 1982/85 and 1985/88: the deficit of fuel exporters increased, and there was a further sharp contraction in the developing countries' deficit (countries who had been heavy borrowers from banks during the 1970s moved from a large deficit to a small surplus).

One of the most significant features of the pattern of imbalances over the 1980s has been between industrial countries with the US running a cumulative deficit of over $800 billion between 1982 and 1988 and Germany and Japan running a cumulative surplus of over $550 billion. The 'financing' of these industrial countries' deficits and surpluses has been via the capital market rather than the banking system.

The overall picture of the period since the breakdown of the Bretton Woods regime has been of historically large and sustained

TABLE 10.1   Current account imbalances ($ billion)

	1978–81	1982–85	1985–88
United States	− 8.2	− 279.9	− 526.6
Germany & Japan	− 16.1	140.5	413.3
Other Industrial countries	− 66.5	− 21.1	+ 6.6
Fuel Exporters	176.0	− 39.7	− 68.4
Other developing countries	− 223.0	− 169.5	− 73.5
of which market borrowers	− 97.1	− 99.9	12.6
Other countries	− 9.1	13.5	4.3
TOTAL	− 146.9	− 356.2	− 244.5

Source: World Economic Outlook (IMF, various issues).

current account imbalances, major changes in the geographical structure of imbalances, and substantial corresponding changes in the form of international financial intermediation. The size of imbalances since the early 1970s have been very large by previous standards suggesting that the adjustment mechanism has changed.

Capital movements

A dominant feature of all aspects of the international monetary system since the early 1970s, but most especially over the 1980s, has been the enormous growth and volume of international capital movements. Historically, long-term capital market flows have been a major part of economic development strategies and can have clear beneficial effects (Lessard and Williamson, 1985). A dominant feature of the 1970s and 1980s, on the other hand, has been the growth of short-term capital movements and portfolio shifts between financial assets in different centres and currencies. Overall, the volume of international financial flows has expanded at a very much faster rate than the volume of trade flows. A survey by the Bank of England indicated that in 1985 around 90 per cent of the value of transactions in the London foreign exchange market were not related to trade. There are several reasons for this growth: (i) the abolition of exchange control and the general trend towards financial deregulation in most industrial countries, (ii) the rise in most developed economies in the size of wealth portfolios relative to income, (iii) the general internationalisation of portfolios, (iv) the development of information and trading technology and the low level of transactions costs, and (v) the acceleration in the pace of financial innovation involving the creation of new financial instruments many of which relate specifically to foreign currency transactions (see BIS, 1986).

The environment of foreign exchange markets being dominated by capital rather than current account transactions has major implications for the extent of international financial integration, the determination of exchange rates and their volatility (see MacDonald, 1988 for an excellent survey), for the direction of causation between current and capital account imbalances, and for the role of the exchange rate in the adjustment process (see Roosa, 1984).

A major implication of very sensitive speculative and arbitrage capital movements is that it raises the degree of international financial integration and compromises the extent of monetary policy autonomy. These are fundamental issues in that, at the outset, it was noted that a major factor making international as opposed to national monetary issues of particular significance is that the degree of integration between countries is less than that between regions within a country. The greater is the extent of international financial integration the closer the global system (or some subset such as the EEC) approximates to the conditions found within national financial systems. The experience of the post-1970 regime is that financial integration has increased: the volume of capital movements has greatly expanded, their interest rate sensitivity has risen, and the conditions of *global parity* (Llewellyn, 1980 and 1983) have become more general (Kneeshaw and Van den Bergh, 1985).

Financial integration has also been extended through the accelerated pace of financial innovation: the creation of new financial instruments. A Group of Ten study (BIS, 1986) has demonstrated how this has contributed to a greater degree of international financial integration by linking financial markets, as new instruments (swaps, etc.) mean that very small arbitrage differentials induce substantial volumes of transactions. For instance, interest rate and currency swaps have had the effect of facilitating access of both borrowers and lenders to markets which would otherwise have been closed to them. (See also Llewellyn, 1988.) Thus not only has international financial integration increased, its scope has been extended.

Thus exchange rate determination has come to be dominated by capital rather than current account transactions. The domination of capital transactions is not surprising given that they are conducted in organised asset markets where information is disseminated very quickly, transactions costs are low, and there are no lead-times as with the production of goods. Above all, the rate of return can be very high in the short run if expectations about exchange rate movements are correct.

Under current conditions, the emphasis is that exchange rates, rather than being the equilibrating mechanism for current-account imbalances, are determined by capital transactions. Between 1982 and 1985, for instance, there was a trend and substantial appreciation of the US dollar (Figure 10.1) while the current account deficit widened sharply indicating that the autonomous capital inflow exceeded the contemporaneous *ex ante* current-account deficit.

Overall, the evidence suggests that the exchange rate does not move to adjust the current account, with the result that the 1980s have experienced large and persistent current-account imbalances. However, this is partly because interest rates have frequently been set so as to avoid the exchange rate adjusting to current-account imbalances (e.g. in the case of the UK in 1989) and so the result is largely policy-induced.

This raises the issue of volatility and misalignment of exchange rates. The evidence (IMF, 1985) suggests that the former is not a serious problem given that there are markets through which the uncertainty associated with volatile spot rates can be removed. *Misalignment* is more serious than volatility as, for instance, persistent overvaluation has important implications for long-run competitiveness and hence employment in an economy. There is also an asymmetry problem in that markets lost during a period of overvaluation may be difficult to regain even after an eventual exchange rate adjustment. Changes in relative prices can induce costly resource reallocations, and Meershwam (1989) argues that permanent losses of productive capacity can emerge due to a sustained overvaluation of an exchange rate.

Structural change: privatisation

A particular feature of the international monetary system in the 1970s was the substantially increased role that came to be played by international banking and the consequent shift in the balance of roles of the official and private sectors. In terms of the provision of international liquidity, the financing of the transfer of real resources to less developed countries, and balance of payments financing, the private international banking sector increased its role both absolutely and relative to the traditional official sector.

The demand for international financial intermediation rose substantially in the 1970s with the absolute size of global financial imbalances. In many developing countries, internal factors such as the evolution of large-scale investment projects and budget deficits in an environment of domestic financial constraints also increased the demand for international finance. The apparently high real rates of return on capital projects, coupled with negative real rates of

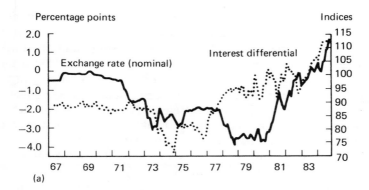

(a)

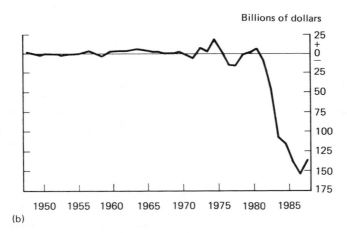

(b)

FIGURE 10.1   **(a) Long-term nominal interest differential**
                  (b) US current account

interest for much of the 1970s, also induced an increase in demand for external finance over the decade.

The portfolio preferences of both surplus and deficit countries are relevant in determining the forms of international financial inter-mediation. The portfolio preferences of OPEC have been analysed in detail elsewhere (Amuzegar, 1983). Banks were a convenient intermediary and had the general advantage of being able to meet the conflicting maturity preferences of depositors and borrowers through maturity transformation. OPEC depositors could also gain the implicit advantages of a diversified portfolio by sharing in the wide asset structure of banks and in the benefit of their economies of scale in such services as risk assessment. To the extent that there is an assumed lender of last resort to banks which does not exist to ultimate borrowers, the risk of holding bank deposits is reduced, which acts as an implicit subsidy to financial intermediation by banks (Swoboda, 1985; and Llewellyn, 1990).

Borrowing countries, by contrast, had a strong demand for long-term finance. But the terms of different financing options were also relevant. One particular example of the importance of terms was the experience with the type of conditionality provisions imposed by the IMF. While the Fund's lending capacity was increased over the 1970s (albeit by a considerably smaller amount than the size of financial imbalances), for much of the decade the Fund was under-loaned while countries were borrowing heavily from banks at considerably higher rates of interest. There seemed to be a strong preference to avoid Fund conditionality provisions, particularly when the amounts that could be drawn from the Fund were small compared with some countries' access to private facilities. In effect the increased supply of private financial intermediation mechanism was perceived as reducing the pressure for adjustment.

Banks are not passive agents, but have balance-sheet objectives and act to secure them. International lending became part of a general and simultaneous process of balance sheet growth and portfolio diversification, and in turn had a significant impact on the international monetary system. However, the strategic objectives and portfolio behaviour of banks changed during the early 1980s, as they began to feel increasingly limited by capital and exposure constraints and the volume of international bank lending declined sharply after 1982 (Llewellyn, 1990).

This development of international banking had substantial implications for the international monetary system. The change in the balance of pressures as between balance of payments adjustment and financing had two dimensions. To the extent that it became easier to finance deficits, and governments had confidence in future financing facilities, there was correspondingly less pressure on them to adjust their balance of payments. Whether this is regarded as beneficial depends upon whether the balance of pressures for adjustment versus financing was previously optimal. A second dimension is that the change in the balance of pressures as between adjustment and financing had a distributional effect in that it moved more towards financing for those countries with ready access to bank finance. Thus not only did the increased financial intermediary role of banks alter the global balance of pressures as between financing and adjustment, it did so differentially as between countries. The international banking sector also contributed to a substantial transfer of real resources to developing countries and thereby contributed to their development. To the extent that this international financial intermediation allocated world savings to where rates of return were highest, it would in the process have contributed to world economic growth.

A further implication is that a potential systemic problem was created resulting from the exposure of banks to a small number of heavily-indebted countries. Although this exposure has been reduced (and hence the potential systemic problem has become less powerful) because banks have raised additional capital, the arrangements of the 1970s did create a potential systemic problem in national financial systems. This did not arise in the same way in the 1930s as international financing was conducted predominantly through the capital market rather than the banking system.

Cohen (1981) also notes that in some cases access to bank credit had an adverse effect on the efficiency of the adjustment process itself and the mechanisms chosen. On the basis of a series of case studies of different borrowing countries, Cohen makes a distinction between those which used access to credit markets to postpone needed adjustment and other countries which adopted an integrated approach and developed a borrowing strategy as part of a programme of balance of payments adjustment. Some countries appear to have used borrowing as a substitute for adjustment, while in other cases it was complementary. If efficiency is measured in terms of the costs imposed by particular adjustment mechanisms, Cohen observes that efficiency had in some cases been reduced by borrowing because, by delaying the ultimately necessary adjustment, the eventual adjustment mechanism had to be more severe and costly.

Exchange rate management

There has been no universal exchange rate system since the early 1970s and six types of exchange rate arrangements have been applied by different countries: (1) independent floating though in practice with varying degrees of intervention; (2) pegging to a single currency in a similar fashion to the Bretton Woods procedure; (3) pegging to the SDR (a currency composite of six of the world's major currencies); (4) maintaining a constant effective exchange rate value; (5) changes in pegged rates on the basis of a formula such as the rate of inflation, and (6) membership of a joint exchange rate system such as the European Monetary System. There is substantial variety even between the major currencies: six are independent floaters (Canadian dollar, US dollar, Japanese yen, Swiss franc, the Deutschemark and sterling), the Belgian franc, Italian lira and Netherlands guilder are part of the EMS exchange rate mechanism, and the Swedish krona is pegged to a composite. Although Germany is a member of the EMS it behaves like an independent floater in that other EMS currencies are pegged to it while the exchange rate policy of the group is effectively determined by Germany. Virtually all currencies of developing countries are pegged in one way or another.

In practice even the independently floating currencies are seldom left totally free and from time to time governments seek to influence movements by interest rate policy and official intervention in the foreign exchange market. There have, however, been periods where the US dollar and sterling have been left free; the latter for a long period between October 1977 and 1981. The experience of the major currencies is given in Tew (1987 and 1988). Several studies have considered the rationale of intervention, whether it has on balance been stabilising, and the profitability of it to the central banks; the issues are reviewed in Mayer (1982) and Mayer and Taguchi (1983). Intervention has usually been 'smoothing' in nature with central banks intervening to moderate fluctuations rather than to prevent any trend emerging. There have been two major periods when internationally concerted action has been made to influence exchange rates. In the Plaza Agreement (September 1985) five major governments agreed that the dollar was substantially overvalued. They agreed to sell dollars (on a sterilised basis) on a concerted basis in order to expedite the currency's decline. A second example of concerted action was the Louvre Accord in February 1987 which was in effect a reversal of Plaza in that the major countries agreed to support the dollar by massive intervention purchases in the foreign exchange market. It also contained an undertaking that a series of indicators (growth, inflation, current accounts, budgets and monetary conditions) would be monitored with a view to coordinated policy action when appropriate and feasible.

Though not enshrined in any agreement, something of a concerted policy also emerged during 1989. In the first half of the year the Deutschemark and yen were under downward pressure (though both countries had large current-account surpluses) while the US dollar was tending to rise in the context of a massive current-account deficit. Central banks acted in the foreign exchange market to restrain the dollar and support the yen and Deutschemark. At the same time intervention was supported by domestic policy adjustments: German and Japanese interest rates were raised while in the US they were allowed to fall slightly.

It would seem, therefore, that while there is no formal exchange rate system, and intervention obligations are not well-defined, central banks do seek both to limit fluctuations but also to prevent substantial misalignment. However, this has not extended as far as the Bergsten and Willamson (1983) proposal for a system of explicit target zones for the major exchange rates. Official action seems in general to be aimed at exchange rate stability rather than at seeking a structure of exchange rates to adjust current account imbalances.

Aspects of international reserves

Table 10.2 shows the broad composition and growth of identified reserves over the 1970s and 1980s. The obvious features are the relative insignificance of IMF-based sources of liquidity (Reserve Positions in the Fund and Special Drawing Rights, with the latter being the only source of planned creation of reserves) and the sharp rise and rising proportion of reserves in the form of foreign currency holdings of central banks.

Most of the absolute increase in reserves since 1982 has been in US dollars and the unique role of the US balance of payments position is particularly relevant to the analysis. Dollar reserves rise when central banks (other than the Federal Reserve) purchase dollars on the foreign exchange market to support the dollar or prevent their own currencies appreciating. The link between dollar

TABLE 10.2   Global reserve developments ($ billion)

	Foreign exchange	IMF reserve positions	SDRs	Gold[1]	Total
1969	33 (42)	7 (9)	—	39	79 (49)
1980	329 (34)	22	15	609	975
1982	285 (36)	28	20	456	789
1983	290 (39)	41	15	398	744
1984	315 (41)	41	16	324	769
1985	352 (47)	43	20	339	754
1986	411 (47)	43	24	402	880
1987	598 (51)	45	29	500	1172

( ) is percentage of total valued at current market prices.

reserve growth and the US balance of payments position is, how-ever, complex. Dealtry (1988) notes that between 1983 and 1987 the US had a cumulative current account deficit of $572 billion. Within that period, between 1983 and 1985 there was little growth in dollar reserves though in 1986 and 1987 reserves rose substantially (Table 10.2). In the former case the deficit was covered by substantial autonomous private capital inflows to the US, while in the latter case the inflow was substantially reduced and replaced by central bank purchases of dollars to prevent a substantial depreciation. Thus the link between the US deficit and reserve growth is determined largely by the portfolio behaviour of the private sector and central banks.

Table 10.3 shows that the currency composition of foreign currency reserves has been changing, though the US dollar still dominates. This raises the issue of whether a multiple reserve-currency system is potentially unstable due to changes in the desired currency composition of reserves. Since the mid-1970s there has been a trend decline in the proportion of reserves held in dollars

TABLE 10.3 Currency composition of foreign exchange reserves (percentage of total)

	US dollar	Deutschemark	Yen	Swiss franc	Sterling	French franc
1970	77	2	—	1	10	1
1973	76	7	—	1	6	1
1976	80	7	1	1	2	1
1980	69	14	4	3	3	1
1982	71	12	5	3	2	1
					Others	
1985	66	14	7	—	12	
1987	69	15	7		9	

(Table 10.3) and a rise in the significance of the Deutschemark and yen. Developing countries were the first to diversify in the early 1970s and there was some switch away from the dollar by industrial countries after 1978. This is considered in detail in Horrii (1986) and the BIS (1988).

The other major issue with respect to international liquidity centres on the concept of 'reserve adequacy' which was a central issue of dispute under the Bretton Woods system. As in that period, there is still no conscious control of the supply of international reserves though it is not an issue that currently features in official discussions of international monetary arrangements. The concept of 'reserve adequacy' is now difficult to define and more so than in the Bretton Woods era for three main reasons: (i) the exchange rate system is less precise and hence the need for reserves for intervention purposes less determinate; (ii) the substantial growth in international capital movements both adds to potential exchange rate pressure (implying a greater need for reserves) and offers an alternative way of 'financing' current-account deficits (implying a lesser need); and (iii) some countries have substantial capacity to borrow reserves in the international banking and capital market such as with developing countries in the 1970s (from banks) and the UK government which has borrowed in the international capital market.

Williamson (1986) notes that because of the well-developed capital market the supply of international liquidity to industrial countries has become endogenous. Liquidity can be satisfied from the liability as well as the asset side of the balance sheet because 'an assured ability to borrow provides a near-perfect substitute for holdings of an asset that can be assuredly realised'. A more formal analysis of the same issue is given in Dooley (1985) who argues that foreign reserves are in elastic supply to industrial countries. His analysis suggests that reserve holdings are, for most countries, an element in a more general financial strategy. Each country faces a schedule that determines the terms under which reserves are supplied to that country, which in turn are determined by the terms on which the country can obtain credit in international financial markets. Thus for countries which have access to the markets the effective cost of obtaining reserves is the small difference between the borrowing cost and the rate of interest earned on the foreign currency borrowed. For countries excluded from international credit markets the effective cost of acquiring reserves is measured by the real resources forgone by securing a balance of payments surplus. Thus reserve holdings are a more important issue for countries which do not have access to international credit markets such as developing countries (Williamson, 1984).

Confidence problem

An earlier section discussed the 'confidence problem' inherent in the gold-exchange standard. We may identify two analogous potential 'confidence problems' of relevance to the 1980s in a totally different international monetary regime: the debt problem of developing countries and the emergence of the US as a net debtor. Both centre on the debt implications of international financial intermediation, and for illustration we restrict the discussion to the US case.

The origin of a potential 'confidence problem' centred on the US is the substantial and persistent current-account deficit of that country since 1982 (Figure 10.1). This has been financed predominantly by autonomous and interest-rate induced capital inflows. This has substantially raised the external liabilities of the US, albeit denominated in its domestic currency. This has changed the US from being a major net creditor in 1982 to the world's largest net debtor nation (Figure 10.2) over only three years. The counterpart is a corresponding rise in the net asset position of Germany and Japan. This creates a potential 'confidence problem' for if the capital inflow

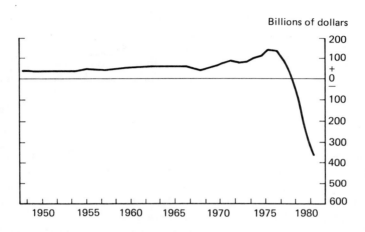

FIGURE 10.2 US net international investment position

were to cease (foreigners reached a portfolio limit to their desire to hold dollar assets) and even more so if dollar assets were liquidated, massive pressure on the dollar would emerge which would induce either a sharp depreciation of the dollar in the foreign exchange markets or massive support intervention by central banks.

There is a parallel between the confidence problem experienced in the early 1980s by developing countries and that likely to be experienced eventually by the US. Concern at the *stock* position of external indebtedness of the US is likely at some stage to constrain the future *flow* of current account financing just as it did earlier with developing countries. How the required current-account adjustment is made (either through income or exchange rate adjustments) will have powerful effects upon the world economy and has the potential for inducing substantial exchange market instability. Although the net external liabilities of the US at the end of 1987 were only 8 per cent of GNP as against comparable ratios of 25 per cent in heavily indebted developing countries, Howard (1989) notes that assuming a US nominal GNP growth of 6 per cent per annum and net external debt increases in increments equal to the 1988 nominal current account deficit, the US debt to GNP ratio would approach 25 per cent in the late 1990s.

The central dilemma is that if there is no planned policy adjustment by the US external debt likely to rise inexorably. Eventually a confidence problem will emerge which forces adjustment, as finance is not forthcoming to facilitate the continuing net absorption of real resources. Given the size of the actual and projected current account deficits, the adjustment requirement will be substantial. Indeed a US balance of trade surplus is required in order to halt the rise in the volume of external liabilities.

This is not the first time the dollar has been seriously misaligned. There is a parallel between the current position of the US dollar and that which prevailed at the end of the 1960s and early 1970s. The potential significance of the parallel derives from a consideration of how the *confidence problem* of the late 1960s and early 1970s was eventually resolved. In the earlier period concern developed over what was then termed the 'dollar overhang': the volume of external liabilities exceeding the value of the US gold stock. In the face of demands by some central banks (the Banque de France in particular) for a gold guarantee to their dollar assets, President Nixon in August 1971 declared the US dollar to be non-convertible (into gold) and threatened an import surcharge in the event that Europe and Japan would not facilitate a dollar devaluation. It was largely this that was the proximate cause of the breakdown of the Bretton Woods system.

ASSESSMENT

Historically international monetary arrangements have oscillated between structured systems and flexible, market-based arrangements. The evolution of the international monetary system is fashioned by the changing weights attached to the alternative organising mechanisms identified earlier.

The gold standard and, to a lesser extent the Bretton Woods system, were structured systems. But both were crisis-prone at various times in their history. In the current environment (most especially in the context of voluminous international capital movements and in the absence of a high degree of *ex ante* policy coordination) there is probably no alternative to the current flexible arrangements. Indeed, in the context of major shocks to the world economy, and in the conduct of monetary policy, the system has worked remarkably well. It has not been subject to the frequent crises experienced during the 1960s, and neither has the system reverted to the anarchy of the 1930s after the collapse of the previous formal and structured system. If anything, current arrangements have facilitated a more liberal economic order.

Given past history it is tempting to ponder whether current arrangements are in some sense transitional. The author's judgement is that they are not and that the basics of the present system will remain. Nevertheless, the chapter has highlighted three areas where future problems may arise: (1) the size of current imbalances and their adjustment; (2) the role of capital movements in a world economy with different degrees of international integration between different groups of countries, and (3) a potential 'confidence problem' associated with the US external debt position in the context of a continuing large deficit. If there is to be a modification to the system it will likely centre on these three issues.

The likely focus on the first will be attempts and mechanisms at more formal policy coordination, and this is the area where the more exciting developments could emerge. There does seem to be some official recognition of this even though the practical and political problems are formidable.

As for the second issue, there could be movement along the lines advocated by Bergsten and Williamson (1983) and McKinnon (1984). The former relates to the idea of 'target zones' for exchange rates. The latter is based upon regional blocs. The most obvious example of this is to be found in the EEC. Towards the end of the 1960s a European monetary initiative was taken and in 1979 the European Monetary System (EMS) was formally instituted. Acording to official statements at the time several factors in the world economy and financial system prompted this move: (i) a general disillusionment with the operation of floating exchange rates; (ii) the longstanding European concern at the hegemony of the US dollar in the international monetary system, and (iii) a rather imprecise view that a coordinated policy approach by European governments would be a more effective means of improving the general performance of the European economies, and for reducing unemployment and inflation in particular. But above all else it was the substantial pressure on the dollar in the exchange markets that was the dominant factor. As already noted, when the dollar came under pressure it was largely into the Deutschemark that speculative funds flowed. The predominant motive was to mitigate the disruptive effects on intra-EC exchange rates that results from this pressure. This is related, however, to the more general and longstanding objective of EC countries of securing a higher degree of monetary independence from the US without having to accept the implications of floating exchange rates between themselves. The broad objective of the EMS was to create a 'zone of monetary stability' in Europe. However, such a scheme, while collectively enhancing the monetary independence of the EMS group as a whole *vis-à-vis* the US, implies even less monetary independence between members. Nevertheless, there might be a greater chance of members of the EMS being able to coordinate and agree upon monetary targets between themselves than with the US.

Perhaps the most vulnerable area centres on the potential 'confidence problem' of the dollar. An analogy has been drawn with the problem of the 'dollar overhang' in the late 1960s. It is instructive to recall that the last time this problem surfaced the solution was found in a major change in the structure of the international monetary system. A more market-orientated system was viewed as the solution and yet this seems not to have prevented a similar problem re-emerging. *Plus ça change, plus c'est la même chose*!

End-Notes

CHAPTER 2

1. This paper draws in part on my 'Exchange Rate Economics: 1986', published in the March 1987 issue of the *Economic Journal*, but additional material has been added.
2. See Johnson (1969, p. 199).
3. See Dornbusch (1976; 1980). Some of the extensions are considered in Dornbusch (1986a).
4. The formula for the risk premium here omits wealth terms. It also focuses on debt rather than all nominal outside assets.
5. In a model with a risk premium there is a serious difficulty in linking goods and assets markets. There is certainly no excuse for using the interest rate on bonds in home currency as *the* domestic interest rate used as a determinant of domestic spending. The *ad hoc* model becomes a liability. The correct treatment, drawing on an optimisation model, would use the marginal cost of capital, which is based on the marginal financing pattern, which in turn is derived by solving the firm's and household's complete intertemporal optimisation problem.
6. See especially Frankel (1985, 1986b).
7. See especially Baldwin (1986), Krugman (1986) and Baldwin and Krugman (1986) and Krugman and Baldwin (1987).
8. See Dornbusch and Frankel (1987) for a more detailed review.
9. Let $_tf_t + 3$ denote the three-month forward rate prevailing at time t and e_t the spot rate. The left-hand side is defined as: Error $= 100^*$ $(_tf_{t+3} - e_{t+3})/e_{t+3} - 1)$ and depreciation $= 100^*((e_t - e_{t-3})/e_t - 1)$. In the regression the depreciation variable is entered as a 4-quarter distributed lag.
10. In fact, I could not get satisfactory results for the longer sample period.
11. The following are data for the real yield differential on long-term debt and the full employment budget (as a percent of GDP) in the US and the major trading partners:

	Differential	*US budget*	*Foreign budgets*
1984	2.03	− 1.02	− 1.23
1985	3.5	− 2.5	− 1.17
1986	1.3	− 2.9	− 1.35
1987	1.09	− 2.04	− 1.06
1988	0.3	− 2.04	− 1.01

Source: OECD and DRI, Inc.

12. See Dornbusch (1985b), Krugman (1986), Feinberg (1986), Mann (1986) and Flood (1986).
13. This analysis draws on Dixit (1986) and Seade (1983).
14. See Sachs (1985) and Woo (1984) on the exchange rate effects on US inflation.
15. See Cooper (1969), Hamada (1985), Buiter and Marston (1985), Oudiz and Sachs (1984), Canzoneri and Edison (1988) and McMillan (1986).
16. For a further discussion see Fischer (1986).

CHAPTER 3

1. The author wishes to thank the Lady Davis Trust, Jerusalem for its generous financial support.
2. A bubble arises when agents believe that there will be self-fulfilling expectations of exchange rate movements regardless of the fundamentals. Unstable roots in rational expectation models reflect such behaviour.

CHAPTER 4

1. See, for example, Friedman (1953).
2. A nominal effective exchange rate is simply the index of a currency against the currencies of its main trading partners. A real effective exchange rate, in turn is the nominal effective rate multiplied by the ratio of a corresponding effective price level to the domestic price level.
3. See Hallwood and MacDonald (1986) for a fuller discussion.
4. See Frenkel (1987) for a further discussion.
5. See Balassa (1964), Samuelson (1974) and Hallwood and MacDonald (1986).
6. See, *inter alia*, Frenkel (1976), Bilson (1978), and Putnam and Woodbury (1979).
7. See, for example, Hooper and Morton (1982) and Frenkel (1984).
8. See Frenkel (1982b), Cumby and Obstfeld (1984) and Loopesko (1984).
9. The real rates have been calculated using consumer price indices.
10. Figures 4.1 and 4.3 are also supportive of the findings in Dornbusch (1979).
11. See, for example, Frenkel (1981) and Krugman (1987).
12. Thus Roll (1979), Frenkel (1981), and MacDonald (1985) find in favour of the EMPPP, whilst Cumby and Obstfeld (1984) and Frenkel and Froot (1985) are able to reject the hypothesis.
13. Where in equation 7, α_2 and β_2 are the semi-interest rate elasticities.
14. See MacDonald (1988) for a further discussion.
15. On this topic, see Domowitz and Hakkio (1985) and Hodrick and Srivastava (1984).

16. See Bilson (1981) and Cumby and Obstfeld (1984).
17. See Frankel and Froot (1985) for the US and MacDonald and Torrance (1988) for the UK.
18. See MacDonald and Taylor (1988) for a further discussion.
19. The attempts by researchers to empirically model the risk premium have been largely unsuccessful.
20. Thus the portfolio balance model, which is the relevant model in the presence of risk, suggests that a swap of domestic bonds for foreign bonds – sterilised intervention – can affect the exchange rate.

CHAPTER 7

1. Although the author has received helpful advice and comments from colleagues at the OECD, the views expressed in this chapter are the sole responsibility of the author and should not be attributed to the OECD. Special thanks are due to Val Koromzay for his inspiration and encouragement.

CHAPTER 8

1. In this 'rational actor' literature, these motives are attributed interchangeably to the government or to the 'representative citizen'. In reality most bank lending has been to, or guaranteed by, governments, and the validity of this equivalent treatment is questioned below.
2. The demand curve indicates the maximum loan demand at each interest rate charged and thus passes through the indifference curves at the point of zero slope (e.g. Jaffee and Russell, 1976).
3. 'Risk' arises when the possible future returns on an investment can each be assigned a probability 'weight' with the sum of the weights adding to unity. The 'expected' return is then the sum of those weighted probabilities. In contrast, the future is 'uncertain' when there is no basis for assigning such weights.

CHAPTER 9

1. The gold standard might be dated from 1694, when the Bank of England was established; the requirement was that its note issues be convertible into gold at a fixed price. An alternative date is 1880, about the time when the United States, Germany, and France pegged their currencies to gold; for the United States, pegging gold in 1879 was a return to the pre-Civil War parity.
2. The convertibility of the British pound into gold was suspended just before the First World War in April 1914. From April 1914 to March

1919, the British authorities supported the pound at a US dollar price which was 5–10 per cent below the price inferred from the 1914 gold parities.

3. The Belgian franc and the Italian lira were pegged after the French franc in 1927 and 1928 (Brown, 1940). In this chapter the system of exchange rates is defined by the currency-pegging practices of the four or five larger countries.

4. Some countries had stopped pegging their currencies to gold even before Great Britain. Uruguay stopped pegging its currency in October 1929, and Argentina in November 1929. Brazil stopped pegging in January 1930, Bolivia in February, Australia in March, and New Zealand in August 1930. In 1931 Venezula stopped pegging in January, Mexico in August, and Great Britain, India, Canada, Denmark, Norway, and Sweden in September. For the sequence of suspensions and subsequent currency values, see League of Nations (1935).

5. See Yeager (1969) and Myhrman (1976) for surveys of some of these earlier experiences.

6. Similarly the United States suspended the convertibility of the US dollar into gold at $20.67 parity in March 1933. A new parity of $35.00 was established at the end of January 1934.

7. One monetarist proposition is that monetary shocks have no structural consequences; the cliché is that 'Changes in monetary variables have no *real* effects'. This proposition is tested by a number of the subsequent observations.

8. The economic intuition is that the inflation rate could remain stable at a high level, say at 5 or 8 per cent, as well as stable around zero or 1 per cent. The observation is that when the inflation rate is high, it cannot remain stable.

9. To the extent that inflation – or at least the early stages of inflation – is associated with a decline in real interest rates.

Bibliography

Abuaf, N. (1985) 'The effects of monetary and real shocks on the real exchange rate', unpublished PhD dissertation, University of Chicago.

Aliber, R. Z. (1962) 'Speculation in the flexible exchanges: the European experience: 1919–1926', *Yale Economic Essays*, Spring.

Aliber, R. Z. (1980) 'Floating exchange rates: the twenties and the seventies', in *Flexible Exchange Rates and the Balance of Payments*, edited by J. S. Chipman and C. P. Kindleberger, North Holland, Amsterdam.

Aliber, R. Z. (1984) 'Structural changes, monetary policy, and the foreign exchange value of sterling', in *Monetarism in the United Kingdom*, edited by B. Griffiths and G. E. Wood, Macmillan, London.

Aliber, R. Z. (1987) 'Exchange rates', *The New Palgrave: A Dictionary of Economics*, Macmillan, London.

Aliber, R. Z. (1988a) 'The US trade deficit and the US fiscal deficit: which is the cause and which is the effect?, mimeo, Chicago.

Aliber, R. Z. (1988b) 'The foreign exchange value of the US dollar, sticky asset prices and corporate financial decisions', mimeo, Chicago.

Alogoskoufis, G. (1989) 'Stabilisation policy, fixed exchange rates and target zones', in M. Miller, B. Eichengreen and R. Portes (eds), *Blueprints for Exchange Rate Management*, Academic Press, London.

Amuzegar, J. (1983) 'Oil exporters' economic development in an interdependent world', IMF Occasional Research Paper No. 18, IMF, Washington.

Argy, V. (1981) *The Postwar International Money Crisis: An Analysis*, Allen & Unwin, London.

Arndt, H. W. and Drake, P. J. (1985) 'Bank loans or bonds? Some lessons from historical experience', Banca Nazionale del Lavoro, 38, 373–92.

Artis, M. S. and Lewis, M. K. (1981) *Monetary Control in the United Kingdom*, Philip Allan, Oxford.

Backus, D. (1984) 'Empirical models of the exchange rate: separating the wheat from the chaff', *Canadian Journal of Economics*, 17, 4, 824–6.

Backus, D. and Driffill, J. (1986) 'The consistency of optimal policy in stochastic rational expectations models', *CEPR Discussion Paper No. 124*.

Baer, W. (1987) 'The resurgence of inflation in Brazil 1974–86', *World Development*, 15, 1007–1034.

Balassa, B. (1964) 'The purchasing power parity doctrine: a reappraisal', *Journal of Political Economy*, 72, 584–96.

247

Baldwin, R. (1986) 'Hysteresis in trade', unpublished manuscript, Massachusetts Institute of Technology, April.

Baldwin, R. and Krugman, P. (1986) 'Persistent trade effects of large exchange rate shocks', unpublished manuscript, Massachusetts Institute of Technology, July.

Bank for International Settlements (1986) *Recent Innovations in International Banking*, BIS, Basle.

Bank for International Settlements (1988) 'Reserves and international liquidity', BIS Economic Papers No. 22, BIS, Basle.

Bank of England (1983) *Bank of England Quarterly Bulletin*, March.

Barro, R. J. (1974) 'Are government bonds net wealth?', *Journal of Political Economy*, 82, 1095–1117.

Barro, R. J. (1979) 'On the determination of public debt', *Journal of Political Economy*, 87, 940–71.

Barro, R. J. and Fischer, S. (1976) 'Recent developments in monetary theory', *Journal of Monetary Economics*, 2, 133–67.

Beenstock, M. (1978) *The Foreign Exchanges: Theory, Modelling and Policy*, Macmillan, London.

Beenstock, M. (1983) 'Rational expectations and the effects of intervention on the exchange rate', *Journal of International Money and Finance*, 2, 319–31.

Beenstock, M., Blake, D. and Brasse, V. (1986) 'The performance of UK exchange rate forecasters', *Economic Journal*, December.

Beenstock, M. and Dadashi, S. (1986) 'The profitability of forward currency speculation by central banks', *European Economic Review*, 30, 444–56.

Bergsten, C. F., Cline, W. R. and Williamson, J. (1985) *Bank Lending to Developing Countries: The Policy Alternatives*, Policy Analyses No. 10 (Washington, DC, Institute for International Economics).

Bergsten, C. F. and Williamson, J. (1983) 'Exchange rates and trade policy' in Cline, W. R. (ed.), *Trade Policy in the 1980s*, Institute for International Economics, Washington.

Bernstein, E. M. (1956) 'Strategic factors in balance of payments adjustment', *IMF Staff Papers*, 5, 152–9.

Bhandari, J. S. (1982) *Exchange Rate Determination and Adjustment*, Praeger, New York.

Bhandari, J., Driskell, R. D. and Frenkel, J. A. (1984) 'Capital mobility and exchange rate overshooting', *European Economic Review*, 24, 309–20.

Bilson, J. F. O. (1978) 'The monetary approach to the exchange rate – some empirical evidence', *International Monetary Fund Staff Papers*, 25, 48–75.

Bilson, J. F. O. (1981) 'The speculative efficiency hypothesis', *Journal of Business*, 54, 435–451.

Binmore, K. (1989) 'Game theory and the social contract, Mark II', *Economic Journal*, Supplement.

Blanchard, O. (1979) 'Speculative bubbles, crashes and rational expectations', *Economic Letters*, 3, 387–9.

Blanchard, O. J. (1985) 'Debt, deficits and finite horizons', *Journal of Political Economy*, 93, 223–47.

Blanchard, O. J. (1988) 'Why does money affect output? A survey', in B. M. Friedman and F. H. Hahn (eds), *Handbook of Monetary Economics*, North Holland, Amsterdam.

Boughton, J. (1989) 'Policy assignment strategies with somewhat flexible exchange rates', in M. Miller, B. Eichengreen and R. Portes (eds), *Blueprints for Exchange Rate Management*, Academic Press, London.

Boyer, R. S. (1978) 'Financial policies in an open economy', *Economica*, 45, 39–57.

Branson, W. H. (1977) 'Asset markets and relative prices in exchange rate determination', *Socialwissenschaftliche Annalen*, 1, 69–89.

Branson, W. H. (1980) 'Asset markets and relative prices in exchange rate determination', *Princeton Reprints in International Finance*, No. 20.

Branson, W. H. and Buiter, W. (1983) 'Monetary and fiscal policy with flexible exchange rates', in J. S. Bhandari and B. H. Putnam (eds), *Economic Interdependence and Flexible Exchange Rates*, MIT Press, Cambridge.

Branson, W. H. and Haltunen, H. (1979) 'Asset-market determination of exchange rates: initial empirical and policy results', in J. P. Martin and A. Smith, *Trade and Payments Adjustment Under Flexible Exchange Rates*, Macmillan, London.

Branson, W. and Henderson, D. (1985) 'The specification and influence of asset markets', in R. Jones and P. Kenen (eds), *Handbook of International Economics*, 2, North Holland, Amsterdam.

Britton, A. J. C. (1970) 'The dynamic stability of the foreign exchange market', *Economic Journal*, 80, 91–6.

Brown, W. A. Jr. (1940) *The International Gold Standard Reinterpreted, 1914–1934*, 2 volumes, National Bureau of Economic Research, New York.

Bryant, R. *et al.* (1988) *Empirical Macroeconomics for Interdependent Economies*, Brookings Institution, Washington.

Buiter, W. and Marston, R. (eds) (1985) *International Economic Policy Coordination*, Cambridge University Press, Cambridge.

Buiter, W. and Miller, M. (1981) 'Monetary policy and international competitiveness: the problems of adjustment', *Oxford Economic Papers*, Supplement, 33, 143–75.

Buiter, W. H. and Miller, M. H. (1983) 'Changing the rules: economic consequences of the Thatcher regime', *Brookings Papers on Economic Activity*, 2, 305–79.

Cairncross, A. K. (1913) *Home and Foreign Investment 1870–1913*, Cambridge University Press, Cambridge.

Canzoneri, M. and Edison, H. (1988) 'A new interpretation of the coordination problem and its empirical significance', mimeo, Georgetown University, May.

Cline, W. R. (1983) *International Debt and the Stability of the World Economy*, Policy Analyses No. 4, Institute for International Economics, Washington, DC.

Cline, W. R. (1984) *International Debt: Systemic Risk and Policy Response*, MIT Press, Cambridge, Mass.

Clower, R. W. (1967) 'A reconsideration of the microfoundations of monetary theory', *Western Economic Journal*, 6, 1–9.

Cohen, B. (1981) *Banks and the Balance of Payments*, Croom Helm, London.

Committee of Twenty (1974) *International Monetary Reform*, IMF, Washington,

Cooper, R. N. (1969) 'Macroeconomic policy adjustment in interdependent economies', *Quarterly Journal of Economics*, 83, 1–24.

Cooper, R. N. (1971) 'Currency depreciation in developing countries', *Essays in International Finance No. 86*, Princeton University Press, Princeton.

Cooper, R. N. (1984) 'Is there a need for reform', in *The International Monetary System*, Federal Reserve Bank of Boston, Boston.

Cooper, R. N. (1986) 'International cooperation in public health as a prologue to macroeconomic cooperation', *Brookings Discussion Paper No. 44*.

Cooper, R. N. (1988) 'To co-ordinate or not to co-ordinate', in *International Payments Imbalances in the 1980s*, Federal Reserve Bank of Boston, Boston.

Cooper, R. N. and Sachs, J. (1985) 'Borrowing abroad: the debtor's perspective' in Smith, G. W. and Cuddington, J. T. (eds), op cit.

Corden, W. M. (1985) *Inflation, Exchange Rates and the World Economy*, 3rd edition, Oxford University Press, Oxford.

Cornell, B. (1983) 'Money supply announcements and interest-rates: another view', *Journal of Business*, 56, 1–23.

Crockett, A. (1988) 'Strengthening international economic cooperation: the role of indicators', in Eizenga, W. et al. (eds), *The Quest for National and Global Economic Stability*, Kluwer, Dordrecht.

Crockett, A. D. and Ripley, D. (1975) 'Sharing the oil deficit', *International Monetary Fund Staff Papers*, 22, 284–312.

Cuddington, J. (1983) 'Currency substitution, capital mobility and money demand', *Journal of International Money and Finance*, 2, 111–33.

Cuddington, J. J., Johansson, P. O. and Lofgren, K. G. (1984) *Disequilibrium Macroeconomics in Open Economics*, Blackwell, Oxford.

Cuddington, J. J. and Vinals, J. M. (1986a) 'Budget deficits and the current account in the presence of classical unemployment', *Economic Journal*, 96, 101–19.

Cuddington, J. J. and Vinals, J. M. (1986b) 'Budget deficits and the current account: an intertemporal disequilibrium approach', *Journal of International Economics*, 21, 1–24.

Cumby, R. E. and Obstfeld, M. (1984) 'International interest rate and price level changes under flexible exchange rates: a review of recent evidence', in J. F. O. Bilson and R. C. Marston (eds), *Exchange Rate Theory and Practice*, Chicago University Press, Chicago.

Currie, D., Holtham, G. and Hughes Hallet, A. (1989) 'The theory and practice of international policy coordination: does coordination pay?, in R. Bryant, D. A. Currie, J. A. Frenkel, P. Masson and R. Portes (eds), *Macroeconomic Policies in an Interdependent World*, IMF, Washington.

Currie, D. and Levine, P. (1986) 'Time inconsistency and optimal policies in deterministic and stochastic worlds', *Journal of Economic Dynamics and Control*, 10, 191–9.

Currie, D., Levine, P. and Vidalis, N. (1987) 'International cooperation and reputation in an empirical two-bloc model', in Ralph Bryant and Richard Portes (eds), *Global Macroeconomics: Policy Conflict and Cooperation*, Macmillan, London.

Currie, D. and Wren-Lewis, S. (1988a) 'Evaluating the extended target zone proposal for the G3', *CEPR Discussion Paper No. 221*.

Currie, D. and Wren-Lewis, S. (1988b) 'Conflict and cooperation in international macroeconomic policy making', in Andrew Britton (ed.), *Policy Making with Macroeconomic Models*, Gower, Aldershot.

Currie, D. and Wren-Lewis, S. (1989) 'A comparison of alternative blueprints for international macropolicy coordination', *European Economic Review*, forthcoming.

Daniel, B. (1985) 'Optional foreign exchange rate management for a small open economy', *Journal of International Money and Finance*, 4, 523–6.

Darrat, A. F. (1988) 'Have large budget deficits caused rising trade deficits?', *Southern Economic Journal*, 54, 879–87.

Davidson, P. (1972) *Money and the Real World*, Macmillan, London.

De Grauwe, P. (1973) *Monetary Interdependence and International Monetary Reform*, Saxton House, Farnborough.

Dealtry, M. (1988) 'Reserves and international liquidity revisited: 1988', in *Reserves and International Liquidity*, BIS Economic Papers No. 22, BIS, Basle.

Dean, A. and Koromzay, V. (1987) 'Current-account imbalances and adjustment mechanisms', OECD Economic Studies, 8, 7–33.

Delors, J. (1989) *Report on Economic and Monetary Union in the European Community*, EEC, Brussels.

Diaz-Alejandro, C. (1966) *Exchange Rate Devaluation in a Semi-industrialized Country: the Experience of Argentina 1955–1961*, MIT Press, Cambridge, Mass.

Diba, B. T. (1987) 'A critique of variance bounds tests of monetary exchange rate models', *Journal of Money, Credit and Banking*, 19, 104–111.

Dixit, A. (1978) 'The balance of trade in a model of temporary equilibrium with rationing', *Review of Economic Studies*, 45, 393–404.

Dixit, A. (1986) 'Comparative statics for oligopoly', *International Economic Review*, 27, 107–22.

Dixit, A. and Stiglitz, J. (1977) 'Monopolistic competition and optimum product diversity', *American Economic Review*, 67, 207–308

Domowitz, I. and Hakkio, L. (1985) 'Conditional variance and the risk premium in the foreign exchange market', *Journal of International Economics*, 19, 47–66.

Dooley, M. (1985) 'The role of reserves in the International Monetary System', in Posner, M. (ed.), *Problems of International Money: 1972–85*, IMF, Washington.

Dooley, M., Frankel, J. and Mathieson, D. J. (1987) 'International capital mobility: what do saving-investment correlations tell us?, *IMF Staff Papers*, 34, 503–531.

Dornbusch, R. (1976) 'Expectations and exchange rate dynamics', *Journal of Political Economy*, 84, 1161–76.

Dornbusch, R. (1979) 'Monetary policy under exchange rate flexibility', in *Managed Exchange Rate Flexibility: The Recent Experience*, Federal Reserve Bank of Boston.

Dornbusch, R. (1980) 'Exchange rate economics: where do we stand?', *Brookings Papers on Economic Activity*, 3, 537–84.

Dornbusch, R. (1983a) 'Exchange risk and the macroeconomics of exchange rate determination', in R. Hawkins *et al.* (eds), *The Internationalization of Financial Markets and National Economic Policy*, JAI Press.

Dornbusch, R. (1983b) 'Flexible exchange rates and interdependence', *IMF Staff Papers*, 30, 3–38.

Dornbusch, R. (1985a) 'Policy and performance links between LDC debtors and industrial countries', *Brookings Papers on Economic Activity*, 2, 303–56.

Dornbusch, R. (1985b) 'External debt, budget deficits, and disequilibrium exchange rates', in Smith, G. W. and Cuddington, J. T. (eds), op cit.

Dornbusch, R. (1986a) 'Inflation, exchange rates and stabilization', *Princeton Essays in International Finance*, No. 165.

Dornbusch, R. (1986b) 'Flexible exchange rates and excess capital mobility', *Brookings Papers on Economic Activity*, 1, 209–26.

Dornbusch, R. (1986c) 'Special exchange rates for capital account transactions', *The World Bank Economic Review*, 1, 3–33.

Dornbusch, R. (1987a) 'Purchasing power parity', in *The New Palgrave: A Dictionary of Economics*, Macmillan, London.

Dornbusch, R. (1987b) 'Exchange rates and prices', *American Economic Review*, 77, 93–106.

Dornbusch, R. (1987c) 'The EMS, the dollar and the yen', *CEPR Discussion Paper No. 216*.

Dornbusch, R. and Fischer, S. (1980) 'Exchange rates and the current account', *American Economic Review*, 70, 960–71.

Dornbusch, R. and Fischer, S. (1987) 'The open economy implications of monetary and fiscal policy', in R. Gordon (ed.), *The American Business Cycle*, University of Chicago Press, Chicago.

Dornbusch, R. and Frankel, J. (1987) 'The flexible exchange rate system: experience and alternatives', NBER Working Paper No. 2464, December.

Dorrance, G. and Black, J. (1984) *Problems of International Finance*, Macmillan, London.

Driskell, R. A. (1981) 'Exchange rate dynamics: an empirical investigation', *Journal of Political Economy*, 98, 357–71.

Dwyer, G. P. (1985) 'Federal deficits, interest rates, and monetary policy', *Journal of Money, Credit and Banking*, 17, 655–81.

Eaton, J. and Gersovitz, M. (1981a) *Poor Country Borrowing in Private*

Financial Markets and the Repudiation Issues, Princeton Studies in International Finance No. 47, Princeton University, Princeton, NJ.

Eaton, J. and Gersovitz, M. (1981b) 'Debt with potential repudiation: theoretical and empirical analysis', *Review of Economic Studies*, 48, 289–309.

Eaton, J. and Gersovitz, M. (1983) 'Country risk: economic aspects', in Herring, R. J. (ed.), *Managing International Risk*, Cambridge University Press, Cambridge.

Eaton, J. and Taylor, L. (1986) 'Developing country finance and debt', *Journal of Development Economics*, 22, 209–65.

Edison, H. J. (1981) 'Short run dynamics and long run equilibrium behaviour in purchasing power parity', unpublished PhD thesis, London School of Economics.

Edison, H., Miller, M. and Williamson, J. (1987) 'On evaluating and extending the target zone proposal', *Journal of Policy Modelling*, 9, 199–224.

Edison, H. and Tryon, R. (1986) 'An empirical analysis of policy coordination in the United States, Japan and Europe', Board of Governors of the Federal Reserve, International Finance Discussion Papers No. 286, July.

Epstein, E. C. (1987) 'Recent stabilisation programs in Argentina', *World Development*, 15, 991–1005.

Fama, E. (1984) 'Forward and spot exchange rates'. *Journal of Monetary Economics*, 14, 319–38.

Feinberg, R. M. (1986) 'The interaction of foreign exchange and market power effects on German domestic prices', *The Journal of Industrial Economics*, 35, 61–70.

Feldstein, M. (1983) 'Domestic saving and international capital movements in the long run and the short run', *European Economic Review*, 21, 129–51.

Feldstein, M. (1986) 'The budget deficit and the dollar', *NBER Macroeconomics Annual*.

Feldstein, M. (1987a) 'The end of policy coordination', *The Wall Street Journal*, 9 November.

Feldstein, M. (1987b) 'Rethinking international economic policy coordination', mimeo.

Feldstein, M. and Horioka, C. (1980) 'Domestic saving and international capital flows', *Economic Journal*, 90, 314–29.

Fischer, S. (1986) 'Symposium on exchange rates, trade and capital flows: comments', *Brookings Papers on Economic Activity*, 1.

Fischer, S. (1988) 'Recent developments in macroeconomics', *Economic Journal*, 98, 294–339.

Fleming, J. M. (1962) 'Domestic financial policies under fixed and under floating exchange rates', International Monetary Fund *Staff Papers*, 9, 369–79.

Flood, E. (1986) 'An empirical analysis of the effects of exchange rate changes on goods prices', unpublished manuscript, Stanford University.

Forsyth, P. J. and Kay, J. A. (1980) 'The economic implications of North Sea Oil revenues', *Fiscal Studies*, 1, 1–28.

Frankel, J. A. (1979) 'A theory of floating exchange rates based on real interest differentials', *American Economic Review*, 69, 610–22.

Frankel, J. A. (1982a) 'In search of the exchange risk premium: a six-currency test assuming mean variance optimization', *Journal of International Money and Finance*, 1.

Frankel, J. A. (1982b) 'A test of perfect substitutability in the foreign exchange market', *Southern Economic Journal*, 49, 406–16.

Frankel, J. A. (1983) 'Monetary and portfolio balance models of exchange rate determination', in J. Bhandari and B. Putnam (eds), *Economic Interdependence and Flexible Exchange Rates*, MIT Press, Cambridge, Mass.

Frankel, J. A. (1984) 'Tests of monetary and portfolio balance models of exchange rate determination', in J. F. O. Bilson and R. L. Marston (eds), *Exchange Rate Theory and Practice*, Chicago University Press, Chicago.

Frankel, J. A. (1985a) 'The dazzling dollar', *Brookings Papers on Economic Activity*, 1, 199–217.

Frankel, J. A. (1985b) 'Portfolio crowding-out empirically estimated', *Quarterly Journal of Economics*, 100, 1041–65.

Frankel, J. A. (1986) 'The implications of mean-variance optimization for four questions in international finance', *Journal of International Money and Finance*, 5, 53–75.

Frankel, J. A. (1987) 'Obstacles to international macroeconomic policy coordination', *Discussion Paper 8737*, University of California at Berkeley.

Frankel, J. A. and Froot, K. (1985) 'Using survey data to test some standard propositions regarding exchange rate expectations', *NBER Working Paper No. 1672*.

Frankel, J. A. and Froot, K. (1986a) 'Three essays using survey data of exchange rate expectations', unpublished manuscript, University of California, Berkeley, November.

Frankel, J. A. and Froot, K. (1986b) 'Understanding the US dollar in the eighties: the expectations of chartists and fundamentalists', *Economic Record*, Supplement.

Frankel, J. A. and Froot, K. (1986c) 'The dollar as an irrational speculative bubble: a tale of fundamentalists and chartists', *The Marcus Wallengerg Papers on International Finance*, No. 1.

Frankel, J. A. and Froot, K. (1987) 'Using survey data to test standard propositions regarding exchange rate expectations', *American Economic Review*, 77, 133–53.

Frankel, J. A. and Rockett, K. (1988) 'International macroeconomic policy coordination when policy-makers disagree on the model', *American Economic Review*, 78, 318–40.

Frenkel, J. (1976) 'A monetary approach to the exchange rate: doctrinal aspects and empirical evidence', *Scandinavian Journal of Economics*, 78, 200–24.

Frenkel, J. (1978) 'Purchasing power parity: doctrinal perspectives and evidence from the 1920s', *Journal of International Economics*, 8, 169–191.

Frenkel, J. (1981) 'Flexible exchange rates, prices, and the role of "news": lessons for the 1970s', *Journal of Political Economy*, 89, 665–705.

Frenkel, J. (1987) 'The international monetary system: should it be reformed?', *American Economic Review*, 77, 205–10.

Frenkel, J. (1989) 'Capital movements and exchange rate volatility', in *International Payments Imbalances in the 1980s*, Federal Reserve Bank of Boston, Boston.

Frenkel, J. and Razin, A. (1986a) 'The international transmission and effects of fiscal policy', *American Economic Review*, 76, 330–5.

Frenkel, J. A. and Razin, A. (1986b) 'Fiscal policies in the world economy', *Journal of Political Economy*, 94, 564–94.

Frenkel, J. A. and Rodriguez, L. A. (1982) 'Exchange rate dynamics and the overshooting hypothesis', *IMF Staff Papers*, 29, 1–30.

Friedman, M. (1953) 'The case for flexible exchange rates', in *Essays in Positive Economics*, University of Chicago Press, Chicago.

Friedman, M. and Schwartz, A. (1963) *A Monetary History of the United States 1867–1960*, National Bureau of Economic Research, Princeton University Press, Princeton.

Gailliot, H. J. (1970) 'Purchasing power parity as an explanation of long term changes in exchange rates', *Journal of Money, Credit and Banking*, 11, 340–57.

Gavin, M. (1986) 'The stock market and exchange rate dynamics', *International Finance Discussion Papers*, Board of Governors of the Federal Reserve, No. 278.

Gersovitz, M. (1985) 'Banks' international lending decisions: what we know and implications for future research', in Smith, G. W. and Cuddington, J. T. (eds), op. cit.

Ghosh, A. R. and Masson, P. (1988) 'International policy coordination in a world with model uncertainty', *IMF Staff Papers*, 35, 230–58.

Giavazzi, F. and Pagano, M. (1986) 'The advantage of tying one's hand: EMS discipline and central bank credibility', *CEPR Discussion Paper No. 135*.

Giovannini, A. (1983) *Three Essays on Exchange Rates*, unpublished MIT dissertation.

Giovannini, A. (1985) 'Exchange rates and traded goods prices', unpublished manuscript, Columbia University.

Greenwood, J. and Kimbrough, K. P. (1985) 'Capital controls and fiscal policy in the world economy', *Canadian Journal of Economics*, 18, 743–65.

Group of 30 (1988) *International Macroeconomic Policy Coordination*, London.

Guttentag, J. M. and Herring, R. J. (1985a) 'Commercial bank lending to developing countries: from overlending to underlending to structural reform', in Smith, G. W. and Cuddington, J. T. (eds), op. cit.

Guttentag, J. M. and Herring, R. J. (1985b) *The Current Crisis in International Lending*, Studies in International Economics, Brookings Institution, Washington, DC.

Guttentag, J. M. and Herring, R. J. (1986) *Disaster Myopia in International Banking, Essays in International Finance No. 164* (Princeton, NJ, International Finance Section, Princeton University).

Hacche, G. and Townend, J. (1981) 'Exchange rates and monetary policy: modelling sterling's effective exchange rate, 1972–80', in W. A. Eltis and P. J. N. Sinclair, *The Money Supply and the Exchange Rate*, Oxford University Press, Oxford.

Hallwood, P. and MacDonald, R. (1986) *International Money: Theory, Evidence and Institutions*, Blackwell, Oxford.

Hamada, K. (1985) *The Political Economy of International Monetary Interdependence*, MIT Press, Cambridge, Mass.

Harberger, A. (1950) 'Currency depreciation, income and the balance of trade', *Journal of Political Economy*, 1, 47–60.

Haynes, S. E. and Stone, J. A. (1981) 'On the market: comment', *American Economic Review*, 71, 1060–67.

Hekman, C. R. (1977) 'Structural change and purchasing power parity', unpublished PhD thesis, University of Chicago, Chicago.

Helpman, E. (1981) 'An exploration of the theory of exchange rate regimes', *Journal of Political Economy*, 89, 865–90.

Helpman, E. and Razin, A. (1987) 'Exchange rate management: intertemporal tradeoffs', *American Economic Review*, 77, 107–23.

Henderson, D. W. (1979) 'Financial policies in open economies', *American Economic Review*, 69, 232–9.

Hendry, D. F. and Mizon, G. E. (1978) 'Serial correlation as a convenient simplification not a nuisance: a comment on a study of the demand for money by the Bank of England', *Economic Journal*, 88, 549–63.

Hodrick, R. J. (1978) 'An empirical analysis of the monetary approach to the determination of the exchange rate', in J. A. Frenkel and H. G. Johnson (eds), *The Economics of Exchange Rates*, Addison-Wesley, New York.

Hodrick, R. and Srivastava, S. (1984) 'An investigation of risk and return in forward foreign exchange', *Journal of International Money and Finance*, 3, 5–30.

Hoffman, D. and Schlagenhauf, D. (1983) 'Rational expectations and monetary models of exchange rate determination: an empirical examination', *Journal of Monetary Economics*, 11, 247–60.

Holtham, G. and Hughes-Hallett, A. (1987) 'International policy cooperation and model uncertainty', in Ralph Bryant and Richard Portes (eds), *Global Macroeconomics: Policy Conflict and Cooperation*, Macmillan, London.

Honohan, P. (1986) 'Exchange rates do not fail variance bounds tests', *Manchester School*, 54, 308–13.

Hooper, P. and Morton, J. (1982) 'Fluctuations in the dollar: a model of nominal and real exchange rate determination', *Journal of International Money and Finance*, 1, 39–56.

Horrii, A. (1986) *The Evolution of Reserve Currency Diversification*, BIS Economic Paper No. 18, BIS, Basle.

Howard, D. (1989) 'The United States as a heavily indebted country', Board of Governors, Federal Reserve System, *International Finance Discussion Papers*, 353.

Huang, R. (1981) 'The monetary approach to the exchange rate in an efficient foreign exchange: tests based on volatility', *The Journal of Finance*, 36, 31–41.

Huang, R. (1984) 'Some alternative tests of forward exchange rates as predictors of future spot rates', *Journal of International Money and Finance*, 3, 157–67.

Hutchinson, M. and Throop, A. (1985) 'The US budget deficit and the real value of the dollar', Federal Reserve Bank of San Francisco, *Economic Review*, No. 4, Fall.

IBRD (1985) World Development Report 1985, OUP for IBRD, New York.

IBRD (1987) World Development Report 1987, OUP for IBRD, New York.

Institute for International Economics (1987) *Resolving the Global Economic Crisis: A Statement by Thirty-three Economists from Thirteen Countries*, Washington.

International Monetary Fund (1984) 'The exchange rate system: lessons from the past and options for the future', *Occasional Paper No. 30*, IMF, Washington.

International Monetary Fund (1985) *Exchange Rate Volatility and World Trade*, IMF, Washington.

International Monetary Fund (1987a) *World Economic Outlook*, April and October, IMF, Washington.

International Monetary Fund (1987b) *Report on the World Current Account Discrepancy*, IMF, Washington.

Isard, P. (1977) 'How far can we push the law of one price?', *American Economic Review*, 67, 942–8.

Isard, P. and Stekler, L. M. (1985) 'US international capital flows and the dollar', *Brookings Papers on Economic Activity*, 1.

Ishiyama, J. (1975) 'Theory of optimum currency areas: a survey', *IMF Staff Papers*, June.

Ize, A. and Ortiz, G. (1987) 'Fiscal rigidities, public debt and capital flight', *IMF Staff Papers*, 34, 311–32.

Jaffee, D. M. and Russell, T. (1976) 'Imperfect information, uncertainty, and credit rationing', *Quarterly Journal of Economics*, 90, 651–66.

Johnson, H. G. (1962) 'Monetary theory and policy', *American Economic Review*, 52, 335–84.

Johnson, H. G. (1969) 'The case for flexible exchange rates: 1969', reprinted in his *Further Essays in Monetary Economics*, Harvard University Press, Cambridge, Mass.

Johnson, H. G. (1972) *Further Essays in Monetary Economics*, Allen and Unwin, London.

Johnson, H. G. (1977) 'The monetary approach to balance of payments theory and policy: explanation and policy implications', *Economica*, 44, 217–229.

Kawai, M. (1985) 'Exchange rates, the current account and monetary-fiscal policies in the short run and in the long run', *Oxford Economic Papers*, 37, 391–425.

Kearney, C. and Fallick, L. (1987) 'Macroeconomic policy and the balance of payments in Australia', *Economic Analysis and Policy*, 17, 131–48.

Kearney, C. and MacDonald, R. (1986) 'Intervention and sterilization under floating exchange rates: the UK 1973–83', *European Economic Review*, 30, 345–64.

Kemp, M. C. (1964) *The Pure Theory of International Trade*, Prentice Hall, Englewood Cliffs, NJ.

Kenen, P. B. (1985) 'Macroeconomic Theory and Policy: how the closed economy was opened', in Jones, R. W. and Kenen, P. B. (eds), *Handbook of International Economics, II*, Elsevier, New York.

Kenen, P. (1987), 'Exchange rates and policy coordination', *Brookings Discussion Paper No. 61*.

Khan, M. S. and Knight, M. D. (1983) 'Determinants of current account balances of non-oil developing countries in the 1970s: an empirical analysis', *IMF Staff Papers*, 30, 819–43.

Khan, M. S. and Knight, M. D. (1986) 'Import compression and export performance in developing countries', unpublished paper, International Monetary Fund, Washington.

Kimbrough, K. P. (1985) 'An examination of the effects of government purchases in an open economy', *Journal of International Money and Finance*, 1, 113–33.

Kindleberger, C. (1986) quoted in Eaton and Taylor, op. cit.

Kindleberger, C. P. (1987) *International Capital Movements*, Cambridge University Press, Cambridge.

Kletzer, K. M. (1984) 'Asymmetries of information and LDC borrowing with sovereign risk', *Economic Journal*, 94, 287–307.

Kneeshaw, J. T. and Van den Bergh, P. (1985) 'International interest rate relationships: policy changes and constraints', *BIS Economics Papers No. 13*, BIS, Basle.

Krasker, W. S. (1980) 'The Peso problem in testing the efficiency of forward exchange markets', *Journal of Monetary Economics*, 6, 269–76.

Kravis, I. and Lipsey, R. (1978) 'Price behaviour in the light of balance of payments theory', *Journal of International Economics*, 8, 193–246.

Krueger, A. O. (1985) 'Prospects and proposals', in Smith, G. W. and Cuddington, J, T. (eds), op. cit.

Krugman, P. (1978) 'Purchasing power parity and exchange rates: another look at the evidence', *Journal of International Economics*, 8, 397–407.

Krugman, P. (1985a) 'International debt strategies in an uncertain world', in Smith, G. W. and Cuddington, J. T. (eds), op. cit.

Krugman, P. (1985b) 'Is the strong dollar sustainable?', in Federal Reserve Bank of Kansas, *The US Dollar – Recent Developments*.

Krugman, P. (1986) 'Pricing to market when the exchange rate changes', *NBER Working Papers Series No. 1926*, May.

Krugman, P. and Baldwin, R. (1987) 'The persistence of the US trade deficits', *Brookings Papers on Economic Activity*, 1.

Krugman, P. and Baldwin, R. (1988a) 'Deindustrialization, reindustrialization and the real exchange rate', *NBER Working Paper No. 2586*, May.

Krugman, P. and Baldwin, R. (1988b) *Exchange Rate Instability*, The Robbins Memorial Lectures, MIT Press, forthcoming.

Kydland, F. E. and Prescott, E. C. (1977) 'Rules rather than discretion: the inconsistency of optimal plans', *Journal of Political Economy*, 85, 473–91.

Laney, L. O. (1984) 'The strong dollar, the current account and federal deficits: cause and effect', *Economic Review*, Federal Reserve Bank of Dallas, 1–14. Dallas, 1–14.

Laughlin, J. (1918) *Credit of Nations*, Charles Scribner's Sons, New York.

League of Nations (1935) *Commercial Banks: 1929–34*, Geneva.

Leiderman, L. and Blejer, M. I. (1987), 'Modelling and testing Ricardian equivalence', *IMF Staff Papers*, 34, 1–35.

Lessard, D. and Williamson, J. (1985) *Financial Intermediation Beyond the Debt Crisis*, Institute for International Economics, Washington.

Levin, J. H. (1985) 'Does leaning against the wind improve exchange rate performance?', *Journal of International Money and Finance*, 14, 135–49.

Levine, P. and Currie, D. (1987a) 'Does international policy coordination pay and is it sustainable? A two country analysis', *Oxford Economic Papers*, 39, 38–74.

Levine, P. and Currie, D. (1987b) 'The design of feedback rules in linear stochastic rational expectations models', *Journal of Economic Dynamics and Control*, 11, 1–28.

Lewis, M. K. and Davis, K. T. (1987) *Domestic and International Banking*, Philip Allan, Oxford.

Llewellyn, D.T. (1980) *International Financial Integration*, Macmillan, London.

Llewellyn, D.T. (1982) 'European monetary arrangements and the international monetary system', in Sumner, M. and Zis, G. (eds), *European Monetary Union*, Macmillan, London.

Llewellyn, D.T. (1983) 'The Euro-currency markets: credit effects and the dynamics of monetary policy', in Fair, D. E. and Bertrand, R. (eds), *International Lending in a Fragile World Economy*, Martinus Nijhoff, The Hague.

Llewellyn, D.T. (1985) 'US dollar in the international monetary system', Treasury and Civil Service Committee, Appendix 7 to 1985 Report on *International Monetary Arrangements*, HMSO, London.

Llewellyn, D.T. (1989) 'International financial integration: the global dimension', in Fair, D. E. and Boissieu, C. (eds), *International Monetary and Financial Integration: The European Dimension*, Kluwer, The Hague.

Llewellyn, D.T. (1988/89) 'Monetary union in Europe', *Banking World*, November/December 1988, May 1989.

Llewellyn, D.T. and Sutherland, A. (1987) 'Exchange rate variability: a review of theory and evidence', *Loughborough University Banking Centre Research Paper Series No. 35*.

Llewellyn, O. T. (1990) 'The Capital Transfer Process: A Critique of the 1970s', in Bird, G. (ed.) *International Financial Regime*, Guildford, Surrey University Press.

Loopesko, B. (1984) 'Relationships among exchange rates, intervention and interest rates: an empirical investigation', *Journal of International Money and Finance*, 3, 257–78.

Lucas, R. E. (1976) 'Econometric policy evaluation: a critique', in K. Brunner and A. Meltzer (eds), *The Phillips Curve and Labour Markets*, Carnegie–Rochester Conference Series 7.

MacDonald, R. (1983) 'Some tests of the rational expectations hypothesis in the foreign exchange market', *Scottish Journal of Political Economy*, 30, 235–50.

MacDonald, R. (1985) 'Do deviations of the real effective exchange rate follow a random walk?', *Economic Notes*, 14, 63–9.

MacDonald, R. (1988) *Floating Exchange Rates: Theories and Evidence*, Unwin-Hyman, London.

MacDonald, R. (1988) *The Economics of Floating Exchange Rates*, Prentice Hall, Englewood Cliffs, NJ.

MacDonald, R. and Taylor, M. P. (1988) 'Empirical exchange rate economics', in R. MacDonald, and M. P. Taylor, *Exchange Rates and Open Economy Macroeconomics*, Blackwell, Oxford.

MacDonald, R. and Torrance, T. S. (1988) 'On risk, rationality and excessive speculation in the Deutschemark–US dollar exchange market: some evidence using survey data', *Oxford Bulletin of Economics and Statistics*, 50, 107–23.

Mann, C. (1986) 'Prices, profit margins and exchange rates', *Federal Reserve Bulletin*, June.

Marston, R. C. (1985) 'Stabilization policies in open economies', in R. W. Jones and P. B. Kenen (eds), *Handbook of International Economics*, Elsevier Science.

Mathieson, D. J. (1985) 'Comments', in Guttentag and Herring (1985a), op. cit.

Mayer, H. (1982) 'Theory and practice of floating exchange rates and the role of official exchange market intervention', *BIS Economic Paper No. 5*, BIS, Basle.

Mayer H. and Taguchi, H. (1983) 'Official intervention in the exchange markets: stabilising or destabilising?', *BIS Economic Paper No. 6*, BIS, Basle.

McAvinchey, I. D. and MacDonald, R. (1987) 'The efficiency of the forward exchange market', *Economics Letters*, 25, 71–4.

McKinnon, R. (1984) *An International Standard for Monetary Stabilization*, Institute for International Economics, Washington.

McKinnon, R. (1988) 'Monetary and exchange rate policies for international financial stability: a proposal', *Journal of Economic Perspectives*, 2, 83–103.

McMillan, J. (1986) *Game Theory in International Economics*, Harwood, New York.

Meade, J. E. (1951) *The Balance of Payments*, Oxford University Press, Oxford.

Meade, J. E. (1984) 'A new Keynesian Bretton Woods', *Three Banks Review*.

Meershwam, D. (1989) 'International capital imbalances: the demise of local financial boundaries', in O'Brien, R. and Datta, T., *International Economic and Financial Markets*, OUP, Oxford.

Meese, R. A. (1986) 'Testing for bubbles in exchange markets: a case of sparkling rates?', *Journal of Political Economy*, 94, 345–73.

Meese, R. A. and Rogoff, K. (1983) 'Empirical exchange rate models of the seventies: do they fit out of sample?', *Journal of International Economics*, 14, 3–24.

Miller, M. and Weller, P. (1988) 'Target zones, currency options, and the dollar', mimeo, University of Warwick.

Miller, M. and Williamson, J. (1987) 'Targets and indicators: a blue print for the international coordination of economic policy', *Policy Analyses in International Economics No. 22*, Institute for International Economics, Washington, DC.

Milner, C. and Greenaway, D. (1979) *An Introduction to International Economics*, Longman, London.

Minford, A. P. L. (1978) *Substitution Effects, Speculation and Exchange Rate Stability*, North Holland, Amsterdam.

Minford, A. P. L. and Peel, D. (1983) *The New Classical Macroeconomics*, Oxford, M. Robertson.

Mirakhor, A. and Montiel, P. (1987) 'Import intensity of output growth in developing countries, 1970–85', Staff Studies for the World Economic Outlook, International Monetary Fund, August, 59–97.

Moore, M. J. (1989) 'Investories in the open economy macromodel: a disequilibrium analysis', *Review of Economic Studies*, forthcoming.

Morgan Guarantee (1986) *World Financial Markets*, March (Morgan Guaranty Trust Company of New York).

Muhleman, M. L. (1985) *Monetary Systems of the World*, Charles H. Nicoll, New York.

Mundell, R. A. (1962) 'The appropriate use of monetary and fiscal policy for internal and external stability', International Monetary Fund Staff Papers, 9, 70–7.

Mundell, R. A. (1963) 'Capital mobility and stabilization policy under fixed and flexible exchange rates' *Canadian Journal of Economics and Political Science*, 29, 475–85.

Mussa, M. (1979) 'Our recent experience with fixed and flexible exchange rates', *Carnegie Rochester Supplement*, 3, 1–50.

Myhrman, J. (1976) 'Experience of flexible exchange rates in earlier periods: theories, evidence, and a new view', *Scandinavian Journal of Economics*, 78–(2), 169–96.

Neary, J. P. (1980) 'Non-traded goods and the balance of trade in neo-Keynesian temporary equilibrium', *Quarterly Journal of Economics*, 95, 403–29.

Niehans, J. (1977) 'Exchange rate dynamics with stock-flow interactions', *Journal of Political Economy*, 85, 1245–57.

Nurkse, R. (1944) *International Currency Experience*, League of Nations, Geneva.

Obstfeld, M. (1981) 'Macroeconomic policy, exchange rate dynamics and optimal asset accumulation', *Journal of Political Economy*, 89, 1142–61.

Obstfeld, M. (1983) 'Exchange rates, inflation and the stabilization problem: Germany 1975–1981', *European Economic Review*, 21, 161–89.

Obstfeld, M. (1985) 'Floating exchange rates: experience and prospects', *Brookings Papers on Economic Activity*, 2.

OECD (1983) *Development Co-operation*, OECD, Paris.

OECD (1985) *Development Co-operation*, OECD, Paris.

OECD (1986a) *OECD Economic Outlook*, 40, December, 61–2.

OECD (1986b) *OECD Economic Survey of the United States*, November.

OECD (1988) *Why Economic Policies Change Course: Eleven Case Studies*, OECD, Paris.

Officer, L. H. (1976) 'The purchasing-power-parity theory of exchange rates: a review article', *International Monetary Fund Staff Papers*, 23, 1–60.

Oudiz, G. and Sachs, J. (1984) 'Macroeconomic policy coordination among the industrialised economies', *Brookings Papers on Economic Activity*, 1.

Panic, M. (1988) *National Management of the International Economy*, Macmillan, London.

Penati, A. and Dooley, M. (1984) 'Current account imbalances and capital formation in industrial countries, 1949–1981', *IMF Staff Papers*, 31, 1–24.

Persson, T. (1982) 'Global effects of national stabilization policies under fixed and floating exchange rates', *Scandinavian Journal of Economics*, 84, 165–92.

Poole, W. (1970) 'Optimal choice of monetary instruments in a simple stochastic macro model', *Quarterly Journal of Economics*, 84, 197–216.

Posner, M. (1986) *Problems of International Money, 1972–85*, IMF, Washington.

Purvis, D. D. (1985) 'Public sector deficits, international capital movements and the domestic economy: the medium-term is the message', *Canadian Journal of Economics*, 18, 723–41.

Putnam, B. H. and Woodbury, J. R. (1979) 'Exchange rate stability and monetary policy', *Review of Business and Economic Research*, 15, 1–10.

Putnam, R. and Bayne, N. (1987) *Hanging Together: Cooperation and Conflict in the Seven-Power Summits*, 2nd edition, Sage, London.

Razin, A. and Svensson, L. E. O. (1983) 'The current account and the optimal government debt', *Journal of International Money and Finance*, 2, 215–24.

Reisen, H. and van Trotsenburg, A. (1988) *Developing Country Debt: The Budgetary and Transfer Problem*, Development Centre Studies, OECD, Paris.

Robin, J. (1987) 'Are there reliable adjustment mechanisms?', Bank of Japan Monetary and Economic Studies, 5, 1–12.

Rodriguez, C. (1979) 'Short and long-run effects of monetary and fiscal policy under flexible exchange rates with perfect capital mobility', *American Economic Review*, 69, 176–82.

Rogoff, K. (1985) 'Can international monetary policy coordination be counter-productive?', *Journal of International Economics*, 18, 199–217.

Roll, R. (1979) 'Violations of purchasing power parity and their implications for efficient international commodity markets', in M. Sarnat and

G. Szego (eds), *International Finance and Trade*, 1, Ballinger, Cambridge, Mass.

Roosa, R. (1984) 'Exchange rate arrangements in the eighties', in *The International Monetary System*, Federal Reserve Bank of Boston, Boston.

Sachs, J. (1980) 'Wage indexation, flexible exchange rates and macroeconomic policy', *Quarterly Journal of Economics*, 94, 731–47.

Sachs, J. (1981) 'The current account and macroeconomic adjustment in the 1970s', *Brookings Papers on Economic Activity*, 1, 201–69.

Sachs, J. (1984) *Theoretical Issues in International Borrowing*, Princeton Studies in International Finance, No. 54, International Finance Section, Princeton University, Princeton, NJ.

Sachs, J. (1985) 'The dollar and the policy mix: 1985', *Brookings Papers on Economic Activity*, 1.

Sachs, J. (1986) 'Managing the LDC debt crisis', *Brookings Papers on Economic Activity*, 2, 397–431.

Sachs, J. and Wyplosz, C. (1984) 'Real exchange rate effects of fiscal policy', *NBER Working Paper No. 1255*.

Salop, J. and Spitäller, E. (1980) 'Why does the current account matter?', *International Monetary Fund Staff Papers*, 27, 101–34.

Samuelson, P. A. (1966) *Foundations of Economic Analysis*, Harvard University Press, Cambridge, Mass.

Samuelson, P. A. (1974) 'Analytical notes on international real-income measures', *Economic Journal*, 84, 595–608.

Sargen, N. (1985) 'Comments' on Guttentag and Herring (1985a), op. cit.

Sargent T. J. (1979) *Macroeconomic Theory*, Academic Press.

Saunders, P. and Dean, A. (1986) 'The international debt situation and linkages between developing countries and the OECD', *OECD Economic Studies*, 7, 155–203.

Scammell, W. M. (1987) *The Stability of the International Monetary System*, Macmillan, London.

Scheetz, T. (1987) 'Public sector expenditures and financial crisis in Chile', *World Development*, 15, 1053–75.

Schuker, S. A. (1988) *American 'Reparations' to Germany, 1919–33: Implications for the Third World Debt Crises*, Princeton Studies in International Finance No. 61, July.

Seade, J. (1983) 'Prices, profits and taxes in oligopoly', Working Paper, University of Warwick.

Shiller, R. J. (1981) 'Do stock prices move too much to be justified by subsequent changes in dividends?', *American Economic Review*, 71(3), 421–36.

Simonsen, M. H. (1985) 'The developing country debt problem', in Smith, G. W. and Cuddington, J. T. (eds), op. cit.

Smith, G. W. and Cuddington, J. T. (eds) (1985) *International Debt and the Developing Countries*, IBRD, Washington.

Snowden, P. N. (185) *Emerging Risk in International Banking: Origins of Financial Vulnerability in the 1980s*, Allen and Unwin, London.

Snowden, P. N. (1987) 'Chicago schism on banking reforms and debt crisis', *The World Economy*, 10, 219–26.

Solomon, R. (1975) 'The allocation of oil deficits', *Brookings Papers on Economic Activity*, 1, 61–88.

Stanyer, P. and Whitley, J. (1981) 'Financing world payments imbalances', *Bank of England Quarterly Bulletin*, June, 187–97.

Stiglitz, J. E. and Weiss, A. (1981) 'Credit rationing in markets with imperfect information', *American Economic Review*, 71, 393–410.

Stiglitz, J. E. (1983) 'On the relevance or irrelevance of public financial policy: indexation, price rigidities and optimal monetary policy', in R. Dornbusch and M. H. Simonsen (eds), *Inflation, Debt and Indexation*, MIT Press, Cambridge, Mass.

Swoboda, A. K. (1982) 'International banking: current issues in perspective', *Journal of Banking and Finance*, 6, 323–48.

Swoboda, A. K. (1985) 'Debt and the efficiency and stability of the international financial system', in Smith, G. W. and Cuddington, J. T. (eds), op. cit.

Taylor, D. (1982) 'Offical intervention in the foreign exchange market, or bet against the central bank', *Journal of Political Economy*, 90, 356–168.

Tew, J. H. B. (1985) 'The international monetary system', in Morris, D. (ed.), *The Economic System in the UK*, OUP, Oxford.

Tew, J. H. B. (1987) 'Floating exchange rates in the 1980s within The Group of Ten', *Arab Banker*, March.

Tew, J. H. B. (1988) *The Evolution of the International Monetary System 1945–88*, Hutchinson, London.

Thirlwall, A. P. (1988) 'What is wrong with balance of payments adjustment theory?', *The Royal Bank of Scotland Review*, 157, 3–19.

Tobin, J. (1982) 'A proposal for international monetary reform', in *Essays in Economics: Theory and Policy*, MIT Press, Cambridge, Mass.

Tobin, J. (1987) 'Are there reliable adjustment mechanisms?', *Bank of Japan Monetary and Economic Studies*, 5, 1–12.

Triffin, R. (1960) *Gold and the Dollar Crisis*, Yale University Press, New Haven.

Tsoukalis, L. (1985a) 'The New International Monetary "System" and prospects for reform', in Tsoukalis, L., *Political Economy of International Money*, Royal Institute of International Affairs, London.

Tsoukalis, L. (1985b) *The Political Economy of International Money*, Royal Institute of International Affairs, London.

Turner, P. (1986) 'Saving, investment and the current account: an empirical study of seven major countries, 1965–84', *Bank of Japan Monetary and Economic Studies*, 4, 1–58.

Van Wijnbergen, S. (1984) 'Government deficits, private investment and the current account: an intertemporal disequilibrium analysis', World Bank DRD Discussion Paper No. 100.

Wasserfallen, W. (1988) 'The behaviour of flexible exchange rates: evidence and implications', *Financial Analysts Journal*, September–October.

Watson, M., Mathieson, D., Kincaid, R. and Kalter, E. (1986) *International*

Capital Markets: Development and Prospects, Occasional Paper 43, IMF, Washington.

Williamson, J. (1977) *The Failure of world monetary Reform: 1971–74*, Nelson, Sunbury.

Williamson, J. (1982) 'The failure of world monetary reform: a reassessment', in Cooper, R. *et al.*, *The International Monetary System Under Flexible Exchange Rates*, Ballinger, Cambridge.

Williamson, J. (1983) *The Exchange Rate System*, Institute for International Economics, Washington.

Williamson, J. (1984) 'International liquidity: are the supply and composition appropriate?', in *The International Monetary System: Forty Years After Bretton Woods*, Federal Reserve Bank, Boston.

Williamson, J. (1985) *The Exchange Rate System*, 2nd Edition, Institute for International Economics, Washington.

Williamson, J. (1985) 'On the system in Bretton Woods', *American Economic Review*, 75 (Supplement), 74–9.

Williamson, J. and Miller, M. (1987) *Targets and Indicators: a Blueprint for the International Coordination of Economic Policy*, Institute for International Economics, Washington.

Wilson, C. (1979) 'Anticipated shocks and exchange rate dynamics', *Journal of Political Economy*, 87, 639–47.

Winters, L. A. (1981) *An Econometric Model of the Export Sector*, Cambridge University Press, Cambridge.

Wionczec, M. (1979) 'LDC external debt and the Euromarkets: an impressive record and an uncertain future', *World Development*, 7, 175–87.

Woo, W. T. (1984) 'Exchange rates and prices of nonfood, nonfuel products', *Brookings Papers on Economic Activity*, 2.

Woo, W. T. (1985) 'The monetary approach to exchange rate determination under rational expectations', *Journal of International Economics*, 18, 1–16.

World Bank (1985) *World Development Report 1985*, World Bank, Washington.

Yeager, L. B. (1969) 'Fluctuating exchange rates in the nineteenth century: experiences of Austria and Russia', in R. A. Mundell and A. K. Swoboda (eds), *Monetary Problems of the International Economy*, University of Chicago Press, Chicago.

Name Index

Subject Index